Memory into Memoir

An Anthology

Memory into Memoir

An Anthology

Written and Edited by
The Red Wheelbarrow Writers
Bellingham, WA.
2016

Memory into Memoir
An Anthology

Copyright © 2016 Cami Ostman

1ˢᵗ Edition

Printed in the United States of America

Published by:
Penchant Press International, LLC
PO Box 1133
Bellingham, WA 98227

www.penchantpressinternational.com

Library of Congress Cataloging-in-Publication Data

Ostman, Cami 1967 -
Memory into Memoir
An Anthology

ISBN 978-0-9724960-5-6

Cover and Book Design by J. Allen Fielder

So much depends
upon

a red wheel
barrow

glazed with rain
water

beside the white
chickens.

William Carlos Williams
"XXII" from *Spring and All* (1923)

Foreword

So much depends upon community.

THE RED WHEELBARROW WRITERS ARE A LOOSE COLLECTIVE OF WORKING writers who produce independently, and who join together to support, encourage, and sustain one another. This volume, *Memory into Memoir*, our first anthology, demonstrates all these qualities. The pieces are independently written. The editing, marketing, proofreading, funding, organizing, publishing, and peddling are collectively undertaken by our members. Our lengthy Acknowledgments testify to the essential roles played by hard-working writers who volunteered their time and energy, their skills and insights, and to community partners who have offered us space and time.

In 2015 Red Wheelbarrow Writers partnered with Village Books in Bellingham to found Whatcom Memoir Writing Month. During the month of September—that most nostalgic of seasons—memoir writers gathered, supported, and worked together, and attended classes, readings, and outings.

In writing memoir, one gives narrative shape to the past, creates order out of what might have been (as it was lived) chaos. One assesses the past and brings some measure of understanding. For this volume we asked writers to connect their memoir to a line from any poem by William Carlos Williams, whose thoughts on the importance of a red wheelbarrow furnished us with inspiration. The poet would be pleased to see his lines live on in the work of these writers.

Red Wheelbarrow Writers is not a club or non-profit. We have no dues or formal order of responsibility. When we need money, we pass a hat. When we have an important undertaking, we show up. We meet once a month at an Irish pub to drink wine, read what we have in progress, exchange news and views. We have a monthly Writerly Book Club, and our monthly Bored Meetings (yes, that's the correct spelling) are not boring at all. Anyone can attend with a thought, an idea, a project. It was at one of these Bored Meetings when Cami Ostman, one of the RWB Founding Mothers, first floated the idea of the book you now hold in your hands.

The anthology takes its title from *Memory into Memoir*, a course taught for many years by another RWB Founding Mother, Laura Kalpakian. Our third Founding Mother, Susan Tive, enthusiastically joined the effort to bring this book to fruition.

We are publishing our anthology in September 2016 to celebrate the renamed Washington Memoir Writing Month. Because we are readers as well as writers, Red Wheelbarrow will make a contribution from the proceeds of our sales to the Whatcom Literacy Council.

We are proud to present these diverse voices, and narratives of travel, childhood, personal victories, personal losses, astute observations, laughter, tears, and moments of wonder. The past, as they say, is a foreign country; they do things differently there.

Cami Ostman
Laura Kalpakian

Bellingham, WA.
June 2016

redwheelbarrowwriters.com
facebook.com/redwheelbarrowwriters

Table of Contents

Just Say No

Nancy Adair

No defeat is made up entirely of defeat—
since the world it opens is always a place formerly unsuspected.
William Carlos Williams, *The Descent*

MIKE'S COBALT BLUE EYES WERE FILLED WITH MYSTERY, UNNERVING, TO SAY
the least. As our Deputy Ambassador, his words always had
an impact, and on that humid April morning, I could tell that
something big was about to roll off his tongue.

"Nancy Reagan is coming to Malaysia. You are going to be
the Community Control Officer for her Embassy visit." His eyes
began to twinkle, like he expected me to be excited. I wasn't.
Terror lit up the circuits of my brain and raced through my
system, leaving behind scorch marks in my stomach.

The fear wasn't even for myself, but for my husband. He was
a new Consular Officer in the Foreign Service—his dream job
since high school—and we were still learning about the diplomatic life. At that point, all we knew was that the Foreign Service was a family career. A screw-up by any one of us impeded
the career path of the diplomat. And from my point of view,
working with the White House had high potential for screw-
ups.

"I appreciate your confidence, sir, but so many of our Embassy spouses are star-struck over Mrs. Reagan. You might
want to tap them."

"We chose you to be the Community Liaison. That means we
trust you to be the Control Officer." I acquiesced because I'm
one of those introverts who doesn't like to disappoint people.

Feeling affirmed yet nervous, I took refuge in the sanctity
of my peaceful office in the Embassy courtyard. The plum and

federal blue décor soothed me. I gazed through the floor-to-ceiling window and became one with the water flowing through the fountain outside. The White House briefing papers sat on my desk, and one glance told me that this moment of calm would disappear at the arrival of the White House Advance Team, bringing my contact, Christian Malloy. I bolstered myself with the hope that my work would be good enough to shine favor on our family career.

Christian Malloy was a DC lawyer in his mid-thirties, about my age, I guessed. The extrovert strutted into my office and plunked his powerful presence in my plum-colored chair. Not that he was necessarily handsome. He wasn't, but he didn't know it. His persona loomed large, enhanced by the fact that he was a protégé of Michael Deaver, the PR genius behind all memorable Reagan photographs, like the one at the Great Wall of China. The goal for us was to create an equally memorable photo op for Nancy Reagan.

Chris began his assignment by standing in the courtyard every day at three o'clock to study the sun. Like the god, Apollo, he was to control the angle of the rays to cast the most flattering light on Mrs. Reagan's face. She was to deliver a motivational speech while surrounded by children gazing up at her in awe.

I began my assignment in panic. Nancy Reagan was coming to Malaysia to promote her JUST SAY NO TO DRUGS campaign. According to Chris, the photos with our diplomatic children was the most important part of her trip. After she spoke, the kids were to respond in gratitude, as per my coaching. With CNN present, the whole event had to be flawless.

The problem was getting the kids excited about her campaign. Malaysia didn't need JUST SAY NO. It already had the death penalty. Anyone (usually a foreigner) caught with even an ounce of marijuana was hanged by the neck in downtown Pudu Prison, while hundreds of gawkers watched from high-rise hotel rooms, specially rented for the occasion. The locals, including all Embassy children, already knew how to say no.

I soon learned that people don't just show up for a White

House photo op. Every second, every placement is orchestrated, like a performance of *Aida*. Job One was to have our Malaysian staff erect risers at the open end of the courtyard. Job Two was to schedule practice sessions—imagine, practicing for a photo. The children were to arrive in the afternoon just before three. On the first day, my two sons met in my office, and I spiffed them up so their cuteness could land them front and center—Grandma watched CNN. At the rehearsal I, the other Nancy, stood in for Mrs. Reagan while Chris slowly and methodically placed the kids around me. Sadly my adorable sons didn't land in front.

At one point I sensed scuffling over my right shoulder. Chris looked up with a grimace.

"I'm sure I did not put you in that spot," he told ten-year-old Marcie, my boss's daughter.

Her lip curled under. She was a plain little girl, not as yet blossoming into the beauty that was her mother. She twirled her finger on a strand of dishwater-colored hair and said, "I can't see from there."

Chris pointed to the end of the top row. "Go back where I put you." He folded his arms and waited as she slowly retreated to her mark.

After organizing more kids, his face suddenly crinkled as if someone had just cut into a durian, the local fruit that tastes like heaven but stinks like hell. Marcie had sneaked into the second row. Chris fumed, "You cannot stand there either." She moved up one row, and he placed an African American girl in the spot and then two Asian brothers in front of her. When she squeezed in behind my shoulder, Chris exploded. "Move! That spot is reserved—for someone cute."

She moved, all right—down and off the riser—leaving the courtyard and marching straight to her father's office. My heart sank. I'd already lost control, and my boss's daughter was the first casualty.

Chris continued, oblivious to the pain he had just caused. He returned to his task until the arrangement was perfect. He ordered the kids to memorize their places. Then he asked for a volunteer to give the speech. High-school twins stepped forward.

"Here is the speech. Let me hear each of your read."

Oh, God. Is Chris going to make the twins compete? But soon enough they self-deselected over one line, "I am the President of the Just Say No Club." One of the twins—I couldn't tell them apart—looked up, confused. "We don't have a Just Say No Club."

"Well start one."

The twins responded in sync, "We don't want to."

"Why not?"

"It's stupid."

"Don't you want to make Mrs. Reagan happy?"

"We're busy."

"Then just *say* there is a club. And form one later when you have time. Take this speech home and practice." They left.

Chris turned to me. "You need to form a club."

"Me? How?"

"What does a club do? Holds meetings. Just get a bunch of kids together for one meeting and declare yourself a club. Here's what we'll do. We need posters. On Saturday morning you gather kids to make posters and tell them they are in the Just Say No Club. See if you can get those twins to come."

Suddenly my boss, a pit bull of a man, charged into the courtyard to defend his daughter's honor. As an introvert, I don't have the stomach for fights, so I left the two men to duel it out in private while this stupid photo op, like a spoiled roll of film, unspooled itself into the light.

The next day I visited Mike. "I'm sorry to create problems for you," I said. "I know you're busy organizing Mrs. Reagan's visit to the Foreign Ministry. But Christian Malloy is calling kids ugly and asking them to lie. If they refuse, he expects me to deliver the lie." Reduced to a tattletale, I was in essence admitting my lack of control. But Mike was kind and offered to consult the Ambassador.

An ambassador serves at the pleasure of a President. He can be removed at any time. However, our Ambassador was about to retire, and he'd served long enough to keep his title for life, so he had wiggle room. Yet there was no wiggle in his response: "Whatever the White House wants."

I was sure the First Lady did not want people to lie, but to avoid conflict I said, "Okay."

On Saturday morning twelve little kids showed up at the Embassy cafeteria to paint posters. The wife of our Marine Gunnery Sergeant brought a boom box and played a new Springsteen song, *Born in the USA*, which created a lively patriotic atmosphere. For the first time, I felt like I was doing something meaningful for my country. I reveled in the importance and significance of my task and failed to announce the bit about the club.

Then Chris showed up with the big lie. He proclaimed this the first meeting of the Malaysia Chapter of the Just Say No to Drugs Club. The kids didn't have a clue. Not a one was old enough to name a drug more powerful than baby aspirin.

At our next rehearsal, the Louks twins were still MIA, so the speech fell to me. I don't mind public speaking. I can do anything given enough time to prepare, but this was a challenge—I had little time to create a message that was both meaningful and true.

After the rehearsal, I asked Chris if I should be in the photo op. After all, I'd worked hard and deserved a picture with the First Lady as much as anyone.

"We'll see," he said.

In my house "we'll see" usually meant "no." Would I have to pull a Marcie?

At the last rehearsal, I stepped away from the riser to give some feedback. That's what a control officer does, right? A beautiful scene played out before me. A fountain bubbled. The lush green backdrop was like a scene from *South Pacific* where coconut palms swayed before azure skies. On the riser, adorable, shiny-faced kids beamed with the sun at just the right angle, and even the twins showed up. Marcie was now one spot removed from the center. My boss, who monitored from his office door, must have cut her a deal. I stepped back into Mrs. Reagan's place, holding the gift, an expensive Malaysian Selangor Pewter plate with an engraved THANK YOU. We practiced the presentations, mine with the pewter and two middle-schoolers with a giant construction paper card, filled with kids' signatures and true words.

At the end I looked toward Chris to share the moment of joy. He should have been thrilled, but that scowl reappeared. *Oh no.*

"Good," he said, "but not perfect. Something's missing."

"Like what?"

"Like a crippled kid. Does this embassy have any crippled kids?"

"No."

"Go see if your med unit has a wheelchair. We'll put a kid in the chair with a blanket on his lap."

"Are you kidding me?" Without considering my husband's career or the Ambassador's tenure or my future as an ambassador's wife, I just said no. Chris had gone too far. "I will not ask a child to fake a disability." My insides squeezed into a knot as I prepared to be axed.

"Oh well," he said. "Just a thought." He turned to the kids. "See you on Saturday at one o'clock sharp."

The kids left, but I was stuck on pause. *Saying no to the White House was that easy?* I couldn't believe it. Maybe this campaign was on to something. I had a new respect for Nancy Reagan.

On May 3, at 12:45 PM, the real Control Officer—God—tore open the skies and pummeled Malaysia with a warm, tropical deluge of Biblical proportions. Was that Noah floating by? Because the rains usually came in late afternoon, families arrived unprepared. We all scrambled from our cars to the Embassy and got drenched in between. By 2:00 our media room was overrun with soggy, matted children who smelled like wet dogs.

And there I stood with teardrops of rain splotching my green linen blouse. Our beautiful photo op, washed out. Even so, the moment was auspicious. We were about to be showered with wisdom from America's First Lady.

When Mrs. Reagan arrived at 3:02, my husband and other low-ranking diplomats were drafted into the umbrella brigade. They escorted her, drip-free, up the grand staircase. She entered the Embassy with her movie star aura: perfect blond hair, swept back, and flawless skin, smooth as the silk in her dress. Her signature red jacket added a glow. While Chris complained about the riser, hastily reassembled in the wrong location, I met the First Lady in an anteroom to discuss what would happen before and after her speech.

"I'm not giving a speech," she said.

I was dumbfounded. We had practiced for weeks. *Did she want me to disappoint eighty damp people, who had shivered in air-conditioning for two hours?*

"What's wrong?" *Laryngitis? Travel woes?*

"The rain has put us off schedule. We are already two minutes behind. If I don't have time for my whole speech, I won't give one."

"Can't you just cut two minutes?" *It's not like the plane will leave without you.*

"I wouldn't know which part to cut."

My moment of dismay gave her time to reconsider. But then I remembered that actresses work from scripts, and I had just asked Juliet to cut two minutes from the balcony scene, on the fly.

"Okay," I said and mentally deleted half of my own speech. On the spot, I had to come up with a reason to thank her so I wouldn't look dumb giving her an expensive pewter gift for what?

She double-checked herself in the mirror, and I opened the door to the media room. When the Ambassador announced, "The First Lady of the United States," the sea of families parted, and she strode among the applause, regal and refined, in no particular hurry. I followed, like a loser bridesmaid.

The Ambassador spoke some words about her visit and then welcomed her to the microphone. More applause was followed by hushed anticipation. The moment had arrived.

"Thank you for coming," she said.

Silence reigned as the audience eagerly leaned into her speech. Only I knew that it was already over. She gazed at the crowd momentarily and stepped back from the microphone, ceding the stage to me. Me, in front, alone, with eighty muffled sighs of disappointment blowing at my face.

I delivered my abridged presentation, two middle-schoolers gave her the card, and then it was over. The whole thing. Eight minutes. Mrs. Reagan and I stepped back while the Ambassador announced details for a photograph with the First Lady. A line formed at the anteroom even before he finished saying "for a limited time only."

Still on stage, Mrs. Reagan gave me this hazy stare, possibly a generic version of the famous Nancy Reagan gaze. I thought she might thank me, but instead she asked, "What was your name again?"

"It's Nancy," I said, wondering how she could forget.

"I'll see you in the anteroom." The Ambassador helped her down the steps as the sea parted again. Without a glance, they strolled right past the riser of kids, with my youngest son now in the front row.

Alone on stage, I watched people leave, heading for a photograph, a historical record, documenting the moment while belying the lack of substance.

"No. I'm afraid you won't see me in the anteroom."

Novelist, blogger, and now memoirist, Nancy Adair left the United States in the eighties with her diplomat husband, two babies, and an electric typewriter. The Embassy life agreed with her. Not the life of tea parties and special privileges, but the life of intrigue, of partying with the CIA and heads of state, privy to the truth vs. the facade. Through her twenty-five years overseas, her sensibilities were most profoundly affected by the absurdity of political beings, those found in both her memoir and her novel, Beyond the Scope—Truth Turns Deadly in the Congo.

What Not To Do In Afghanistan

Debbie Brosten

If you can bring nothing to this place but your carcass, keep out.
William Carlos Williams, *Dedication for a Plot of Ground*

"WAKE UP! WE'RE LATE! HURRY!" I BARKED DIRECTIVES AT MY YOUNGER
brother, Jay. We were staying at a guesthouse in Afghanistan,
pre-Soviet invasion, pre-Taliban, pre-US Army. The guesthouse
was basic. For about the equivalent of five American dollars,
we shared a room with two small wooden beds, a small table
and a washbasin. The bathroom was down the hall, shared by
the six or seven other travelers on our floor. Most of these travelers, Europeans, Australians, North Americans, were heading overland from Katmandu to Istanbul as we were, although
some were doing the trip in reverse. There was a well-worn path
nicknamed the Hippie Trail, and most of our fellow travelers,
like us, were relying on a Lonely Planet Guidebook, *Southeast
Asia on a Shoestring*. This was before smart phones or even
cell phones. To communicate, we wrote letters home on flimsy
blue aerograms and arranged short expensive phone calls from
crowded call centers. When we needed to be awoken at specific
times, we used travel alarm clocks or relied on management
wherever we were staying.

The evening before, Rashid, the guy manning the hotel desk,
promised he would wake us in time for our early morning bus
to Herat. We had "lost" our alarm clock months earlier. "No
problem," Rashid assured us with an ever-present smile on his
lips. "I will be up. I will wake you in time for you to catch your
bus." We settled our bill and headed to our room hoping Rashid
would keep his word.

As usual, we found the Afghanis quick to offer assistance,

but relaxed about providing it. There was no wake-up call or knock. I looked at my watch. We had ten minutes to get dressed, stash the few last-minute items into our backpacks and make it across town. Possible, but not probable. We dashed down the stairs, through a deserted lobby and into the quiet, dusty street. We sprinted past closed storefronts, small squat colorless buildings, on our way to the bus station. I'd like to say that the bus was still there when we arrived. Or that we saw the tail end of it turning a corner, and we converged on it at a nearby red light. But I can't say that. One, I don't think there were any red lights in that tiny town and two, there was no bus anywhere in our field of vision, only a deserted street in the quiet early light.

We slowly wound our way back to the guesthouse via streets that were quickly coming to life. Old men wore plain, long tunics over loose trousers, dusty shoes, and white rags coiled like cobras on their heads. Women were conspicuously absent other than the young girls heading to school in their black uniforms and white headscarves. Schoolboys grouped together separate from the girls, rubbing their hands against the cold. Their chatter mixed with the cries of hawkers selling their copper pots and woolen blankets. A few braziers heated up the morning naan emanating enticing aromas from makeshift cubicles. Men gathered in front of the storefronts quietly talking, warmed by small clay pots they carried with them. A warm coal burned in the pot, which fit well beneath their cape-like wool coats as they squatted in conversational groups and fought the winter temperatures.

Traveling in a foreign country comes with a bandwagon of challenges, especially when you are doing it on a shoestring. Of course traveling on your own with a vague itinerary and flexible calendar also opens the door to incredible opportunities that arise along the road. That day was not one of our more magical days, nor did it lead to one of those opportunities. In fact, my brother still refers to it as the day I almost got him killed.

Jay and I trudged back into the now lively guesthouse. Bill, a Brit we had met back in Kabul, nursed a cup of coffee in the makeshift dining room. "I thought you would be gone by now," he announced.

"So did we," I answered.

As we drank our own cups of sweet hot liquid, tea for me, coffee for Jay, we related our mad dash through the empty streets to the bus station. While we ate our breakfast of naan, eggs, and beans, Bill could tell I was mad. He excused himself as I continued to fume. Jay, as usual, adjusted to the situation as it was. He had learned our father's philosophy of "Don't worry," far better than I had. He was easy going. I tended to fret and angst over things.

"Damn Rashid," I said as I watched him drinking coffee at a corner table with another local man. Slouched back in his chair, he looked as though he didn't have a care in the world. Jay followed my gaze. "Let's just figure out what to do while we wait for the next bus," he suggested. I shifted my glare to him. He sighed.

"Let's just get out of here," I said, "I don't even want to look at Rashid anymore." I started putting on my coat and backpack.

"Wait, we need to pay for breakfast," Jay countered.

"No we don't. They owe it to us for not waking us. For making us miss the bus. Screw them. I'm so tired of people saying one thing and doing another. Let's just go." I didn't check for agreement, just headed out.

We hadn't even made it out of the dining room before Rashid, sporting the ubiquitous black moustache of that region, yelled out. "Hey, where are you going? You haven't paid." The backpacks on our backs only increased the urgency in his voice.

"I don't think we should pay. You said you would wake us this morning and you didn't. We missed our bus," I said. As he stood in front of me, fists clenched at his sides, his red face appeared ready to explode. Spittle sprayed from his lips as he sputtered, "You ate breakfast. You pay!"

I stood my ground, trying to inflate my five-foot, two-inch frame. We stared at each other. As he raised his left hand toward me, I noticed Jay out of the corner of my eye. He was brandishing a chair above his head, no longer remotely resembling my baby brother. Suddenly visions of a full-on bar fight, or at least the Afghani restaurant version of it, filled my brain as fully as cigarette smoke filled the air. If Jay broke that chair over anyone or anything, I was convinced we would end up dead. Or rotting in an Afghani jail, which might be worse. When we crossed the border into Afghanistan, there were graphic displays of backpacks and cars torn apart in a search for illicit drugs. Photos of the poor jail conditions accompanied the images of the cars opened to the wheel wells. We had been extra careful to never carry anything that could possibly cause scrutiny and questioning. Yet there we were doing something just as reckless as carrying drugs.

"Shit, put that down!" I shrieked at Jay. My outburst worked as well as if I had pushed the pause button on a remote. Everyone froze. Granted by that time, everyone else in the dining room was already silently watching us, waiting for the drama to play itself out. Jay lowered the chair, Rashid dropped his hand, I began shaking uncontrollably.

A second later a policeman walked in. He was dressed in a baggy green uniform, pistol holstered in his black belt, scuffed boots on his feet, worn cap on his head. Steel black eyes surveyed the situation as he spoke in rapid Pashto to Rashid. We watched Rashid's hand gestures, the nodding of the policeman's head. Even though we didn't understand a word of their conversation, we knew exactly what was being said. My shaking increased.

"Pay the man and walk outside," the policeman instructed us in British-accented English. Jay fished some bills out of his pockets. We walked from the guesthouse, afraid to meet anyone's eye, unsure what would happen next. The policeman followed us.

"Where are you headed?" he asked.

"Herat, on the next bus." Jay answered. The policeman nodded and suggested we wait at the bus station. Gratefully we agreed.

In fairness, if fairness deserves to be in this discussion, we were tired. We had been traveling for seven months by this time. Living out of backpacks, pinching pennies or rupees or baht or, in this case, afghanis. We were exhausted from unfamiliar beds, working out foreign customs and languages, acquiring needed toiletries, visas, supplies. The time it took to accomplish simple tasks we performed automatically at home astounded us. Traveling with newly made friends who had a bit more money to spend resulted in arguments that would have been ridiculous at home. Fatigue was a constant companion along with my unsettled stomach.

Don't get me wrong. It had been a great trip so far. Among other adventures we had hiked in the Himalayas, rode an elephant on safari in the Chitwan National Park in Nepal, stayed with a tribal leader in remote hills outside of Chiang Mai, Thailand, got our first glimpse of an almost deserted Taj Mahal under a full moon, and spent Christmas on a houseboat in Kashmir opening presents around an ingeniously decorated "tree."

I calmed myself down and examined my motives, as my trembling lessened. I discovered I was embarrassed. Ever since my first trip to Indonesia a few years earlier, the first foreign country I visited, I had tried to separate myself from the Ugly American tourist. When I traveled, I did not rely on organized tours, but instead used guidebooks to help me discover places. I took the time to learn at least a few words of the local language. I delighted in meeting the locals, being invited into their lives, no matter how temporarily, and I tried to be respectful of mores that differed from my own. Yet in Afghanistan, I found myself acting just as ugly as the tourists I disdained. How had I morphed into the Ugly American? I was more than embarrassed, I was ashamed. Ashamed of myself, ashamed of what I had bullied my brother into doing and saddened to see the crack widen between who I was and who I wanted to be.

I was not the center of the universe. Others were not put on this planet to serve me, to promote my agenda. Much as I wanted it to be so, the world is not a fair place. This was a heady thought for a young woman who had been brought up in a loving American family where she was given as much as possible in order to make her life better than that of her parents. My family tried to shelter me from the harsh realities of the world. The trip my brother and I were undertaking was as much an education as the one we had in school. In fact, we learned how to live in a world with compassion, to see how much people around the world strive for the same things regardless of their language, customs or religion. Unfortunately, it took provoking an incident for me to realize that the power I have for good can just as easily be used for bad.

When I was young, my parents often recited the children's poem about a little girl who had a little curl. When she was good, she was very, very good, but when she was bad, she was horrid. Like the girl in the poem, I too vacillated between those two extremes. That experience in Afghanistan propelled me toward removing horrid from my repertoire.

Debbie Brosten is a retired teacher addicted to travel. William Carlos Williams' poem "Dedication for a Plot of Ground" prompted her to recollect experiences she had traveling home from her first teaching position. Overseas teaching and the subsequent travel changed the trajectory of her life. Now retired and resettled in Bellingham, she finds joy by sharing laughter with friends, exploring new places and ideas, and discovering the commonalities that exist between writers and their writings. Connecting all her observations and musings into coherent stories is her current practice.

Lost Virginity

Nancy Canyon

I am alone.
The weight of love
Has buoyed me up
Till my head
Knocks against the sky.

William Carlos Williams, *A Love Song*

THE URGE COMES FROM LOW IN THE SPINE. MY FRIEND, ALICE, SAYS IT'S called Kundalini rising, the serpent energy. She knows about metaphysical stuff and says that lots of sex will make my legs strong and blend Jack's aura with mine. She says sex is good for me, which is a completely different message from the one my mother gave me: *You have to do what your husband wants.* And Dad's message: *Don't go getting all bent out of shape.* That's what he said when my first boyfriend moved to Alaska. After that Dad tried to keep me from dating—practically turned me into a nun—until I met Jack, that is.

Jack wanted me naked almost immediately. Got a little pushy even. It was exciting at first and then I got scared. I barely knew how *it* happened let alone did I know if I wanted *it* to happen. I was only seventeen, he a year older. He said he could be thrown in jail for statutory rape, if caught. Dad was a catcher, I knew that for sure. Anything I did was suspect. We eventually carried on despite the danger.

Anyway, Kundalini rising comes from deep inside. It must be fickle as the first time it rose, I was surprised. "Don't stop," I'd begged. Jack looked excited. Afterward he said, "Haven't you ever had one?" I shook my head no.

Even then, I'm no prude; it's stupid to say that about a person when you don't know where she's been. You know what I mean? Have you ever had your father feel you up? No, I didn't think so. So calling me prude is dumb. And so is suggesting I would lie about being hurt by my father. "Oh, he wouldn't do that." Or even more insulting, "You're crazy."

I'm afraid I'll upset people by talking about the abuse. Besides, Dad made me promise not to. Yet, one night after I started living at the campground at Priest Lake with Jack and his buddies, Jack said, "Go ahead; tell them what happened." Everyone was quiet as I relayed the story of the abuse. I felt much better afterward, like the *weight of love* had *buoyed me up*. Then I started to shake. Hard. Real hard. The next day, Jack's best friend asked if I'd been drunk when I said those things. I said no. That's how I remember it, not drunk; oh, I may have had a beer or two, but drunk I wasn't. The shadows of the night woods surrounded us and the beach sand took on a yellow caste from the licking campfire flames. Everyone was silent as I broke the secret: "Dad touches me every chance he gets."

I've heard that some folks who've been molested don't like sex. To my best friend's face when asked what the big deal about sex was, I said, "I wouldn't know." Hopefully nothing bad had happened to her, but I was embarrassed to talk about the pleasure of sex with anyone except Alice. And I didn't want to give away the fact that I'd been doing it with Jack since I was seventeen. Yes, statutory rape if caught, but who would know? Well, Dad, of course, but fortunately he didn't figure it out until I turned eighteen. Then he forbade me from seeing Jack. "No, I haven't seen him," I lied when asked.

Now I'm twenty-one and living on a lookout tower with hubby. The baby we made when I was twenty died after three months. I still cry over losing it. Things happen for the best, the doctor said. The egg probably didn't attach correctly to the uterus wall. I don't know—should I give back the booties and crocheted baby blankets friends and relatives made for me, or keep them for the next baby? Well, in any case, they are safe in the chest with the towels from our wedding, stowed in Mom's basement; the basement where Jack and I slept before heading to Grangeville for this job keeping fire watch at six thousand feet. That night in the basement we made love on the foldout bed that Mom got in the split with Dad, the same one we *stained with love* the night it snowed a skiff.

The night I lost my virginity, I swept the snow off the front porch afterward. I didn't want Dad to see Jack's footprints. Such a sleuth, right away asking, "Was someone here?"

I lied. "No, no one."

He stared, his eyes saying he didn't believe a word of it. And somewhere deep inside I felt a terrible transparency. He knew exactly what I was up to.

Tonight, forty-five feet in the air, we entwine beneath a brilliant starlit sky. Heat pulses our spines as the shivering serpent readies to uncoil. The curse may or may not come this month, but I don't think about that right now. Ordinary life is as far from my thoughts as Kundalini rising is from my understanding. I close my eyes and let go.

Nancy Canyon's prose is published in Raven Chronicles, Songs of Ourselves, Water~Stone Review, Fourth Genre, Exhibition, Main Street Rag, Floating Bridge Review, Labyrinth, Clover: A Literary Rag, *and more. She holds the MFA in Creative Writing from Pacific Lutheran University and a Certificate in Fiction Writing from UW. Canyon teaches writing and art classes through Village Books and WCC Community Ed, and in her art studio in Historic Fairhaven. She lives near Lake Whatcom with her fiancé, Ron, her dog, Olive, and her tuxedo cat, Sid.*

Rooms of My Own

Susan Chase-Foster

> *. . . a doorway*
> *opens for you—*
> *like some great flower—*
> *a room filled with lamplight . . .*
>
> William Carlos Williams, *Keller Gegen Dom*

WHEN I WAS SIX, WE LIVED IN A LARGE ENGLISH TUDOR HOUSE IN DETROIT with a ballroom on the third floor. One winter when it was too snowy to ice skate on the neighborhood pond, my brother and I strapped on our steel-wheeled roller skates and engraved a series of curlicue designs on the polished oak floor of the ball-room. Our saintly mother, who had been busy praying the Rosary in her second-floor bedroom, heard us grinding away and stomped up the stairs, spitting mad.

"Cease!" she screamed, banging open the ballroom door, her heavenly halo of holiness somewhat dimmed. We stood frozen, locked in her death-ray of guilt, but she glared hardest at me because I was the elder of her two little devils and, therefore, responsible.

She sent my brother to our book- and toy-filled bedroom and then marched me down to the first-floor telephone room, where I was incarcerated for an eternity just outside the kitchen so she could keep her eye on me. I was given a writing tablet with thick black lines, a yellow No. 2 pencil with a clean eraser, and sentenced to write a letter of apology to my father who would need to hire a craftsman at great expense to restore the ball-room floor to its former condition. Upon satisfactory completion of that task, I would be paroled.

The telephone room was more like a cozy closet than a room, with a tiny wooden desk that had belonged to my grandmother, a bronze gooseneck lamp, a black rotary dial phone and a fat telephone book with curled up pages. The chair had a green velvet cushion that slipped off when I squirmed, which was constantly.

Now, a good girl might have quickly scribed a heartfelt letter, but even as a child, my muse was untamable. She'd scream, jump up and down, hammer her inspirations into my head until I could no longer resist. Thus, after spending several minutes reading the telephone book and folding its pages into fans and paper airplanes, I wrote my first story.

One day a meen mama loked her sweet little girl in a room until she called the polis who sent her mama to jale so she had to rite leters all day. The end.

I exhaled, and about then my mother looked in on me like a prison guard checking on her charge. Seeing the enthusiasm with which I had attacked the paper, she gave me a thumbs-up. I waved. She entered.

"Looks like you're making progress, Suze. Are you about ready to come out?"

"Yep. Here you go, Mama." I handed her my story, which she read, her head bobbing up and down as she took in each word. She handed it back to me.

She frowned. "Well, not what I asked for or expected, but I will say this. It's a start, a good one, but you can do better. Was the mama always mean? Who feeds the sweet little girl while the mama is locked up? And how does the dad feel about all this? I'm afraid you've got a lot more writing to do before breakfast tomorrow . . . after you finish your letter to Daddy, of course."

"Breakfast tomorrow?" It wasn't even dinnertime today and I was starving. "Can I have a snack first?" I asked, trying to look as hungry as possible.

"I'll bring you a plum, and that's it until you finish your letter, Princess." My mother closed the door behind her. She returned with one purple plum on a tiny white plate, placed it on the desk, and left. As I ate the plum in the glow of the gooseneck lamp, I looked around the telephone room, at the tablet on the desk and the No. 2 writing pencil, and realized it was a pretty good place to write a story, a whole bunch of stories, and maybe even a letter to my father.

* * *

As I moved through the elementary grades, I was never without my red-and-blue plaid book-pack with its deep pouch for Big Chief writing tablets and two front pockets stuffed with pencils and ballpoint pens, a perfect complement to my pleated Catholic school jumper. My classroom desk replaced the telephone room during the week, and slipping notes to my best friend Barbara during Sister Mary Elizabeth's lectures on the dangers of boys becoming aroused by the reflection of our undies in our black patent leather shoes, eclipsed letter writing.

Me:
    "Can't wait to put Vaseline on my shoes, so they'll reflect even more!"

Barbara:
    "I'm actually gonna glue mirrors on mine so I can see Sister M.E.'s panties when she walks by!!"

Me:
    "Yuck. Have fun staring at her *you-know-what.* Everyone knows nuns don't wear panties!!!"

By the time I reached high school, my writing room had become more portable. I wrote short stories on a typewriter in the school library, and poems in journals in the backseat of our Chevy while my mother bought fish on Fridays. I penned my own obituary leaning against a tombstone at the cemetery behind our church, and composed prayers in pews during Mass as our priest delivered his life-affirming homily. I once wrote the beginning of a sonnet in my head while paddling out on my surfboard at Malibu before a wave knocked me off.

Shall I compare thee to a 10-foot wave?

During college, my first husband, Gary, an artist and my high-school sweetheart, was accepted into a study abroad program and we moved to Florence, Italy, for a year. We lived in the basement apartment of a 14th century villa near Porta Romana. He painted in the kitchen, sometimes for days at a time, while I took lonely walks along the Arno River. In the doorless bedroom/living room/whatever-we-needed-it-to-be room next to the kitchen, I sat on a straw mattress writing gloomy poetry in my blue leather journal with gilded pages, purchased from a thief on the Ponte Vecchio. But the fumes from Gary's paint wafted into that eclectic space and made me feel drunk. He blasted *Jumpin' Jack Flash* a million times each day over our tiny stereo, which drove me so crazy I couldn't write, even with earplugs. Worse, our best friend, Tamio, a Japanese American sculptor with an Afro, arrived each afternoon with several bottles of chianti, drank himself into a stupor and passed out on my lap as he sprawled across our bed. I tried hard to write with my journal propped on his head, but Tamio's vino breath was too distracting.

I began to hang out in cafés and bars near our apartment, dreary, low-light places filled with cigarette smoke and the slap-tap of pissy smelling old men moving chess pieces across their boards. Here, the cappuccinos and wine were cheap and I could write in peace at a wobbly table that had probably been around since the Renaissance or earlier . . . maybe even occupied by Dante Alighieri himself! But then came lunchtime when a local younger man or two or ten, their mouths stuffed with twirled balls of spaghetti and drunk on Nastro Azzurro beer, would discover the American blonde sitting in the corner. Their whistles and propositions and laughter would force me to grab my journal and head to Chiesa dei Santi Apostoli, an almost unknown medieval church near the Arno River.

Santi Apostoli was a tiny Romanesque temple illuminated by flickering votive candles and, I imagined, haunted by the ghost of Michelangelo whom I'd read had fought for its preservation. Being almost always empty, Santi Apostoli had the atmosphere of monastic silence I craved. I would hide in the shadows behind one of its marble pillars, my back leaning against the arm of a pew, my sockless feet resting on wood polished by centuries of worshipers like Blessed Villana who turned to prayer after seeing a horrific dragon in the same mirror in which she had admired herself one too many times. There, undisturbed, I wrote in my journal and when an idea for a short story or poem came to me with the ferocity of a vision, I would glance over at the painting of fat baby Jesus in his Virgin Mama's lap. Once, I swear, she smiled at me, extended her hand and said, "You're welcome!" in a voice that sounded like a dove cooing.

* * *

Thirty years after Florence, our daughter drove her red Volvo north to begin pre-med studies at the University of Alaska. Gary and I sobbed in the driveway as she pulled away, and a few days later hauled a large travel trailer filled with household essentials—red licorice, peanut butter, surfboards, and running shoes, about 300 books and our thirteen-year-old son—south to a fishing village near Puerto Vallarta, Mexico. We quickly found an apartment and enrolled our boy in the American School. The trailer, which we parked in a beach court once owned by Elizabeth Taylor and Richard Burton, was directly across the cobblestones from our apartment and became the room in which I wrote each morning. But, as in Florence, there were complications. In this case it was my neighbor.

As I sat at a small table by the window, drinking Nescafé and writing in thick spiral binders about arroyos filled with baby diapers and the proliferation of scorpions along the Bahía de Banderas, I noticed that Jim, the Hawaiian-shirted, crew-cutted American in his early sixties who lived next door, had a curious daily routine. Each morning, he received a different young woman into his trailer for an hour, and then she would leave. The woman was invariably Mexican, in her mid-twenties, and gorgeous. Maybe I should have been minding my own business, but I found the comings and goings unsettling. One day, Jim knocked on my door.

"Do you want to come over for a beer?" he asked, staring at my boobs, when I opened the door.

"You mean like the women who come to your trailer each day, Jim? No, thanks. I need to be writing, not fooling around."

Jim looked up. He studied my lips for a second. I looked at his hairy chest. He hadn't bothered to re-button his Hawaiian shirt after today's visitation. I couldn't wait for him to go away. "It's not what you think," he said. "Those girls are my Spanish tutors."

I rolled my eyes. "A different one each day? That's some special tutoring, Jim."

Turned out, my suspicions were not entirely imaginary. The "girls" *were* teaching Jim Spanish and he was teaching them English, but they were also supplying Jim with large quantities of *mojo*, or pot, which he, in turn, sold to the local expats at inflated prices. Jim and the gorgeous young women were making a bundle on this enterprise until the local drug mafia showed up with machetes and threatened to feed his brains to the herd of hammerheads circling the bay. Jim flew back to Los Angeles the next day, and I found a quiet little studio on the grounds of our apartment complex with a view of the sea. Miraculously, the sale of our trailer more than covered the rent. In that sweet room, there was an air conditioner that, when it worked, kept me from melting and walls covered with dozens of chirping geckos. There was even a tiny refrigerator to keep my Pacificos and lime chilled, and a toilet that only broke twice.

One afternoon when it was cool enough to open the window, a confused, raven-black, multilingual *zanate* flew into the room. I'd heard the story about how the *zanate*, being created without a voice, stole songs from the sea turtle and one of them was about rage. This explains why the bird slammed into the walls of my studio squawking something like, "What are you going to write about? Get going! *¿Qué vas a escribir? ¡Ándale!*" until I committed my hands to the keyboard and wrote the first words of my novel, *Gringa Tales.* And then she flew out.

When Rosi woke up, the first thing she noticed was she wasn't sweating.

Not one gotita. *She was on her back, watching the sky pink up through the* parota *trees, but there was no sensation of heat on her face and no salty, stinging dampness under her breasts.*

* * *

It's 5:00 AM and still dark as my flashlight beam bounces through the gauzy fog hanging over the garden path to Ravens Roost, the small cottage my second husband, Robert, built for me several years ago. The Roost, named just after my mother died when two ravens soared over our backyard one morning as we pinched out tomato suckers, takes up much of the middle of our garden. It resembles a Japanese teahouse we discovered in one of Robert's architecture books, basically a cube of cedar walls with paned windows on all four sides and a sloped cedar shake roof that looks like a rice farmer's straw hat covered with grapevines. If I look carefully, I can just make out the half-barrels of staked tomatoes and wooden boxes of bell peppers, carrots, and the ubiquitous tendrils of Chinese lanterns that seem to grow a foot or more each night.

I hear a familiar rustle coming from the grapevines.

I open the door, flip on the heater and the Shogi lamp, and grab my purple shawl from its hook below the framed and illustrated poem I wrote about a squirrel for a local writing contest. I plug in my electric kettle, boot up my computer, and sit at my black triangle of a desk wedged in a corner between two windows. On the wall above my desk, *La Mano*, a large framed poster of a hand, waves at me. The image is from a Mexican lottery card that I first encountered on a restaurant tablecloth in our fishing village when Gary and I drove our Volkswagen camper bus around Mexico searching for the perfect wave and/ or place to live. Back then, I was silly enough to think the hand might have something to do with the famous Zen koan, "What is the sound of one hand clapping?" Today, though, the only hand sound I'll hear will be my own fingers tapping computer keys.

When the water gurgles and the kettle shuts off, I steep oolong tea in the celadon green cup I found at the jade market in Taipei, where my son now lives. I take a sip, and immediately a raspy raven voice pops into my head.

"You're late."

"Don't you ever sleep?" I ask her, pretty sure I'm just talking to myself.

"Don't you ever write? Hey, check out that black cat."

There's a small porch with a loveseat outside the window to the left of my desk. The black cat from two doors down is perched there now, staring at me. She comes nearly every day. What does she see through those thin slits in her yellow eyes? I stare back at her and meow as though I speak Cantonese, until I feel twitchy, like she's looking into my soul, knows my secrets, is controlling my mind. When I can't take it anymore I growl like a lion and jump out of my chair. She leaps off the porch. I get to work on a poem.

> *Black cat*
> *stopped by this morning*
> *tried to steal my soul*
> *with her eyes*
> *again.*

"That sucks," the voice in my head croaks. "You've got this

beautiful cottage that most writers would kill for, and all you can come up with is a five-liner about a cat. Jeeze!"

"Thanks for the encouragement," I tell her, taking another sip of my tea. It's cold.

"You're welcome," she says, but her voice is sweeter now, kind and patient. More like the dove I heard cooing in that small church in Italy.

"Hey! Wait a minute! I've heard your voice before," I say. But before I can spit out a flurry of profound and probing questions about muses and virgins and why I wake up in the middle of the night with an asteroid shower of images shooting through my mind, my hands begin to type as if they have a mind of their own, and something new to say.

When I was six, we lived in a large English Tudor house in Detroit with a ballroom on the third floor.

Susan Chase-Foster writes poetry and magical realism in her backyard cottage in Bellingham, Washington, in coffee cafés in Fairbanks, Alaska, and in teahouses in the hills above Taipei. Her work has appeared in Clover, Peace Poets, Noisy Water, *and* Cirque *among other publications, and she is a two-time winner of the Sue C. Boynton Poetry Contest. Susan is currently working on a collection of poems and photographs from Taiwan. She blogs at* stilllifewithtortillas.com.

Thank you, Grace Paley

Barbara Clarke

*There is
no good in the world except out of
a woman and certain women
for certain things.*

William Carlos Williams,
To A Friend Concerning Several Ladies

IMAGINE, GRACE PALEY IN MY KITCHEN!

Well, not exactly *my* kitchen. It was during a writers' workshop in the Rowe Conference Center's kitchen in western Massachusetts. The Center was basically an old house expanded to host weekend events for a limited number of people.

In the mid-1980s phase of my writing life I attended most workshops by getting dishpan hands.

"The kitchen is all yours this weekend," the facility manager said in an overly cheerful voice when I arrived early Saturday morning. "Your coworker canceled at the last minute."

The fact of being so broke I couldn't afford a workshop fee at age forty was discouraging. It only took a few minutes sitting in a classroom to make me not care how I got there. I had dropped out of corporate life to become a writer and took any job, performed any chore, in order to learn the craft.

It was late and I was tired of working in the steamy kitchen where the old appliances and grimy open shelving looked like they'd never been wiped clean. I was hurrying to put the last dishes away and turning off the overhead light when I heard a faint knock on the doorframe. *Oh, now what*, I thought, *someone who just has to have a cup of tea before they could possibly go to sleep.*

I wasn't feeling that kindly. Besides, I had my notes to copy from Grace Paley's craft talk that afternoon and was still captivated by her after-dinner reading from her new book *Later That Same Day.*

"I'm so sorry to bother you," *the* Grace Paley said, standing in the doorway. She was backlit by the hall light and looked even more petite, barely filling the doorway. "I see the kitchen's closed. I was hoping that they left the makings of tea out. I'm sorry to bother you. I know it's late."

"Oh, it's not too late for you," I said, turning the light back on and offering her a seat at a small wooden table. "Please. Tea it is."

"Yes, but only if you'll join me." Suddenly, lingering in the kitchen seemed like winning a literary prize, but what could I possibly have to say to Grace Paley, a goddess among feminist writers and not one to mince words?

We managed a bit of conversation about the writing assignment and why there weren't more men at workshops, and then switched to how strange it was to have an aging nuclear power plant next door. She had noticed the unnerving and unmistakable towers on her drive up to the Center.

"I know all about nuke plants," she said. "Too cheap to meter is what they touted. I've got one in my backyard in Vermont, too." We both shook our heads in mutual misgivings.

"Ms. Paley, what kind of tea would you like?"

"It's Grace," she said, tapping the box of chamomile that was one of the many choices in the wicker basket I set on the table. "Does it bother you to live next door to a nuke plant?"

I told her about the picture in the local paper of the seven-leaf clover the plant's security guard had found. Only the kettle's whistle brought us back to why she was in my kitchen. I found two unchipped mugs that were free of mundane sayings like HANG IN THERE and silently sipped the steaming tea.

Up close, animated by the topic, she looked just like the picture I had seen of her wearing her knitted HELL NO! cap with her wiry gray hair sticking out. She was so many people sitting across from me—the famous writer, ardent feminist, community advocate, and friend for the time we had together in the kitchen. I didn't want her to leave. I asked her what advice she would give to a beginning writer.

"Here's the answer I always give out. You become a writer because you need to become a writer. You're on the right track by working at places like this. You're not likely to ever make a lot of money as a writer."

I tried to take in every word, and then I stumbled. I was embarrassed—no, mortified—that I'd never read any of her books, and spooned more sugar into my mug, forgetting that I'd already done so. I could see *The Little Disturbances of Man* sitting on my bookshelf in my apartment, a gift from a friend who said, "You have to read this," but I had never made the time for it.

"Learn your craft," she said. "Send things out and get used to rejection. It's all part of the process. Sooner or later, if you keep working at it, you'll start to get published."

While I refilled her mug, I tried to imagine seeing a book I'd written on a bookshelf. She brushed a few crumbs that I'd missed off the table and turned her bright searching eyes on me.

"What are you writing?" she asked.

I did some verbal handwringing—"Oh, I'm just getting started writing fiction . . . Only write for the local alternative newspaper"—until I screwed up enough courage.

"I was working on a collection of family stories until I was advised to stop," I said.

"Who told you to do that?" Her voice deepened in anger, the anger I had been too demoralized to feel for myself. Her eyes held mine, her small presence rising to fill the chair. "Has this person seen your work?"

"No. I didn't get that far."

"Well then, how could he or she say that?"

I told her how a professor from an MFA program in the Midwest had prescreened me by phone for his program.

"When I told him that I was working on family stories, he stopped me and said, 'That's domestic fiction and it's over.' "

"Oh, fuck him," she said. "Typical. What he thinks is irrelevant. You have to be faithful to the stories that stick with you. These are the ones you need to write. We can always use well-written family stories that connect writers with readers. Just keep going."

Somehow it was important to me that she not see how teary I was out of relief and encouragement, and busied myself straightening the tea packages in the basket. I didn't dare look up until the waterworks behind my eyes had subsided.

"Well," she said, "I've delayed you long enough. That was a lovely cup of tea and a chat. Good night and thanks."

"Oh, no, thank you." I was so choked with feelings I could hardly breathe. Maybe I said, "Goodnight, Grace," but more likely I said "Goodnight, Ms. Paley."

While I hurriedly washed out our teacups and closed up the kitchen, *keep going* played in my head like a mantra given by a sage. I turned off the light and dashed to my room, working late into the night on a new family story.

Months later I found a quote from Grace Paley and wrote it on a small card and taped it to my monitor: *Write what will stop your breath if you don't write.*

Of all the tips and advice I've received over the years, that quote is what I take out and tape to my monitor whenever I start a new writing project. Thanks, Grace.

Barbara Clarke works as a freelance grant writer and has written extensively for corporate clients, trade magazines, and newspapers on a variety of topics. Her memoir, Getting to Home: Sojourn in a Perfect House, *was published in 2009. "How Many Writing Books Does It Take to Write a Novel, Memoir, Nonfiction or Something besides an Annual Holiday Letter?" appeared in the 2010 debut issue of* Line Zero, *a literary arts magazine. Her personal essay, "Good Vibrations," will be published in the online magazine* Full Grown People *this fall. She is currently completing a novel,* Breathing Room, *which includes socially* *relevant topics of the health insurance industry, the pre- and post-*Feminine Mystique *generations, and the many ways of love. She uses Beckett's "Ever tried. Ever failed. No matter. Try again. Fail again. Fail better," as her personal and writing guide.*

Garden-Variety Grace

Victoria Doerper

O marvelous! what new configuration will come next?
I am bewildered with multiplicity.

William Carlos Williams, *At Dawn*

A SMALL SEA OF GREEN SURROUNDS OUR TWELVE-HUNDRED-SQUARE-FOOT
saltbox cottage near the shore of the Salish Sea. If you stand
with me on the flagstones, a thousand splashes of color in
hues of green, umber, gold, scarlet, and sapphire wash over
us like an Impressionist painting. You may have difficulty at
first in seeing the picture while you stand close to the thickly
bedaubed details. Where do the chartreuse hazelnut leaves end
and the greeny-gold grape leaves begin? Does that branch to
your left have as its parent the katsura tree reaching across the
front walk, or is it part of the ginkgo tree twirl of branches that
rise before you?

If you could somehow magically sprout wings and soar up
into the clear summer sky, you would have the same view as the
gulls, terns, and great blue herons that glide over our house,
and you would see a small grey expanse of smooth roof encir-
cled by an infinite texture of trees. Looking down from that vantage point, you might parse the pricking tops of the bamboo in
the back yard from the round swell of magnolia canopy above
the back deck. You'd be able to see our eastside neighbor's stiff
ponderosa pine keeping company with our own pliant wutong
tree that flashes candy-green leaves as large as platters. You'd
notice the soft puffy shapes of the cherry, hazelnut, pear, and
apple trees that float like low-hanging pale green clouds above
the front yard.

Nearer the street you couldn't help but take in the feathery
teal of the towering sequoia, grown tall from a four-inch-high

seedling my husband bought for a dollar twenty-five from the Georgia Pacific nursery in Fort Bragg, California, and which he patted into our streetside soil many years ago. And as long as you have wings, you might as well perch in one of the topmost sequoia branches and rest for a while, enjoying the warm sun on your back, watching the lush sway of the star magnolia below, or turn to take in the far view of the Salish Sea two blocks away. As you moved from one vantage point to another, you would come to learn more about the garden as it looks today. But no perch would help you see back in time, where stories always start.

My husband's childhood in Germany spawned this Pacific Northwest garden. He was born in a jewel box of a town, the baroque Bavarian city of Würzburg, where the intersection of time and place couldn't have been less auspicious. This city on the Main River, between Frankfurt and Nuremberg, was one of the final casualties of World War II, and like Dresden, was swept into the last circle of firebombing targets. On March 16, 1945, at 9:30 PM, three hundred and eighty thousand bombs and fiery incendiaries rained down in a precise and terrible synchronized pattern for maximum destructive impact. In seventeen minutes, the time it would have taken to hard cook an egg, the terror-bombing raid laid waste to ninety percent of the town.

My husband, not yet two years old, was receiving treatment for diphtheria, and was buried under the rubble of a hospital. A week and a half later, the patients were finally pulled from under the debris and out into a traumatized world.

With their home destroyed, my husband's parents eventually found shelter for their family in an abandoned anti-aircraft barracks on a hill overlooking their ruined town. Here in a small, stark building they set up housekeeping with my husband's aunt and her son. In the spring, sloe trees on the hilltop near their dwelling exhaled clouds of white blossoms, and rabbits nibbled nearby. Down the slope, a swath of Silvaner grapevines cascaded toward the river, the ripe grapes like little treasures for the future harvest, crush, and making of wine.

So important were the post-war vineyards that security guards patrolled the plots to protect them from hungry intruders who might slip in and strip the vines of their precious grapes.

When my husband talks about these times, he tells of rubble-filled streets, the desolate look of the bombed-out buildings in town, the swastika still painted on one of the walls he passed as his father walked him to school, the sound of tanks crawling across the land, the guns of occupying forces held at the ready. He seems happiest when he recollects the taste of the Mirabelle plums from his grandfather's leased garden, the wildness of woods, and the hillside vineyards. He talks with most animation and enjoyment about the vineyard on the slope below his anti-aircraft barracks home.

The young boy longed to be in that vineyard, thirsted after the grapes whose heavy perfume wafted in tantalizing breezes across the slopes. And in that vineyard he found solace and sustenance. He was hungry for so many things.

With vigilant security guards walking the vineyard rows, eyes out for interlopers, stealth was required for successful illicit harvesting of grapes. But with the ingenuity and speed of an intelligent small boy, he learned to dart past the vineyard perimeters without detection. The secret to eluding capture once in the plot was to quickly scoot under the vines and their spreading leaves, then lie face up and hidden from view.

I imagine his little heart beating fast as he ran in search of a central sheltering vine, and I can almost feel the heartbeats slowly thumping back to normal as he caught his breath and gazed upward, sky now a blur of green and gold. I can almost see the little boy surrounded by the thick scent of ripening grapes, the soft drape of their leaves, the sun dappling the vines, the earth warm, solid, and imperturbable beneath him. In that quiet, peaceful world, he could shake grapes free from the ripe golden clusters dangling just above his open mouth. He could eat as much as he wanted, eat until the juice ran down his cheeks like sweet tears, eat until he was full.

When we found this cottage and land twenty years ago, after

many months of searching, we rejoiced in the quiet location near meandering trails through parks and woods. Our new place tucked into a neighborhood of small lots in a lower-income area on the verge of the sea, nestled at the foot of hill properties adorned by larger houses with sweeping views of the bay. The neat and compact cottage, a one-and-a-half-story structure, had a view, too. Upstairs in the master bedroom, if I leaned to the right while looking out of the dormer window, I could catch a glimpse of the sea by squinting through a thin slot between the condominiums across the street. But even an impressive view of the sea would have held no interest for my husband. He wanted a house surrounded by a green cloistering garden.

The yard looked forlorn, with a ragged lawn in the company of a few malingering shrubs and an ailing tree. When my husband and I first walked through the front yard, we noticed the absence of birds, the silence a kind of hollowness as the still air folded in around itself. Thin rhododendron bushes drooped dispiritedly near the street, and a few day lilies backed up against the house as if cowering in fear of some clumsy, ignorant hand. The backyard showed a little more pluck, with one valiant wild rose displaying fat scarlet hips and a hint of flowers to come.

On the very first day we moved in, my husband planted a ginkgo tree in the front yard. The small transplant stood spindly and crooked, blinking dazedly into the early afternoon sun, looking lonely and out of place. But my husband has ever been a man compelled to stick things in the ground and cajole them to live. And because he places great store in the history and symbolic nature of things, the first planting of this particular tree was anything but random.

Like all the things of this earth, the ginkgo, too, has a story. As you wander with me a little to our left, along the flagstone path, you'll meet our ginkgo, now a foot thick and thirty feet tall after twenty years of living here. Look up, and you can see the healthy spread of fan-shaped leaves gracing our garden clerestory and reaching toward the heavens. If you run your hands over the light ridging of rough gray-brown bark on the trunk, you may feel the distant vibration of our tree's progenitors, who once gazed down upon roaming herds of dinosaurs, the creatures who dispersed ginkgo seeds far and wide. Ancestors of this tree stood witness to staggering transformations of the earth's journey through the breakup of continents, the struggles and death of plant and animal species, the endless incremental evolution of man, and the evils and miracles of messiahs, saints, disciples, and fools.

Botanically, our lonely little transplant is a relic with no close kin, bridging a gap between the "lower" order of ferns and the "higher" order of conifers. The ginkgo is the only family member left—the only species in the genus, the only genus in the family, the only family in the order, the only order in the subclass. Though all the close relatives have succumbed and are now extinct, this undaunted one has managed to endure. The oldest tree living in our time is in China, about three thousand five hundred years old, with a sure heartwood that must be full of lessons and wisdom. Perhaps that's why Confucius chose to sit under a ginkgo when he taught.

Our own less-experienced relic seems to be happy here as we stand under its summer abundance of tea-green leaves. If we had been born and grown up in Asia, we would have learned as children that this tree is revered for endurance, longevity, strength, and hope. And we probably would have played with the leaves, twirling them by their stems, fanning the two lobes, watching the separateness in the unity, the yin and the yang. Perhaps we would have walked by the wise old ginkgoes as we entered a temple or shrine, because so many eastern places of holiness join their spirits and share their land with this ancient tree.

My husband claimed our garden and home with this ginkgo. Four ginkgo trees survived the 1945 bombing of Hiroshima, victims of the same war that my husband survived. Is it any wonder that this tree was the first for a child of war to plant as a stake in his new home territory?

After planting the ginkgo, my husband commenced digging into our new land, his goal to discover what type of soil might lie beneath the wan and tattered lawn. What he unearthed, as he poked and prodded out in the yard day after day, was compact clay soil studded with unexpected bits from human predecessors—a small, thick-glassed apothecary bottle, minus the cork; errant shards of blue-and-white porcelain. We learned that this humble three-street neighborhood had sustained many of our town's sawmill and cannery laborers in the 1800s and, indeed, represented the only area Chinese workers were allowed to live. Community leaders at that time forbade this undesirable foreign influence from infiltrating the center of town. A few blocks up the shore-side street paralleling our own, a stone marker denotes the exact boundary beyond which the Chinese workers could not step.

Those early residents lived simple and hard—grueling, loud, and stinking manual labor in the mills and fish canneries. Workers slogged through the seasons, trying to stay healthy so they could keep sending money home to families depending upon their toil. They carried on daily lives in a grinding routine, confined to the unwanted fringe of town, but with hopes and dreams for their families, despite the ill will that swirled, crested, and broke over them daily like the tide.

I like to believe that on an early summer evening here in the late 1800s, some young Chinese man walking home from a long day of work, sweaty, aching, and tired, looked up and was surprised by the tenderness of the sky, felt the soft breath of the wind on his face, saw the fresh rush of the incoming tide bathing the purple sea stars, and walking on, that he found comfort in the firm support of green land beneath his feet. I hope that he put on this beauty like a coat, protection from the grime of bigotry and discrimination. I like to believe he tended a tiny garden in our neighborhood, and found relief in the company of lacey ferns and the small hard buds of plum trees opening into fragrant pink blossoms.

My husband always finds relief and comfort in this garden. If you sit with me on the stone bench in our small, thickly green place, you may feel the sheltering arms of the land wrapping about us, encircling our world with sparrows fluttering through the katsura branches, squirrels scampering down the ginkgo trunk in search of peanuts, the fragrance of golden honeysuckle, bright pink of blooming rhododendron, and surely at least ten thousand other growing things, breathing in and out together with us. You may forget for a time your heartaches, worries, and wounds as you melt into this rich and close cosmos of detail, becoming for a few moments part of the multihued community of our fellow plants and creatures who are making their way in the world, too.

Our companions are not homogenous members of a species, but individuals whose spirits animate their specific cellular constellations. They have their own idiosyncrasies and scars, those distinctive marks the world makes upon bodies and psyches. We'll see the jay with the broken wing feather swoop in, or the one with the missing tail feathers, an intrepid survivor who now perches on the magnolia above the back deck and screams for peanuts. "Girly," the old raccoon with the milky blind eye, wanders in with confidence laced with subtle caution, but "Foxy" will always spook and sprint at any sudden sound, then slyly tiptoe back to drink, two feet plunged in the water tub, before finally sauntering away, leaving delicate raccoon footprints to dry on the deck.

Our plants are distinct individuals, too. The wutong tree near the eastern fence lists to one side because the big windstorm tore away the balancing branches last fall. The tall bamboo stalks along the alley tilt low into our south backyard ever since the snow last winter bent them down beyond their capacity to bounce back.

The garden is a mixed and changing swirl of burgeon and wane, and we ourselves grow, rejoice, and struggle along with it. Through our vulnerabilities and scars, we connect with one another as kin here in this yard's close quarters. We find the grace to make peace with all that's gone before. We take heart, too, in the exuberance, triumph, and dignity of the beautiful and wounded present we inhabit. Here we glimpse exultation, acceptance, and the brave endurance of the world. What more can be asked of a garden?

Victoria Doerper is a Bellingham writer of memoir, nonfiction, and poetry. Her poetry appears in Sue C. Boynton 2013 Winning Poems; Noisy Water: Poetry from Whatcom County, Washington; Clover: A Literary Rag, *and* Cirque. *Her prose appears in* Orion Magazine. *She is currently writing a memoir,* My Husband's Garden.

Injustice

Seán Dwyer

Sorrow is my own yard
where the new grass
flames as it has flamed
often before but not
with the cold fire
that closes round me this year.
  William Carlos Williams, *The Widow's Lament in Springtime*

MOM WAS SICK AGAIN, AND MY HEART ACHED FOR HER.

She had taken to her bed on New Year's weekend a year ago, and she had gone to the hospital for a week in March. In July, an ambulance took her away in the morning, and she was gone for another week. Dad threw away a bunch of empty pill bottles then.

This year, we canceled Christmas dinner because I brought chicken pox home from school. My younger sisters and I shed our remaining scabs in time to return to our babysitter, Mrs. Daimler, after New Year's Day. Mrs. Daimler had taken care of us the whole year Mom was sick, except when school was out.

Dad was at work already when I started organizing today's trek across the street to Mrs. Daimler's house. The sun had just risen, and yet, when I checked the weather through the picture window, its glare on the snow struck my eyes. Purple spots made it hard for me to see Beth's coat to zip it. She couldn't do it herself, even though she was seven, two years younger than I was. Zipping it was like tying the legs of a stuffed turkey. Once she was set, I turned and helped Karen and Kelly tie their boots. At four, they didn't have many dressing skills.

Now came the hard part of the routine. "I'm going to check on Mom one last time. Don't walk on the carpet." The girls nodded gravely. I hoped I could get back before they overheated or started to bicker. I stepped over the toys they had scattered while I cooked their oatmeal, trotted down the hall, and slipped into Mom's room. Here, it was still so dark that the sun might not have risen. I kissed her cheek. Her skin was cool, yet sweaty, her light-brown hair flat against her head. She hardly left her bed, but the whole room smelled like her. Not just up close, like when I used to come in and snuggle in the morning, but everywhere. And now the room smelled just a little bit like the locker room where I changed to play basketball. She stirred and mumbled something, maybe my name. I checked the level of her water glass; she hadn't touched it since last night. Her pill bottle, orange with a white cap, was half-full of blue-and-yellow capsules.

Her eyes opened. They were green, like mine. I always saw my eyes reflected in hers, and it made me happy. But now hers were bloodshot and glassy.

"Do I have water?" Her voice was creaky, but her words were clear.

"Yes, Mom."

"Can you make me a piece of toast?"

"Sure." My heart raced; I could actually do something for her. I took the plate that had held her toast from last night. On the way to the kitchen, I told the girls what she wanted. They accepted the delay with grace. It was going to be a good day.

I made the toast, spread Chiffon on it, and felt my way back down the unlit hall. I didn't want the light shining in her eyes. "Here it is."

"Thanks. Are the girls ready to go to Mrs. Daimler's?"

"Yes. Do you want me to bring you a second glass of water?"

"I'll get one if I need it." I hoped she wouldn't try. She could barely walk when her medicine was in her system.

"Do you need me to call Dr. Mason today?" Dr. Mason was Mom and Beth's psychiatrist. Beth flew into rages sometimes. I figured Mom went so she could learn how to help Beth.

"I have an appointment with her Monday. Have a good day."

She fell asleep in an instant, her toast untouched. I tiptoed to the bedroom door and looked back. Her clothes lay in heaps on the floor, like a string of white hills. There were a couple of books on the dresser, next to her collection of tiny ceramic horses. One book was *Valley of the Dolls*. The cover showed capsules like the ones Mom took every day. Her alarm clock ticked slowly, as if time ran differently in this room.

When I reached the living room, Karen was clomping in tight circles on the plastic runner by the door. "I'm hot," she whispered. I slammed my boots on.

"I know. We'll cool off outside," I said.

After Beth and the twins stepped out, I closed the front door and made sure the screen door shut tightly. I led the girls down the sidewalk, which was rough with graying snow. When I shoveled the walk, sometimes I missed spots, and they froze. Maybe today would be warm enough for me to scrape off the ice.

They scuffed their boots on the gravel drive. I reminded them to stop at the street to look both ways. Beth was hyper at the best of times, and the twins were not yet in school. I worried that they would get run over someday.

Once we crossed the street, we walked up the clean, dry concrete driveway of the Daimler house. Mr. Daimler had a snow blower. I knocked on the door, and Mrs. Daimler opened it a second later.

"Good morning, kids," she said. "Oh, it's not so cold today."

We stepped in, sat, and removed our boots in the foyer. My left shoe and sock got stuck in the boot, and Beth giggled. The ceramic tile by the front door was cold on my bare foot. I dug around and fished out my sock, but I left the shoe inside my boot. I wouldn't need it until five o'clock.

"Did you eat already?" Mrs. Daimler asked. She looked really tall from where I was sitting.

"I made oatmeal for us."

"Good, Seán. I'll make you some toast if you want it."

"Thanks." I beckoned to Beth and the twins. "Come on."

We sat at the dining-room table, where the two Daimler girls,

Mary and Nancy, were having toast and chocolate milk. They didn't stir the chocolate powder into their milk; they scooped it off the top and drank the milk white. Mrs. Daimler always gave me and the girls just white milk. I tried not to stare at the chocolate powder as it disappeared into the Daimler girls' mouths.

Mrs. Daimler served the toast. It always smelled good, but I liked more margarine on mine. I used my finger to smear the three melting pats farther out.

"Maybe about ten o'clock you kids can go play," Mrs. Daimler said. "It's supposed to hit forty-five today."

Beth clapped her hands. *Forty-five?* I thought. In two hours, I'd be out in the sun. I chewed my toast and imagined the warmth on my face.

I had a book in my coat pocket, so I pulled Saki out and sat on the couch to read. I had ordered the book from the Scholastic flyer in the fall. Mrs. Berg had said it was more appropriate for sixth-graders, but she knew I had read all of the fourth-grade books in the school library. I laughed a lot at the story about the talking cat.

Mrs. Daimler sat next to me, and I jumped. "Do you want to go for a walk with the girls?"

"Yeah!" I set down the book and joined the girls, who were in various stages of readiness. I zipped Beth's coat and helped the twins pull on their boots. I stuck my foot into my boot and managed to get my shoe on without having to dig it out. When I had all of my winter gear on, I zipped Karen's coat and tied her hood. She smiled at me.

"This will be fun," she said.

"Yep."

We all stepped outside. The sun shone even more blindingly than before. The air had added a hint of moist earth to its sterile winter scent. The blanket of snow had melted into white islands, but the water that separated them was green, not blue, glinting like strings of cold, fiery emeralds. I stretched my mittened hands to the sky and jumped in the air. The girls chattered among themselves.

"First, we'll go to the gas station for some candy," Mary said. She was eleven, and she always chose what we would do. I had hoped we would take saucers to the hill and do some sledding. But a candy bar was okay, too.

"Sounds good. Let's go!" I said. I started across the yard, energized by the sun. The girls were still talking.

"Don't run ahead of us, Seán!" Mary called.

I heard Beth splash her way up to me. "Yeah, don't run, Fatso!" She punctuated each syllable by pounding me on the back. Four electric jolts ran through my limbs.

I turned and pushed her arms away and yelled, "Cut it out!"

She reeled backward and landed on her butt in the snow. She jumped to her feet, her blue eyes blazing. "I'm telling!"

"So am I." I crossed my arms and waited as she stomped back to the porch and opened the door. With Beth, it was always something. She stepped on my neck once and suffocated me. Another time, she went into the shed and put her leg through a storm window. Now, she was going to get us grounded.

Mrs. Daimler stuck her head out the door. Beth started to sniffle. "Mrs. Daimler, my butt's wet because Seán pushed me down."

Mrs. Daimler's mouth dropped open. "Seán! Did you push her?"

I stepped onto the porch. "Yeah, but she hit me on the back, really hard. So I pushed her, and she fell."

She turned to Beth. "Beth, did you hit Seán?"

"No."

I stared at her. She'd never lied like that before. "Yes, you did."

"No, Mrs. Daimler, I didn't hit him." Beth didn't look at me.

"You said, 'Don't run, Fatso' and pounded on my back. Four times."

Mrs. Daimler shook her head. "Why would she call you 'Fatso' when you're so skinny? All right, Seán, you come inside. Girls, you can go on and play."

I stepped into the house. "She hit me. It's not fair."

"You shouldn't push her anyway."

"But she should be inside too." Mrs. Daimler didn't settle problems the way Mom did. Beth would be inside with me if Mom had anything to say about it.

"She says she didn't hit you. Now, sit down, and you can read your book." I took off my boots. This time, both shoes came out. I grabbed the book and sat in the corner of the living room on the floor. "Aren't you going to take off your coat?" Mrs. Daimler asked.

"It seems cold in here to me," I mumbled. Mrs. Daimler disappeared into the kitchen.

I read, frowning, for a few minutes, but I couldn't keep my mind on the story. I got up and went to the door. I was pulling on my shoes when Mrs. Daimler came around the corner.

"Where do you think you're going?"

"I'm going over to tell my mom about this."

Mrs. Daimler sighed. "Seán, you can't do that. Your mother is sick. She needs to sleep." I started tying my left shoe. "You are *not* going over there." I finished tying my left shoe and started on the right one. "Take off your shoes, Seán. *Now.*"

I looked up and saw anger on a face that was always pleasant. I stared at her as I slowly untied my shoe. I took them off and walked back to the corner. I sat by an end table. "It's not fair."

Mrs. Daimler stomped back into the kitchen. A moment later, I heard her on the phone. She returned to the living room. "Seán, I called your mother. She says that if you go over there she will spank you."

"No, she won't." I didn't look up from my book.

"You can tell her about this later. Just please don't bother her now. She's not handling stress well, and you know that."

"Because I brought home chicken pox, right?"

She hesitated. "That's part of it right now, maybe."

I read a couple of sentences over and over, wondering all the while if Mom would really spank me just for going over there.

She had hardly ever spanked me. It never hurt. She let Dad do it if he was home. If he was at work, she asked if I wanted my spanking then or later, from Dad. I always took it from her. Mrs. Daimler was probably exaggerating, anyway. Mom could barely stand, much less spank me hard. Even if she did spank me, I was willing to take it to make my point. This was the most unfair situation of my life.

I stood and tiptoed to the door. I was putting on my shoes again when the door popped open and the girls filed in, rosy-cheeked, giving off waves of cold.

I turned my back and sat again. Beth came over to me. "We had fun." I ignored her. "We went to the gas station, and I got M&Ms. I was going to buy you something, but Mary said you were being punished."

I closed the book and stared at the cover. A dark cloud settled over me. I always stood up for Beth when something happened at school. Now she was mocking me, and there was only one person I could trust to make things fair. Mom wouldn't spank me. Not for this.

The girls were wandering around the dining room, waiting for sandwiches. I walked quietly to the door and gathered my shoes yet again.

"Bye, Seán," Karen said. She waved.

"*Seán!*" Mrs. Daimler yelled. I dropped my shoes, opened the door, and ran out in my stocking feet. I heard Mrs. Daimler's angry words behind me as I ran across the yard, dodging snow and jumping from one soggy green patch to the next. My wet socks slapped on the asphalt of the street, and then I hit the welcoming grass of our yard. No one followed me. I gasped for air when I reached our front porch. I leaned on the wrought-iron railing and took several deep breaths before I opened the door.

I looked around the room at the beige carpet, the maple coffee table, the oak dining-room table, the Zenith console TV. I sat on the couch and removed my sopping socks. I tucked my feet under my legs to warm them. I would go wake Mom when I could feel my toes.

I heard slow, heavy footsteps in the hall. Mom, clad in a sleeveless nightgown that hung to mid-thigh, stopped before entering the living room and leaned on the wall, glaring at me. Her hair hung in her face, and I had never seen her look so old. She had always been slender, but now she looked bony. I didn't know how I had not noticed before.

"Hi, Mom," I said. I swallowed hard.

"I told Mrs. Daimler you were not to come over here."

"But Beth hit me, and I got in trouble for—"

"I know all that," she snapped. Her face flushed with rage, and she trembled. I thought she might fall, and I was going to run to her, but when I saw the look on her face, I realized that she was just furious. "And she told you what I would do if you came here." She wobbled across the living room, holding one hand behind her back. When she reached me, she showed her hand. She was grasping one of Dad's belts, the brown one he wore with his jeans. I was in for it. This one might hurt. Still worth it. I stood so she could spank me.

"Sit down," she said. I sat. Maybe she wasn't going to spank me.

She raised her hand. I saw the anger in her eyes, but there was no way she would hit me. Then she swung her arm back. Again, she wobbled, and I almost jumped to catch her. But her hand started forward, the belt unrolled like a snake, and that belt flew toward my mouth in slow motion. I heard the sizzle of the leather as it cut the air. The grain of the leather gained detail as it neared my face.

The belt caught me in the lips, and my head recoiled from the impact. Stunned, I couldn't duck as she followed up with a backhand swing at my mouth. One more forward swing, leather slapping my lips, and she dropped the belt.

"Now, get back over there," she said in a threatening monotone. She pointed to the door. She swayed before me, her arms crossed. I leaned forward slowly, so I wouldn't startle her, and reached for a sock. It seemed far away, and I cringed as I picked it up. She didn't hit me again, but her heavy breathing filled my ears. I wanted to wring out the sock, but I didn't dare. The icy water made my skin crawl, but I grabbed the other sock and slid it over my toes. Apart from the coldness on my feet, I felt fire on my face. I stood, head down, and padded out of the house. I closed the door, taking care not to bump it against the jamb.

Relief flooded me when the door clicked shut. She would go back to bed. The sun-heated concrete of the porch was the only comfort I had. I didn't want to go back across the street. I stared at the tree that stood before me, a yellow birch, leafless, lifeless. I could not think. I wanted to understand what had just happened, but I had no brain. So I just walked. I walked across the grass again, avoiding the snow, dreading the I-told-you-so I had waiting for me. My toes grew numb, then the soles of my feet. All I could feel was the throbbing in my lips.

To my left, the four elms still followed the property line. Mom used to panic when I climbed the elms. I remembered how careful she was then, keeping us safe. I wanted her to care about me again.

I crossed the street without looking. The asphalt was warmer than the grass, but the gravel in the street felt like dull points against my frozen skin. I walked up the Daimler lawn, around their weeping willow and onto the porch. Mrs. Daimler opened the door. I didn't have to knock.

I stepped inside and began to shiver, but not so much from the cold. The five girls stood looking at me. I felt my lips. They had swelled to the thickness of my thumbs. I pulled my hand away and saw blood on it. Mrs. Daimler looked scared, probably from the blood. Her face grew as red as Mom's. She reached to pull me to her, but I backed away.

"Oh, honey, she hit you in the face?"

I tried to smile, but my lips wouldn't stretch far enough. "Well, yeah. She hit me in the face with a belt."

"My God. I'm so sorry." She cleared her throat. "Seán, Beth told me she hit you hard. I'm sorry I didn't believe you."

Beth ran forward and hugged me, squeezing me tightly enough to make me grunt. I hugged her back.

"Can you wear some of Mary's socks?" Mrs. Daimler asked. "Your feet must be freezing. Sit on the couch. Mary, get Seán a towel and some white socks." Mrs. Daimler disappeared and returned with a washcloth. It was cool on my lips as she dabbed at them, and when she handed me the cloth, I realized there was an ice cube wrapped up in it. "The girls just had lunch. Do you want a sandwich?" she asked. She leaned toward me, her hands on her knees. I looked up, she held out her hands, and I let her hug me.

"Sure. But I don't know if I can eat with my lips like this."

"If you can't, I'll get you some broth. Ham?"

"Yes, please." I picked up my book again. Beth sat next to me and asked me to read to her, so I started reading "Sredni Vashtar" aloud. My words sounded mushy. I couldn't make *p* and *b* sounds.

Mrs. Daimler handed me my sandwich. I slid the sandwich between my lips and took a small bite, chewing slowly. After a couple of bites, Mrs. Daimler brought me a glass of milk and a spoon. Floating on top of the milk was a mound of brown powder. I thought for a minute, then I spooned one small lump of chocolate into my mouth and stirred the rest into the milk, the way Mom used to make it.

Seán Dwyer is a Spanish instructor at Western Washington University. He has won awards for short fiction and essays from the Philadelphia Writers' Conference, as well as from Chanticleer Book Reviews for a nonfiction manuscript and for his novel, Chocolates on the Pillow. *He has published extensively as a music journalist. His blog,* dwyercafe.com, *explores venues where he can follow one of his passions: Writing Out, be it alone or, preferably, with a group of writer friends. A native of Indiana, he is on the verge of becoming a longtime resident of Bellingham, Washington.*

An Azure Year

Marian Exall

And dost thou remember the orange and fig,
The lively sun and the sea breeze at evening?
William Carlos Williams, *Sicilian Emigrant's Song*

MEALS IN MY CHILDHOOD HOME IN THE INDUSTRIAL NORTH OF ENGLAND were nourishing, and came in a range of neutral tones: white (mashed potato and semolina), beige (gravy and suet pudding) or grey (tinned peas). Wartime rationing persisted into the fifties, as did the spirit of "making do" and "waste not, want not." Food was fuel, and its preparation a chore, not an art form.

Even after I left home, value and volume still mattered more to me than taste and presentation. By 1974, Graham and I were newlyweds playing house in Balham, a marginal neighborhood squeezed between up-and-coming Clapham and the West Indian ghetto of Brixton in southwest London. I laugh now when I think of us picking our way fastidiously through the ethnic street market, averting our eyes modestly from erotically shaped vegetables with unknown names, ignoring the aromatic enticement of jerk chicken roasting on an improvised oil drum barbecue, in order to purchase frozen fish sticks and instant mashed potatoes in the fluorescent glare of the local Sainsbury's supermarket.

The British newspapers labeled the early months of that year "the winter of our discontent." As well as more than usually depressing weather, a miners' strike resulted in frequent power black- and brownouts. Spring seemed a long way off; summer, an impossible dream. The advertisement in the Sunday paper for a financial auditor at a Westinghouse Electric plant in Nice looked like a shortcut to paradise, although we never imagined Graham would get the job. The position required a French speaker. We had both taken French to Advanced level at school, but seven years of irregular verbs and the ability to spout random quotes from Molière did not equip either of us to hold a conversation in colloquial French. However, nothing ventured, nothing gained, so he applied.

As it turned out, the American executive who interviewed my husband in the bar of the Hyde Park Hilton spoke no French. After multiple Scotches consumed before and during the meeting, he could barely speak English. Thus, it was not difficult for Graham to impress him with his *savoir faire*, and he landed the job at the princely annual salary of $16,000—about four times our joint income at the time.

A month or so later, we stumbled down the steps of the plane at the Nice airport, into dazzling sunshine. We couldn't believe our luck. Not only had we escaped the remnants of a dismal British winter, complete with economic crises, political unrest, and social malaise, but we were going to be paid handsomely to live on one of the most beautiful coasts in the world, with the blue of the Mediterranean at our feet and the grandeur of the Alpes-Maritimes at our back. Better still, until we found a place to live, we were to stay in a luxury hotel, all expenses paid.

The Sofitel was not one of the rococo *grandes dames* like the Negresco or the Metropole that face the sea from the Promenade des Anglais. Tucked away a block or so back, its quiet opulence thrilled me. Graham had to leave for work at some ungodly hour, but I could linger over a second bowl of coffee, brushing the last flakes of my croissant from the duvet. After dressing that first morning, I set out to explore the town, quickly finding that I preferred the twisting alleys of old Nice to the smart boutiques and boulevards behind the Promenade. I bought my lunch from a street vendor: a slice of *pissaladière*— onion tart striped with anchovies and studded with black olives. Then back to the Sofitel to work on my tan by the minuscule rooftop pool.

Graham returned to the hotel after work each day armed with restaurant recommendations from his new colleagues. One evening, we ate at *L'Esquinade*, reputed to be the best in Nice. It occupied an unimpressive house next to the port where the ferries to Corsica docked. I am ashamed to say I can't remember a thing we ate, as I spent most of the time staring at Aristotle Onassis dining at the next table with a woman who was *not* Jacqueline. He looked like an old brown tortoise, spoke little and very quietly, forcing the waiter and his companion to lean protectively toward him.

We bought a car: a one-year-old white Renault. Graham soon became adept at steering with his knees as he made emphatic and universally understood hand gestures to motorists who cut in or stole his parking space. It was amusing to see my mild-mannered accountant transform into a Gallic Godzilla once he donned his automobile armor. He also purchased a small "man-purse" to carry wallet, keys, and small change without ruining the line of his pants, which fitted closely over the *derrière* and flared at the ankle. He started wearing his shirt collar outside his jacket too. Although he had been more nervous about the move to France than I was, his daily immersion in the workplace quickly gave him confidence. I remained more obviously a foreigner.

But that would change once we moved into our castle! La Bastide, the name of an imposing mansion built for some English lord a century ago, *does* translate as castle. It sat on thirty acres of sweet-smelling Mediterranean pines and scrubby oaks high above the town of Beaulieu-sur-Mer, with stunning views over Cap Ferrat, and, on a clear day, all the way west to the Esterel Peninsula beyond Cannes. The current owner, Madame Sabin, had acquired it through one or other of her three former husbands. She now lived alone in the best suite, having divided up the other high-ceilinged rooms, added rooftop studios, and squeezed in sleeping lofts in order to maximize rental income. Our apartment was tucked away on a back corner of the building. I loved it, especially the balcony from which we could watch the craggy face of Cap d'Eze blush pink in the sunset's reflected light.

Françoise Sabin was a well-preserved seventy, with expensively coiffed hair in a shade of light brown that might have looked entirely natural on a woman thirty years her junior. She possessed excellent posture, allowing her to look down her nose at me, even though we were the same height. She was one of those Gorgons who have appeared from time to time in my life. They flirt with your husband and say acidly sweet things like "What an interesting color on you," then lean forward to inform you in a stage whisper that you have the teensiest brown stain on the back of your skirt. In the years since, I have learned to shrug these women off, but back then I was intimidated— sometimes to tears—by Madame Sabin's random cruelty.

When we first moved in, however, all was sweetness and light. She seemed eager to show us off to the friend who was staying with her at the time. Julia Harriman, an elderly lady with frothy white hair and merry blue eyes, was a member of a prominent New York family. While Mrs. Harriman was around, we were cooed over and spoilt like a pair of newly acquired puppies. At Madame Sabin's suggestion, the four of us went out to dinner at a restaurant in the mountains whose specialty was crayfish prepared à l'amoricaine, a spicy, garlicky rub that stained our fingers red. We never would have found the place on our own. Madame Sabin drove us in her ancient Mercedes, chatting animatedly with Julia in the front seat, as she swung the car around hairpin curves with utter disregard for other road users. After Mrs. Harriman returned to New York, Françoise made it clear she was now Madame to us. We were not to expect any further chummy excursions.

Life settled into a pleasant routine. Graham left early each morning to drive over the mountain to the Westinghouse plant at Ariane, the industrial hinterland behind Nice. I did some cursory housekeeping—our apartment covered only 400 square feet—and then set out with my basket down the hill to Beaulieu. La Bastide's lower driveway emerged onto a street opposite the cemetery, which, after a couple of turns, ended at a square where a market was held six days a week. On five of those days, this consisted of a few stalls selling produce from the little farms that clung to the south-facing hillsides toward Italy. On Fridays, other vendors appeared, displaying Provençal pottery and table linens, Italian leather purses and jackets, and immense pink satin brassieres. The stalls filled the square from the fruit and vegetable sellers at the lower end, up to the bandstand where an accordion group provided dance music for the citizenry on Bastille Day and other festivals.

I saved the market until last. First, I bought groceries, wine, and water at the tiny supermarket. Next I went to one of the three or four bakeries this town of about a thousand people supported. I was one of the few housewives who did not buy fresh bread twice a day. It was hard to resist breaking off a nubbin of crusty baguette to savor right there. I completed my order with two croissants or a small brioche for tomorrow's breakfast. The butcher's shop was located back at the market square. There was always a line, as the proprietor took great pride in helping his customers select exactly the cut of meat they needed for a particular recipe. I was intrigued to see him pacify a whining four-year-old with a wafer-thin slice of steak. The child sucked happily on the raw meat as if it were candy.

Finally, I crossed the street to browse the market: misshapen tomatoes big as boxing gloves, fennel, fava and green beans, tiny red potatoes, braids of garlic bulbs, a dozen different types of olives, peaches, plums, pears—not all at the same time, but a seasonally changing medley of color, shape, and smell. Having made my careful selections, I approached the vendor. I quickly learned that it is considered rude to offer your purchases to be weighed and paid for, without first engaging in a polite ritual of comments about the weather, the arrival of the apricots, or the end of artichoke season. This was equally true in the shops and restaurants: food was too important to hurry, whether you were buying, cooking, or eating. The exchange invariably ended with Madame tucking a handful of parsley or basil in with the purchases, a delightful grace note accompanied by a cheerful "*Bonne journée!*"

My basket now heavy, I fortified myself for the long climb back to La Bastide with a *pastis* at the Brasserie Beaulieu, conveniently located across the street. Even in winter, the weather permitted me to sit outside at a sidewalk table, so I could enjoy watching the market activity between scanning the headlines in *Nice-Matin*, the local paper.

Our daily routine continued with a picnic lunch. Graham had a two-hour break at midday, enough time to rush back to La Bastide and pick me up. We took our baguette sandwiches smeared with liver pâté, apples, perhaps a hunk of cheese, and certainly a bottle of wine, down to the beach in front of the casino, or, if the wind picked up, to the sheltered little harbor where we sat with our backs against a sun-warmed stone wall. After the tourists went home at the end of August, we got to know other lunchtime habitués by sight. Two women *d'un certain âge* sunbathed topless with religious determination no matter what the temperature. One had hair the improbable crimson that French women favor, while the other was a bleached blonde. They oiled themselves, then lay rigidly without talking, breasts spreading out to rest over their armpits. A large man in a battered straw hat rowed a small dinghy out to the center of the port, and drifted there while he ate his lunch. We made up elaborate lives for these characters, and missed them if they failed to appear, but, except for a nod and the required "*M'sieurdames*" when we passed, we never exchanged a word.

After Graham went back to work, the afternoons sometimes dragged. Unless I made an excursion on the bus into Nice, I read or sunbathed until it was time to start preparing the evening meal. I possessed no cookbook other than Marguerite Patten's *Step by Step Cookery* that served me well with instructions on basic techniques. I set out to copy the dishes we ate in the local restaurants. Mediterranean food relies largely on the freshest ingredients, mainly vegetables, in traditional peasant dishes that gain their flavor from a liberal use of herbs, garlic, and olive oil. I gradually learned to trust my senses, and to improvise: tricks like placing a lemon stuffed with garlic cloves in the cavity of a chicken, and tucking fresh rosemary sprigs under its loosened skin. Trial and error eventually produced a repertoire of dishes I was proud of.

Not all our food experiences were enjoyable. One Sunday evening in spring, Madame Sabin came to our door bearing a gift: mushrooms gathered that morning in the mountains. She gave us detailed instructions on how to cook them: the correct amount of olive oil made aromatic with garlic, how to crush the thyme, not chop it, etc. Then off she whirled, leaving us open-mouthed in amazement. She had not bothered with us for a while, except to shout at me for parking too close to La Bastide's main entrance. We should have been suspicious, but we so wanted to believe she liked us that we followed her instructions to the letter, and proclaimed the dish delicious. We ate every one of those damn toadstools, sopping up the juices with our bread. By 4:00 AM we were sure we were going to die, deciding it was not even worth calling an ambulance. After our recovery, we never raised the issue of the poisonous mushrooms with Madame. What was the point? She would shrug off our story with some accusation that we had cooked them the wrong way, or say she had eaten from the same crop with no ill effects. I still wonder, did she really want to kill us? High season was approaching, and maybe she calculated how much more rent she could charge for our apartment, once the tourists arrived.

Nevertheless, if we kept out of Madame Sabin's way, life was idyllic. Most weekends, we ventured out to a new destination: east into Italy, west to the nude beaches of St. Tropez, north to the hilltop villages that dotted the Alpes-Maritimes. Each excursion provided its memorable culinary moments: Sunday lunch in Portofino that lasted until 5:00 PM; a picnic in a wildflower meadow on the way to the art museum at St. Paul de Vence.

But labor strife was brewing over in Ariane, disturbing our serene lifestyle. Westinghouse had mismanaged the factory since its acquisition. A revolving cast of American managers, few of whom spoke more than a smattering of French, had failed to understand or communicate effectively with the French workforce. It should not have come as a surprise when the union called a strike. The workers mounted a picket line that veered toward violence any time a manager's car attempted to enter the gate. For a few days, Graham met with other salaried staff in a nearby café where they played *fussball* and drank coffee until it became clear they would not get into their offices that day. Then, some remote administrator lined up a series of auditing assignments for Graham at other Westinghouse facilities to keep him busy while the strike dragged on. These assignments took him to Milan, Paris, and even Tokyo. I accompanied him whenever possible.

Inevitably, the light dawned back at the head office in Pittsburgh that the venture in Ariane, known informally as Westinghouse's summer camp, was never going to turn a profit. The sale of the factory to a Finnish outfit was announced, occasioning a further business trip for Graham to Helsinki as part of the handover process.

We sat on our balcony in the waning heat of a July evening, watching the car lights twinkle along the Basse Corniche toward Monte Carlo. It was hard to imagine leaving this place, even though we always reminded each other it was a fantasy.

"I'm pretty sure I could get back into the accounting firm, and you could work for one of the London boroughs. But perhaps we should look outside London—somewhere we could afford to buy a house?" Graham ticked off our options morosely.

"Tell me what they said about the Brussels job again."

"There's a bump in pay, but I'd be away a lot. Everyone says Brussels is a great place to live—easy to get to Paris, Amsterdam, Frankfurt. . . ."

"What about the food?"

"Fabulous restaurants!" Graham's eyes lit up with memories of the couple of times he had been there.

I lifted my glass and chinked it against his.

"Okay. Done! Let's move to Belgium!"

After a career as an employment lawyer, Marian Exall now writes what she loves to read: mysteries. She has published two novels in the Sarah McKinney *series. Like her series' heroine, Marian was born and raised in England. She lived in France and Belgium before moving to the United States. She is a graduate of the London School of Economics and Emory University Law School. She lived for thirty years in Atlanta before moving to Bellingham in 2006. She is married with a son, a daughter, and two granddaughters. Contact her at* MarianExall.com.

Four Generations of Hope

Ben Frerichs

Times when love cannot smooth the road
Nor friendship lift the heavy load,
But just to know you have a friend
Who will "stand by" until the end.

William Carlos Williams, *The Friend Who Just Stands*

I SIT AS AN AUDIENCE OF ONE, A BOY, AT THE TOP OF WOODEN STEPS IN OUR basement, watching as my father performs in his workshop as on a stage. We don't talk, there is no applause. Our basement is basic, utilitarian, dominated by a large metal octopus of a coal furnace that warms our small home with four, not eight, heating arms. The dingy basement is crowded with laundry equipment, furniture waiting to be repaired or cannibalized, gardening tools oiled for the winter, boxes of bulbs packed in mulch waiting to be planted in spring. The basement is damp and cool year-round. The smell of mold mixed with coal dust and laundry products reminds of its purpose.

In the Midwestern neighborhood of my youth, mid-century 1950s and '60s, evidence of aspiration to Middle Class luxury is the conversion of basements into "family rooms" or "rec rooms" for social and family gatherings. Not for us. My father's considerable skills are not applied to that purpose. Ours is a blue-collar basement with mostly work happening. My father put his talent and energy (and some of mine) to improving the exterior of our home and its yard, but not accommodating space in it for entertaining or recreation.

The vignette of me watching in the basement unfolds months short of my twelfth birthday during the Eisenhower era. A time before blue jeans were de rigueur and ubiquitous. High-top black Keds show below my gray corduroy pants. The modest Keds are not a fashion statement—Keds are what boys wear as "play" shoes. Keds are not worn by girls, nor by adults; these cheap canvas shoes are our "everyday shoes." Our other shoes are shine-able and worn only when dressing up. Under a wool plaid jacket, two sizes too small, a faded brown sweatshirt is worn unadorned with a logo, no sports team insignia, no souvenir of a tourist attraction. My hair is uncombed dishwater blond that flops over an oval face; wire-rim glasses tilt crooked across my nose, breaking up the egg shape of my head. I am this boy, quiet and watchful, an audience of one looking down at his father on the stage of his workshop.

The focus of my attention is a tall spare man who works at a cluttered workbench. My father does not smile or make eye contact with me. He, too, wears wire-rimmed glasses, his dark brown hair is combed straight back in the pompadour fashion of the era, long on top, short on the sides. He moves with dispatch. If he follows a script there are no words spoken, they may be in his mind. No drawings, no instructions or plans are visible. His demeanor, quietness, and concentration belie his occupation as a salesman. I wonder if he used his daily quota of words at work with none left for his family or for the son who watches. Maybe he does not see me, but he must. It is a small basement.

My father goes about his work and gradually the project takes shape as a crèche to be placed under a Christmas tree. The basement is scarcely lit. What light there is, is focused like a spotlight on his performance within the surrounding darkness. The choreography in this play is not accompanied by the music of electric tools; the fine work is accomplished by hand tools and muscle. Am I participating? Does the audience take part in a play? The audience doesn't know what the conclusion will be; this work drama unfolds like a play. I marvel as the product takes shape, but there is no applause. It is slow and quiet magic. If someone spoke, would the magic end?

I can't recall ever playing with my father. I can remember only a handful of conversations that were not about chores to be done, chores not done, or chores not done well enough to suit my old man. His idea of play was me pushing a lawnmower, hand-clipping grass at edges of the sidewalks, raking the fall color off our lawn, smashing rocks with an eleven-pound sledge, beating dusty rugs, swinging a paintbrush, or thrusting a spade into the Midwest clay baked to concrete under the summer sun. I was on our school's baseball team. If there was a game when my father had chores for me, I had to skip the game.

When I recount stories of my early years as a parent, I point out that my son, Dan, and I did not have a lawnmower, sledge, clippers, rake, nor shovel. What we did have were tents, sleeping bags, nested cooking kits, hiking boots, coolers, cross-country skis, and bicycles. Other than household chores, we were all about play, recreation in the out-of-doors. Until he was well into teenage years, we did most of these activities together. We rented homes that were sparsely furnished. The spaces allowed us to roll on floors, wrestle, and mock-fight indoors. I was always careful to gently win, until the last time we wrestled. That time my son won. He was in junior high school and doing well in his weight-training class. He flipped me over his shoulder; my butt bounced painfully off the carpet. Except verbally, we have not wrestled since.

As a father, I have immense pride in who my son is and what he accomplished now as he approaches mid-life. Though I would like to, I cannot claim credit for heredity's contribution to his being. We adopted Daniel at birth. I can only lay claim to the nurture part of the yin and yang of his development. Of course, there were struggles, mostly with the schools. My son is a boundary tester, an accomplished one. We managed to navigate the challenges that skill presented benignly.

The most significant event in my own development as a person happened when my wife, Daniel's adoptive mother, fled "to find herself" in the late 1960s. She left me with the son we had adopted twenty months before. Her flight was devastating. We have not seen or talked to her since. Her decision to leave and to leave "full care and custody" of our son with me compelled me to reinvent myself and reject patterns inherited from my father. Being a solely in-charge parent made my parental challenges simpler, though not easier.

I retain few recollections of spending time, at work or play, with my father. My relationship with my son was and is dramatically different than what I experienced with my father. I can easily compare those experiences after the recent experience of a two-week visit in my son's home in Montana. I observed my son, Daniel, and compared how we relate now as father and son; and also observed his style as a parent.

Much has changed since I became a father: a half-black, half-white man is president; several revolutions—cultural, social, financial, and technological—have marched through the intervening years since I sat on those basement steps. The world is left changed, at least our part of it. Much of my own development as a person changed as a result of being thrust into the role of a father.

Now in Montana, I watch my son as a man. I sit on a sturdy sawhorse made of two-by-sixes in his garage while he works. The roles are reversed now as I watch my son's skills in action. The setting is less like a performance with audience and stage; more like theater in the round, more like a colloquium of peers, or perhaps an improvisational nightclub.

Some things have not changed much; now I wear worn jeans and sneakers with high mileage, and a faded navy sweatshirt, still unadorned with logo, with no touted tourist attraction nor an indicator of sports team loyalty. My visage may still be egg-shaped, but we wouldn't know that because longish white hair and a beard distort the oval if there is one. Gray-blue eyes observe the world without glasses thanks to cataract surgery.

My son's garage is more than a place to store cars. It tells us much about the family that lives there. Their garage is stuffed with sports equipment, bikes, and skis, building supplies, electric tools, and lawn and garden maintenance equipment. Prominent are two large freezers: one for elk and deer, the other filled with the produce and bounty of a tennis-court-sized organic garden behind this modest house. A glass door provides a portal to view a separate space, a studio with a massive kiln furnace in my son's fused-glass art studio.

The contents of the garage reflect the skills and interests of my son, his golden-haired wife, Mary Beth, and my granddaughter, Mary Ellen, who has just attained her first teenaged year, thirteen. My son's muscled arms and back wield his power tools as easily as paintbrushes. He wears threadbare jeans, a stained hickory shirt, low work boots. A smile dances on his face and in his eyes. His curly, gray-flecked dark crown is capped by a bill-forward baseball hat that has never seen a baseball game. He makes his living as a master electrician (his second career; formerly he was an accomplished cabinet maker). His organic garden is more than a hobby; it provides sustenance for the small family. In this scene, the father and son demonstrate familiarity and comfort like the old clothes they wear.

My son is constructing a cold frame (a small hothouse) for his garden. The cold frame is being made out of glass windows rescued from a home demolition. This structure will protect the seedlings on the cool days and nights in early summer in the Bridger Mountains. Work on the project progresses; there is no apparent plan except in the mind and talent of its builder.

As father and son, we interact like old friends, like peers, like buddies. We verbally joust, smile, cajole, tease, and laugh. We have a beer. We discuss various aspects of the project du jour, ideas are exchanged, questions are asked, suggestions made and mulled over by both. Other topics of conversation range from Taoist thought to national politics, to weather, to where my son will take his regular Friday mountain bike ride, on to what we might cooperatively fix for the family's dinner. The roles are reversed now in this setting compared to that basement of long ago. The son would be in the spotlight if there were one. I am the father, still the watcher, but now also participant. If this were a play, the audience would participate now and help shape the outcome. Perhaps, this is less like a play and more like a video of a father watching himself participating in life.

This is not the first time I have reflected on the changes in my life and in my small family. Now I am filled with more hope, less trepidation. I worry little now about perpetuating the patterns of my father. I am confident now that model is banished and replaced by a more effective style. The "gift" of re-invention allowed me to explore and adapt a different way to be a parent, to be a human. Watching my son as a parent now, I can be confident with the hope that parental styles can change over generations.

The next day the cold frame project is installed in the garden. I walk through the house when another experience churns my reflections. The degree of difference in parenting over generations is highlighted as I watch my son in his role as a parent.

At breakfast, Dan is adamant about completing his ambitious list of "have-to" chores that he needs to accomplish that day. Later in mid-afternoon as I wander through the house, I see my son and Mary Ellen kneeling head-to-head on the living room rug, noses down, butts up, with twenty fingers working together on her project to turn colorfully patterned duct tape into flip-flops. My granddaughter is a slender dark-eyed girl with a single dark-haired braid that hangs below her waist. She is the age I was when I perched on that wooden top step in the basement and watched my dad work. She works together with her father on her project. She is a participant, not an observer. Her father allows himself to be sidetracked from his work-man-like efforts and family chore responsibilities of his "to-do list" to take time for her project. He just returned from an eight-mile drive into town to get more duct tape for her project.

Later that day father and daughter work side-by-side in the garden. She helps her father accomplish his agenda. I recall the countless times I was dragooned into assisting my father's yard work agendas and having to give up something important to me, but never voluntarily. That evening while my daughter-in-law and I prepare dinner in the kitchen, father and daughter chase each other laughing loudly in a circle through the house: from hallway to living room, to dining room and through the kitchen, back to the hall. Their rescued greyhound, Greta, runs with them, her bark adding to the cacophony—screams of fun, rock music pulsing from the stereo, laughter bouncing off the walls.

Mary Beth, my daughter-in-law, yells with a smile in her voice from her work at the stove: "Honey, remember who's the adult!"

My granddaughter has skills my son and I don't have. Mary Ellen is able to melt her dad and her grandfather with her smiles. She laughs at Dan's jokes, at my jokes, the family's jokes. She laughs when her joke skewers one of us, or she is skewered by one of us. During this visit, I draw with her; we read together and cook together. I chauffeur her to soccer practice, to harp lessons, and to her friends' homes. While Mary Ellen and I are involved in competitive Easter egg dyeing, her father is annoying us like a little brother who seeks attention. Her eyes crinkle at the corners and light up as she says: "Sometimes I feel like I have two brothers!"

I am in that reflective time in my life having navigated the ironies, vulnerabilities, juxtapositions, contradictions, uncertainties, surprises, mysteries, marvels, and the wonders of life as a son, father, grandfather. Many times the light of hope guided me when the good-sense route wasn't obvious. I used the opportunity given to me inadvertently by a woman trying to find herself to find myself. It would be a lie to say I had a plan, but I tried to keep it simple: do opposite what my old man did; remember that my son was just a short, young human being; and just be there for him when neither one of us could change what confronted us.

Ben Frerichs is reinventing himself as a creative writer. He likes to balance the creative freedom of fiction with the truthiness of nonfiction and welcoming do-ability of short forms. He participates in two writers' groups, takes writing classes, and has volunteered with the Chuckanut Writers Conference for five years. His short pieces were accepted for inclusion in the annual Whatcom Writes *anthology in 2014, 2015, and 2016. He is one-third short of a novel, has a plan and big handful of scenes for a memoir as well as a couple dozen short pieces waiting to be revised for possible submission. In a former life, Ben taught Economics (high school through graduate courses), managed the economic development program for the city of Tacoma, and provided economic consulting services. He has lived two-thirds of his life in Washington State, one-third in Bellingham.*

Marooned in the Liberian Revolution

Shannon Hager

These things astonish me beyond words.

William Carlos Williams, *Pastoral*

THE LIBERIAN GOVERNMENT HANGED PEOPLE ON THE BEACH THE DAY I AR-rived in Monrovia, Liberia's capital, in September 1978. Their crime was practicing witchcraft, and the hanging was a foretelling of what was to come. I just didn't know it.

I went to Liberia as a Peace Corps Volunteer to work as a nurse in a rural clinic in the small bush town of Giablee, fifty miles from the coastal city of Buchanan. The little government clinic had almost no medicine or medical supplies but I did my best. Like most volunteers, I lived in an *uncivilized* manner without electricity or plumbing in a mud hut surrounded by the tropical, claustrophobic forest. The other closest volunteers were teachers who lived twenty miles away.

In the year and a half I'd lived in this West African country, I'd been through riots, witchcraft, beachfront hangings, ritualistic murders, secret society activities, army ants, termites, malaria, dysentery, and fevers of unknown origin. I didn't much care for the hot and humid climate, which was like breathing soup.

Liberia was founded by freed slaves from the United States in 1847 and had since been ruled by their descendants, the Americo-Liberians. Over the years, the tribal people's increasing dissatisfaction with this government led Master-Sergeant Samuel Doe and a gang of renegade soldier-thugs to assassinate President William Tolbert on April 12, 1980 and take over the country. The news media called it Liberia's first coup. Well, it was my first coup, too.

In a biographical sketch broadcast on the radio a day later, we learned that the new Head of State was a high-school dropout. God, he could hardly read his government's Ruling Proclamation. "In the Cause of the People, the Struggle Continues," said Doe at the end of his disjointed and rambling speech.

The following day the military dumped Tolbert and other murdered high-ranking former government officials into a big hole and people threw stones on the bodies. Then a bulldozer covered their common grave with dirt.

Doe sealed the borders. Nobody was allowed in or out of the country. Even if Peace Corps wanted to evacuate us, they wouldn't have been able to do so. Banks were closed and a week later, Master-Sergeant Doe, now General Doe, announced a price freeze on all products imported or manufactured in Liberia. That covered just about everything and shortages began almost immediately. Soon there was little fuel and almost no rice.

The first few weeks living in post-coup Liberia under martial law was stressful and frightening. Drunken soldiers terrorized citizens and expatriates alike, looking for anything they could extort from us. But, dodging the military, stockpiling food, and dealing with transportation problems soon seemed rather normal.

When the borders opened again and life calmed down, Peace Corps gave us the choice of staying or leaving. I chose to stay because life in the bush seemed peaceful and Giablee was safe because the villagers protected me. They hid me in their huts when soldiers drove through town. As a six-foot-tall white woman, I stood out too much in an African village.

My boyfriend, Harry, whom I'd met nine months earlier at a dinner party of Brits, Danes, Swedes, and Americans, worked for an iron mining company in Buchanan. Harry, a tall and slender European pilot, wore mostly khaki shorts and hiking boots. He owned a four-seater Piper Cherokee plane that he kept at a small airfield outside of Buchanan. He had been working in Liberia for many years. He often drove his jeep to Giablee to spend time with me, if I wasn't in Buchanan spending time with him.

One Sunday morning three months after the coup, Harry and I sat on small wooden chairs outside my mud hut in Giablee while I made our morning coffee, which was thick as mud. I used a brass Arab-style coffee pot over a wood fire. We waited for the water to boil the coffee grounds. The coffee pot had a patina of resin on the outside of it from many wood fires. When the pot heated up, the wood resin smell mixed with the smell of the cardamom in the coffee and the tobacco of Harry's cigarettes, creating a satisfying blended odor.

The villagers were in church and we heard their voices singing hymns in the background. Our quiet morning was interrupted by army men from Monrovia driving through Giablee, taking their families to the safety of the bush. Before Harry and I could duck into a hut, the soldiers spotted us and stopped. Our quiet morning was over.

A big, fat captain got out of his car and addressed us in an arrogant manner. "You got ham radio here? No more ham radio contact with Monrovia. Shut down your ham radio and bring it quick!"

"Got no ham radio here, man," Harry said in an artificially respectful tone. "I no live here in the bush. I a Buchanan man. The woman here, Peace Corps. She got nothing. No ham radio, no money, no car." Harry spoke to the captain in Liberian English, so I knew he was annoyed.

"Bring fuel for my car, quick now," the captain demanded.

"Here, take five dollars. Go buy palm wine. Have a nice day," Harry replied, extending his hand with a bill between his long, slender fingers.

The captain snatched the money from Harry's hand and got back into his car. He led his five-car convoy up the dirt road to the palm wine shop.

"Man's an idiot; everything's being monitored on ham radio.

Who's going to talk anything on ham radio?" Harry grumbled and lit another cigarette from the one he just finished.

We drank our coffee in silence.

When I knocked back my third little cup of Lebanese coffee as if I was doing shots of tequila, I said, "Harry, I'm better off back here in the bush, in Giablee, but all you white men with gas, trucks, food, and money are too vulnerable. I think it would be better if I went to Buchanan more often instead of you coming up here."

"Yeah, you right, honey," Harry agreed. He gave me a prolonged hug and a sweet kiss and reluctantly returned to Buchanan.

On my next visit to Buchanan, Harry asked me to stay with him for my own safety. I told him I couldn't do that because I had to work in the Giablee clinic where Peace Corps and the Liberian Ministry of Health had assigned me. However, I now had the habit of keeping my passport and health card on me so I wouldn't need to go back to Giablee if I had to evacuate suddenly. Sometimes I worried too much to want to stay in Liberia, but I was reluctant to leave Harry.

General Doe instituted a witch-hunt for high-ranking members of the former government. Over the radio, lists of names were read of all those arrested, and another list of those wanted by the military. Trials began at a military compound up the coast near Monrovia. Former officials were charged with treason, corruption, and crimes against humanity. The condemned were quickly executed.

Boy, that created plenty of outrage among both the Liberian people and foreigners. The American government called the executions an "atrocity in the civilized world."

"In the Cause of the People, the Struggle Continues," responded the People's Redemption Council.

A fucking civil war was coming, and I asked myself, *Why am I still here?* My nerves got all jammed up but I continued to make the decision to stay because I had little reason to return to the States and I was fond of Harry. I tried to project how it would be to get out of Liberia when life reached the point that I got too spooked to stay.

Harry and I went to visit my old Lebanese friend named Papae. He owned a large grocery store and helped me obtain food during the rice shortage. He lived above the store with his brother and his brother's family. Papae told us that two days earlier, armed soldiers broke into his house and stole beaucoup money and jewelry.

Papae's brother said, "Look at the bullet holes they put in the ceiling," and pointed upward. "They held my wife and kids hostage until we gave them money."

I wanted to cry when I heard such news.

To prevent a hard currency hemorrhage, Doe's government put a limit on the amount of money people could take out of the country. A few weeks later, two planes from some Middle Eastern airlines flew into Liberia's international airport and took Lebanese women and children to Beirut. Plenty of American dollars left Liberia wrapped around the bellies of the women and in the diapers of the children.

One of the Peace Corps Volunteers in Buchanan was having a nervous breakdown. Every day she had bad experiences with soldiers. She told me fifteen or so soldiers hung around a restaurant where we often ate. They drank liquor and refused to pay. They acted stupid and made sexual suggestions to her, so she was afraid to go out of her house.

I heard worrisome rumors of an attempted counter-coup and fifty or sixty soldiers were arrested. I expected they would soon be executed. It was enough to send a sane person over the edge. Sometimes I thought I was quietly going mad and if it wasn't for Harry, I would have cracked up.

By September, I felt too isolated in Giablee and received permission from the Ministry of Health and Peace Corps to relocate to Buchanan and work at the county hospital. And, I'd be close to Harry. We went to lunch every day at one of the few restaurants still opened in Buchanan. Armed soldiers continually paraded through the restaurant, strong-arming food and liquor from the Lebanese proprietor. This did nothing to aid my digestion.

"Honey," Harry said one afternoon after another unpleasant encounter with the soldiers. "We need to formulate evacuation plans. How are you at shooting a gun?"

"I never shot a gun in my life," I said. "Why would I need to know how to shoot a gun? Besides, Peace Corps prohibits us from messing with guns."

"If we have to evacuate, and the army or police tries to prevent us from leaving, your job will be to hold off whoever wants to stop us, while I do the pre-flight check on the plane," Harry said.

I looked at Harry with astonishment. "Where would we go?"

"We'll go to my friend's logging camp over in Ivory Coast," Harry said. Apparently he'd given some thought to this plan before he brought it to me.

Although guns were outlawed by the military government, the Liberians buried their guns in the ground and the Lebanese hid theirs in fake walls. "Remember," Harry said, "I have permission to carry and use my guns for security purposes because I'm a pilot." I suspected there was some army man up the gun-permit chain-of-command who wanted Harry to teach him how to fly a plane, and facilitated Harry's gun-carrying permit.

Every afternoon when he knocked off work, Harry and I went target practicing at the firing range adjacent to the little air-field. Harry taught me how to shoot every firearm he had—a couple of Colt .45 pistols, two Magnum .357 revolvers, and a semi-automatic police riot gun. At twenty-five yards, I could hit the target in four out of five shots using the competition one-arm side stance. We trained in the combat-shooting stance, standing toward the target using both hands on the weapon. Harry couldn't believe I'd never shot a gun before.

"Well, In the Cause of the People the Struggle Continues!" I said, chanting the revolution slogan and laughed.

We took pictures for my mother. I thought it would relieve her to know that I could at least prepare myself for the worst, since I insisted on living in unstable circumstances.

After the sun went down and it was too dark to shoot, I sat with Harry while he melted down lead and cast his own bullets in the airfield's workshop. "I have to replace the bullets we use, because I can't buy ammunition anywhere," he said.

I loved this guy who knew how to take care of himself. . . and me.

Sometimes, if I thought about what we were doing, I'd be afraid. Things might go badly for us if the military or police came to the airfield to investigate all the shooting we were doing every afternoon.

Harry decided it was time for a practice run to the logging camp in Ivory Coast. While he did the plane's pre-flight check, I pretended to hold off whoever might prevent us from leaving. We taxied down the runway and, as we ascended into the air, Harry said, "See, woman, we can do this."

We flew in circles for an hour looking down at the bush country resembling heads of broccoli and then we returned to the small airport.

Class conflict continued and soldiers tore up the Masonic Lodges of the hated former government and upper class. Soldiers claimed they found human bones and frozen human blood inside the lodges. *The hell . . . !* After soldiers removed bones and blood, people stole the rest of what was there. That night looters poured into the streets carrying Masonic flags and banners.

People were afraid to say anything against what was happening. This was Africa—no such thing as freedom of speech. Just when life was calm again, Head of State Doe arrived in Buchanan for a visit with a horde of soldiers and police. The streets filled up with uniforms. Scared white people locked themselves up in their houses, but we Peace Corps Volunteers went nervously about our business trying to act like nothing was abnormal. We lived at the poverty level of the people and had no vehicles or compound walls behind which to secure ourselves.

I went to a small cane-juice shop to see the owner who was

a friend of mine. A bunch of fucking-ass soldiers were sitting on the porch. I didn't want to speak to them, so I lowered my eyes and walked into the shop. I raised my eyes to speak to my friend and found myself looking down the barrel of a submachine gun. It startled me, but my heart didn't skip a beat. I had gotten used to living under martial law with these assholes. My friend and I went out the back door to sit under a tree to have a chat.

Well, what to do? I had learned how to survive with soldiers and police as numerous and obnoxious as army ants by ignoring them.

The People's Redemption Council issued more decrees. For me, the most important one was that anyone talking against the government would be arrested and jailed. I guessed it would be best not to talk at all. The military and police enforced the dusk-to-dawn curfew in the capital city of Monrovia and people were agitated in Buchanan. Taxes on the few goods coming through the ports increased by an additional 25 to 35 percent and income taxes took a sharp jump.

"Executions will be reinstated soon," Doe said.

I wasn't aware they had stopped.

Once or twice a month, Harry and I went to Monrovia, he on company business and I to be with him. The many roadblocks we'd encounter on the sixty-mile trip made Harry angry and scared me, so Harry decided we should fly there in his plane. The first time we flew into Spriggs Payne Airfield in Monrovia, we disembarked from the plane, blocked the wheels and grabbed a taxi into town. We had no hassles. It was the same when we left the airport. We just left.

The second time, our experience was completely different. All kinds of *yammer-yammer* went on when we arrived. Snarky men in uniform looking for bribes harassed us until Harry gave them money so they would go away. When we were ready to return to Buchanan, Harry filed his flight plan and we climbed into the plane. After the pre-flight check, we began to taxi to the runway. Harry asked for take-off instructions only to be rudely told, "Return to the terminal. You have no security clearance."

We looked at each other. "Damnit, now what?" we said in unison.

Soldiers with submachine guns surrounded us at the terminal. The airport's angry security chief barked, "Just what the hell do you think you're doing, taking off without security clearance?"

There was not one thing we could say.

"Search this plane," the security chief snapped at his subordinates. Irritated and sick of the shit, Harry and I stood side by side in the humid afternoon air while security forces poked their noses here and there. They found nothing and allowed us to re-board, then we were cleared for takeoff.

In December of 1980, I completed my Peace Corps service and made plans to travel overland in West Africa to Timbuktu. Harry decided not to renew his contract, "Twenty years of Liberia *plenty-o*," he said. We planned to meet up in Copenhagen and travel together to the States.

Harry flew me to Grassfield in the mountains near the border with Ivory Coast. The following day, I crossed the border in a bush taxi and traveled on to my next adventure, relieved to be gone from all Liberia offered and glad to see the last of hot and humid weather.

Shannon Hager, author of the award-winning book Five Thousand Brothers-in-Law: Love in Angola Prison, *a memoir, served two stints as a Peace Corps Volunteer: Liberia, West Africa, from 1978-1980; and Zaire, (now called the Democratic Republic of Congo) in Central Africa from 1985-86. Shannon is a retired nurse who specialized in public health, tropical medicine, and infectious diseases. In Liberia, Shannon managed vaccination programs, opened new rural clinics, and taught a national health record-keeping system. In Congo, she worked in a World Health Organization viral research project studying Monkey Pox and viral hemorrhagic fevers such as Ebola. She participated in studies of HIV infection in rural areas of northern Congo's Equateur Region. After living in New Orleans for twenty-two years, Shannon now lives in the Pacific Northwest where she enjoys a cooler climate and the boating culture. She is happy to still be alive!*

The Chosen Day

Sky Hedman

Seeing the leaves dropping from the high and low branches
the thought rises: this day of all others is the one chosen . . .
William Carlos Williams, *Kora In Hell: Improvisations XXVII*

THE FINAL FEW MILES OF THE ROAD UP TO ARTIST POINT ON THE MOUNT
Baker Scenic Byway have no guardrails. Only the thin white
lines marking the edge of the mountainous two-lane highway separated us from the precipitous drop-offs. My partner,
Lynne, drove carefully around the sharp switchbacks, the nose
of our red Sienna van pointing up. I occupied the third seat
with the dog, her furry body pressing against my side. Sand-
wiched in the middle of the van sat my older sister Martha and
her longtime companion David, flatlanders visiting from Texas.
My ninety-five-year-old mother was safely strapped in the front
passenger seat, next to Lynne.

I had planned this day for all of them, hoping it would be the
highlight of Martha and David's weeklong visit with us. Martha was now a fragile, thinner version of her younger self. She
seemed diminished, as if time were chipping away her vigor.
Her shoulders stooped slightly and her white hair was wispy.
She walked awkwardly, feeling for the ground. Only sixty-nine,
she could be mistaken as our mother's sister. David was also
shrinking: his cheeks more gaunt, his back more crooked.

The day was Wednesday, June 15, 2012. Our destination
was Heather Meadows, the highest point of the Mount Baker
Highway that was drivable in June. Deep snow blocked the
road that continued to the top. Today marked six months since
I had moved my mother to Bellingham, her worsening medical

conditions and her stressful living situation in Florida tugging at my heart. Tomorrow Martha and David would travel back to their retired lives in Texas, back to their red brick suburban home, sitting empty in relentless heat.

I felt more like a mother than a sister or a daughter. Based on the forecast for sunny skies, I chose this day to take them up the mountain. This morning, I packed provisions in hopes that our visitors could tolerate the six-hour round trip drive. Calling out "Turkey, ham, or roast beef?" I made sandwiches, customizing the bread, the mayo, the mustard, and the cheese for each person. I had a vision of "happy camper" smiles on their faces when we later stopped for lunch. I added drinks and snacks to the thermal picnic bag that I hauled out to the van. I coaxed Martha, David, Lynne, and the dog out of the house and into the van for a reasonably early start. We headed off shortly before 10:00 AM to pick up one more passenger: my elderly mother.

At my mother's care facility, Lynne and I helped Mom out to the van. She leaned on her walker with every halting step from her room to the parking lot, calling "Hello!" as we coached and steadied her transfer into the front passenger seat. With her limited mobility and the dementia that clouded her mind, she still looked forward to a ride in the car and insisted on being included in our final adventure of Martha and David's visit. We stowed her walker behind the seats with the lunches and provisions, and finally pointed the van east toward Mount Baker.

The forty-two-mile drive there took longer than I thought it would.

The sister who started the family legacy of riding horses and playing the flute, who was afraid of thunder, who never asked for help with anything, sat silently as we headed out of town.

With vistas of Canadian mountain peaks opening up to our left, I asked, "Will you be okay in the second seat?" hoping to kindle conversation as we drove.

"I'll be fine." She stared out the window.

Thinking of her surprise offer to help me mow the day before, I asked, "How is your back?"

"It still hurts."

I tried a different topic. "Do you miss working?"

"I miss the people," she said, at last turning to look at me, waiting for my response.

"The people you worked with?"

"My boss," she answered, then turned forward and back to her own thoughts.

As we drove the curvy road following the course of the tumbling Nooksack River, the farmland gave way to forest, with occasional signs advertising B&Bs and vacation cabins for rent. I could hear the murmurs of Lynne and my mother talking in the front seat, but I was too far away to make sense of their words.

"That's the campground where we stayed in May," I pointed out as we left behind the ski shops and restaurants of Glacier, the last town before we entered the national forest.

"Looks beautiful," Martha said. I was heartened to hear this endorsement, soothing my fears that she would rather have gone shopping.

"Nice," David echoed in his raspy voice, peering through the ample van window. Since his thyroid cancer surgery, David spoke with difficulty through a tracheotomy, forced to push his thumb against the stoma in his throat as he spoke. In his lap, he cradled a new portable weather station, purchased in anticipation of our drive up to 4,250 feet.

Having promised our visitors spectacular mountain scenery, I was relieved when we left behind the level road and began the ascent, slowly rising above the dense forest canopy that had shaded the last twenty miles. Dark green spire-shaped fir trees and mountain hemlock stood gracefully among rocky hills and seeping waterfalls. The tall conifers were dwarfed by the height of mountain peaks behind them. While the temperatures were summerlike in Bellingham, patches of snow appeared and covered the ground on the north-facing slopes. We slowed at each hairpin turn, and then gained speed on the straightaways as we steadily climbed up the steep hills, bringing us closer to Mount Baker and closer to the sun.

I felt the curves more strongly with each switchback, my stomach beginning to protest against the incessant twists and turns. As we rose higher, we all seemed absorbed in the setting. Now looking down on the treetops, we had a broad view across the green valley created by the north fork of the Nooksack River. In the distance rose the snow-capped Nooksack Ridge. The intense blue of the sky was streaked with high white cirrus clouds.

A rising sense of awe stirred in my chest.

"Look, there's snow!" Martha's voice rose out of the hushed silence. "I want to take a picture."

I could hear Lynne call, "Let me find a place to pull off," as she started looking for an opportunity along the shoulder-less road. She drove us around another hairpin turn, and then started up a straight stretch. Ahead on our right lay a gravelly patch, barely big enough to fit our van between the two-lane road and a rocky wall. She slowed to a stop on the narrow pull-over and turned off the engine. We were greeted with ringing silence, reinforcing the fact that we momentarily had the road to ourselves in this alpine wilderness. I felt small amidst the mountainous grandeur.

Martha's voice broke my reverie. "How do I open this door?" she asked. She was determined to get out, fumbling the latches with one hand, her new camera in the other. Lynne pushed a button from the front, and the automatic side door slid open. I felt the cool clear mountain air swoosh across my face as I held back the dog, eager to be free.

David's voice followed Martha like the tail of a kite when she swung her legs out and stood. "Be careful, Martha!" he protested from his seat, straining against his seatbelt.

She tossed back a dismissive "I'm fine" as she proceeded uphill between the van and the rocky outcrop.

David twisted in his seat and appealed to me, "Watch Martha!"

"It's okay," I reassured him, resting my hand on his bony shoulder, insisting that she had enough room to walk safely. I was touched at his protectiveness toward my fiercely independent sister. I was also hesitant to hold her back, dismissing David's fears so that she could experience this memorable moment.

"I'm cold," my mother complained. Lynne closed the door, sealing us in. David's eyes tracked my sister as she passed in front of the van, and stood clicking a few pictures from the edge of the pavement. Taking a step forward, she started to cross the road heading closer to the view, then paused. With her head tilted down, and her forehead wrinkled, Martha's eyes squinted as she studied the camera in the bright light of the mountain atmosphere. I shifted my eyes to drink in the panorama, happy to allow her this moment to capture the scene in photographs.

It took only an instant. A flash of sunlight that reflected in the side view mirror caught Lynne's attention. She glanced back to see a dark vehicle barreling toward us from below, trailed by the faint sound of its motor. She realized that Martha, distracted by her camera while crossing the road, would not register the imminent threat. The driver bearing down on his gas pedal would not see Martha. The car was almost beside us when Lynne yelled "Martha!" and reflexively slammed her hand on the van's horn.

* * *

Martha and I had shared family life until I was twelve. She was the first of my parents' offspring out the door, finding her ticket out of the house by marrying a man eleven years her senior. She reached out to me, her next youngest sister.

Martha faded from my life once she left home. She divorced, and later settled in Texas. She found her life partner, David, but never married him. Her success as a legal secretary and then paralegal was central to her life. With every passing decade, we connected less, a disappointing reality I accepted as I too moved on with my life. I had only seen her twice in the last few years, and even then she had cut both visits short. We didn't realize until after she died that she had been purposefully evading all of our eyes.

This past year, Martha and I communicated a bit more often as I orchestrated my mother's move. We started exchanging emails. I teased her about the temperatures in the cool Northwest compared with the pounding 100-plus degree heat of Texas. In the late spring, she emailed that she and David were coming for a week's visit. I was cautiously excited and surprised. I understood the unspoken subtext: more than to visit me or the Northwest, her trip would be an opportunity to see our aged mother alive one more time. As the oldest child, she shared a unique bond, a mix of loyalty and sisterhood, with our mother.

Only as the week's visit played out did we pick up that Martha herself was losing her memory. When Martha asked what she was seeing from our living room window, I pointed out Bellingham Bay, as well the San Juan Islands that filled our view to the southwest. She asked the same question again later. I gave a shorter answer. When she asked again, I thought she was being intentionally annoying. Each day gave us more clues. She was unable to find chicken in the grocery store or to fill our order at the ice cream shop. She wrote a postcard but had to ask the day, month, and year, answers that my mother was quick to give. Lynne found a time to speak to David on the side. From him, she learned that David had suffered for the last three years while Martha lost her way further with each passing day. She was let go at the job that she had held for many years. She forgot where she lived. She stopped taking her diabetic medication.

While Martha had started the visit as usual, taunting David in an effort to be witty, with each successive day, she became more childlike, stretching out on the sofa and letting David rub her feet. They stayed in our spare bedroom. Martha and David shared the queen-size bed, something they hadn't done for years. Late at night, I heard pleasant conversations through the adjoining wall. He later said that he fell in love with her again that week.

* * *

The blast of the horn interrupted my thoughts. I turned from looking across the valley and mentally scrambled to understand what was happening. In that split second, Martha lifted her eyes from her camera and froze, mid stride, just as the car sped by, missing her by inches. The gust of wind blew up her hair and buffeted her jacket. It rocked the van. She stood momentarily unmoving, her human flesh preserved by her last-minute hesitation. Then her mouth turned down as her face melted from surprise into a look of dismay. I gawked at the dark car that had appeared out of nowhere and then was past. The car receded up the mountain, the sound of its motor fading as it disappeared around the next bend. Mountain quiet returned and relief rolled over us from the front of the van to the back. David's cautionary instinct had been correct. And my mother, I thought, would have witnessed the horrifying drama of her daughter being hit by a car.

Martha didn't die that day. She wasn't hit by the car. But she did die that week, just two days after she and David flew back to Dallas. When they got home, she went straight to bed and didn't get up. She complained of pain in her back. David wondered if she were feeling grief because she might not see her mother alive again. When Martha refused to get up on Friday, even to bring the dogs home from the kennel, he assumed that the long trip had been too tiring.

When I hadn't heard from them by Saturday, Lynne insisted that I call to check on them. David answered the phone. I strained to hear his words. "Your sister is sick," he said. "She hasn't eaten anything or gotten out of bed since we got home."

"Is it her back?"

"She has a fever, and I'm trying to get her to go to a doctor."

In a moment her voice was on the phone. "I'm all right. I'm all right. I'm all right. I'm all right," she repeated in a monotone before I could speak.

"Martha," I interrupted. "What's going on with you?"

"I'm all right. I'm all right."

"David says you are sick. You need to go to the doctor."

"I'm all right."

"Martha, promise me that you will get up and go to a doctor."

After I hung up, David called 9-1-1. The medics sedated my delirious sister to get her in the ambulance. At the hospital, her blood sugar was over 900. She was in ketoacidosis, a life-threatening condition caused by untreated extremely high blood sugar and a kidney infection. The treatment, a rapid infusion of fluid, precipitated a massive heart attack that evening. The staff performed CPR and connected her body to machines to keep some hope alive; her brain activity had ceased.

Martha never did see my mother alive again. The arc of Martha's life had started sixty-nine years earlier in Passaic, New Jersey, when William Carlos Williams delivered her on Christmas Day, 1942. It didn't end that day on the way up to Mount Baker. It ended in a hospital room outside Dallas, Texas, four days later.

We all were shocked. The fragile but stubborn person who had just vacationed with us was gone.

My mother was protected from grief by her own dementia, her mind riddled with holes. When we broke the news to her, Mommy simply said, "She was not known to me," and looked out the window.

I traveled to Dallas in the weeks that followed to help David clear out her belongings. He had not expected to be a widower. I had not expected to be mourning my sister's passing, a huge reminder to all of us of the possibility of mortality.

My grief was compounded because of the degree that my mother's words were true for all of us. The time to know Martha better had passed. I was deeply grateful that she spent her final vacation with us.

When we look back on the near miss just days before Martha's death, Lynne says, "It's almost like she was meant to die."

Sky Hedman's blog, SkyandLynne.blogspot.com, was inspired by her story of attending Barack Obama's first inauguration. The blog continues to be a venue for her personal essays/ stories, and a rewarding connection with readers. She is currently compiling a memoir about her journey of being a reluctant caregiver for her elderly demented mother. She sends a special shout-out to the BUF writers' group, which has been a steady source of writerly help and friendship. Her work at the Alaska Ferry supplies her with a good supply of stories each week while leaving her time to enjoy the beautiful Northwest with her spouse, Lynne, and dog, Winnie. She looks forward to more connections with readers and writers, and thanks the Red Wheelbarrow Writers for their support of the local writing community.

Sperm Runs and Other Lessons in Lesbian Baby Making

Pamela Helberg

In April I shall see again—In April!
the round and perfect thighs
of the Police Sergeant's wife
perfect still after many babies.
Oya!

William Carlos Williams, *The Cold Night*

WHEN SUE AND I DECIDED TO CREATE OUR FAMILY THE OLD-FASHIONED way—that is with sperm and egg and no medical intervention— we only had one problem. No Sperm. Having a baby by do-it- yourself artificial insemination in 1986 meant we would have to find a willing donor on our own. Our small college town north of Seattle did not have a sperm bank or a fertility clinic, and neither my doctor nor Sue's was willing to assist us (medical- ly speaking) in our quest to become lesbian mothers. Though we weren't technically an infertile couple, we found ourselves signed up for their drill: First thing in the morning, before Sue even got out of bed, she took her temperature and charted it on a piece of graph paper. When the graph peaked, we called our donor, George, and he prepped for a week of filling empty film canisters with his seed. And by prepping, I mean he stopped smoking weed for the week and focused on not wasting any bodily fluids.

Generally, before I left the house to pick up the sperm, Sue and I had a ritual. She went upstairs to make her body receptive, to get her juices flowing and her uterus welcoming. Sometimes I joined her, but after several months of negative pregnancy tests, I was getting a bit weary with the whole process. I wasn't some love machine who could just turn on and off at a moment's notice. I had feelings. I preferred to be in the mood, but these days my affections were on demand at the whim of Sue's cycle. This time before I left to collect George's special delivery, I just handed her the vibrator and headed to the kitchen.

While Sue prepped her girl parts, I put a small saucepan of water on the stove to boil. Once the water bubbled, I tossed in a film canister and lid and our sperm syringe. After a minute, I plucked the items from the water with our spaghetti tongs and placed them on a sterile kitchen towel to dry. I called George to let him know I was on my way, grabbed the still warm and sanitized canister, and put it in a plain brown paper bag. When I got to George's house, about three miles away, he met me at the door, took the bag, and disappeared for about five minutes while I waited awkwardly in the foyer making uncomfortable small talk with his wife, Jen. After what seemed to be hours, George returned with the bag, I gave him and Jen a quick hug and headed back to the car where I took the precious plastic vial out of the bag and tucked it inside my shirt, under my armpit to keep the little fellows warm and motile as we made our way home.

I drove quickly but not too fast since I did not want to get pulled over. Not only would a traffic stop endanger the little guys and render them unfit for duty, but I would be hard-pressed to explain what I was doing, exactly: the empty paper bag on the seat, the film canister in my left armpit. I wouldn't even be able to roll my window down without discomfort as my old brown Honda Civic had manual windows. I drove home ever mindful that mine was a serious mission, one requiring swift but careful action.

As soon as I parked in our driveway, I sprinted to the house, to the kitchen for the syringe, then up the stairs to our bedroom where I turned the goods over to Sue. She carefully pried the plastic top off as I readied the syringe, putting the plunger in and pushing it all the way down. She held the vial at arm's length and wrinkled her nose.

"Gawd, this stuff smells awful!" She giggled.

"I know," I said as I put the syringe in the vial and pulled the plunger up until all of George's donation had been sucked up. "Can you imagine swallowing this shit?"

We shuddered in unison. I handed the full syringe to Sue, who had rolled over onto her back and put her feet up over the headboard, her head near the foot of the king-sized bed. She positioned the syringe and pressed the plunger.

"Swim boys!" I urged with diminishing enthusiasm while Sue closed her eyes and visualized the sperm surging toward her egg, the spark of life, the division of cells. I gathered the used supplies, closed the door softly behind me, headed to the bathroom to wash up, and hoped for a miracle, or at least a reprieve from baby making.

* * *

When Sue and I first met, she announced that she wanted to have children right away. At thirteen years my senior, her biological clock was ticking a bit incessantly, and her determination to have a family was a large part of my attraction to her. Since my parents still struggled with me being a lesbian, I thought that giving them grandchildren might go a long way toward winning them over and would certainly legitimize us as a couple. But once we decided Sue would get pregnant, we had to go to extraordinary lengths to make it so. Take for example the matter of asking someone to donate sperm. For a fluid that is so often scattered wantonly about, it is surprisingly difficult to procure. The few men we spoke to were loath to part with theirs. Who knew they would be so proprietary about the stuff? And this being the late 1980s, AIDS was rampant, scary, and still a death sentence. We knew a few gay men who might have been willing donors, but we were reluctant to approach them, thus narrowing our already thin field of options.

We didn't know many single straight men, and when we started scrutinizing them for looks, intelligence, male pattern baldness, and such, the field narrowed considerably. Frankly, we couldn't believe what some of our straight female friends had settled for. But beggars can't be choosers, so we started asking around. Most men feared the implicit commitment, even though we didn't want them to be involved beyond the dona-tion. Others wanted to save their seed for their own children someday, a notion that made no sense to me. How was sperm in my film canister any different from the sperm at the bottom of some dude's tube sock?

It took us about six months to find a willing participant who still had a full head of hair and a measurable IQ, but he was mar-ried and his wife wasn't exactly onboard with the idea. George and Jen were closer to Sue's age than mine, a classic Bellingham couple, slightly crunchy, vaguely activist, athletic, vegetarian, self-employed in the healing arts. George, lean and wiry, had wavy black hair and decent height. He was neither handsome nor unattractive. George had a grown child from a previous re-lationship and didn't want any more kids. The very idea of more women who could claim child support made him leery, and Jen wanted to have children of her own with George. She initially nixed his involvement in our family-making plans, and I could sort of see her point, but his having a baby with us wasn't actu-ally taking anything away from her. Turns out straight women could be oddly possessive with their men's sperm.

In order to convince Jen to help us, we held a series of sperm summits. The four of us met to discuss the project's parame-ters, repercussions, paperwork, and possibilities. We met sev-eral times, in cafés, on hiking trails, at the beach, and in our living rooms. We discussed sperm ad nauseum. Eventually, we wore Jen down, or won her over. I'm still not sure which, and after nearly a month of intense sperm negotiations, we reached an agreement, ecstatic to have a sperm supplier.

Thus my little ritual commenced. I boiled syringes and film canisters and carefully trafficked the little swimmers across town. Pregnancy and mucus viability tests became normal discussion topics in our home, over dinner with friends, and before we fell asleep at night. Each month, the pregnancy test loomed, the fate of our family at the mercy of the little pink stripe. This part of our baby-making ritual, initially exciting and full of promise, became ominous and futile. Self-blame ensued, for Sue and for me. I figured the little buggers had to be dying somewhere between their exit from George's man organ and their introduction to Sue's hoo-hoo. Of course, I faulted my armpit. It wasn't warm enough. It wasn't nurturing enough. I wasn't visualizing live sperm enough. Maybe something in the syringe was killing the little guys.

But then success! A trip to the doctor confirmed it—a baby was growing in Sue. We were going to be parents. Mothers.

Our euphoria lasted only a short time as Sue miscarried about three months into the pregnancy. I made a few more forays across town to George's, but with no success. As Sue approached forty, a dangerous and difficult age for pregnancies, we decided to let well enough alone and look into other options. Even though I was younger and in my prime childbearing years, my womb was not an option. I grew up listening to my mother's horror stories about birthing me: her extra long episiotomy. Her tipped uterus and blood transfusions. Days in the agony of labor. The doctor finally pulling me out with forceps. Her hysterectomy at twenty-eight years old. I'd spent my lifetime avoiding sperm. There was no chance any of the stuff was coming near my girl parts. I even built a pillow barrier in our bed on insemination nights in case any intrepid little guys escaped the syringe and tried to find their way to me across the sheets.

So, adoption seemed a reasonable solution. My mother was adopted, as were my brother and a cousin. Once we started thinking about it, adoption seemed like a responsible choice. Lots of children needed homes, and we knew a few other lesbians who had successfully navigated the adoption process. We decided to give it a try.

Again, we started from scratch and reviewed all of our options. I began to envy heterosexual couples. Not only did so many of them get pregnant by accident (by *accident!*), but they had the advantage in adoption as well. No one questioned their motives. No one asked them if they were planning to raise heterosexual children or if they had a Gay Agenda. Traditional adoption was expensive—agencies demanded big fees—and with only Sue gainfully employed, our finances looked sketchy at best. Even if we added in my itinerant income as part-time bookstore employee and a wannabe writer, the two of us together didn't make as much as one straight man or a heterosexual power couple.

As a way to save on the big fees, we initially decided to try adopting through the state of Washington. Child Protective Services (CPS) placed children in potential adoptive homes through its Foster/Adopt program all the time.

Again, we threw ourselves into the process. We attended workshops and met with social workers. We opened our home for investigation and paid for a home study. We bought fire extinguishers and outlet safety covers. We childproofed our kitchen cabinets and relocated our liquor cabinet. We moved toxic cleaning products to the top shelves. We tested our smoke detectors and sprinkled the refrigerator door with colorful Fisher-Price alphabet magnets.

We told the social workers that while we were open to foster/adopting an older child of any race, we would prefer an infant. We also let them know that we didn't feel capable of parenting a child with developmental delays or physical limitations. They thanked us for our honesty, indeed applauded us for knowing our limits and for not trying to be saintly rescuers. And then we waited.

For six months we waited for the phone to ring and tried to reconcile the silence from CPS with their initial assurances that there were hundreds of children who needed homes. We had believed them when they told us our sexual orientation did not matter in their decision to place a child with us. But as we saw straight couples from the workshops we attended getting healthy infants, we struggled not to become cynical and skeptical about our chances.

As another year went by while we tried to add a child to our family, we both grew restless. I felt like I had put my career on hold while we focused on babies, and I sensed Sue growing frustrated with my waning commitment to the process as she began to explore adopting as a single woman. We knew a handful of lesbians in committed relationships who had successfully navigated this route via international adoption, and Sue reached out to them for advice. While she researched this new and relatively uncharted territory, I started looking for a location in which to open a bookstore. I'd finished graduate school nearly three years ago, and I needed to launch myself into the world. Babies could wait. If we were meant to be parents, I told Sue, a baby would find us. Besides, she was putting enough effort into becoming a parent for the both of us.

I started learning all I could about bookselling. Sue contacted a private adoption attorney and introduced herself as a single woman. She arranged and paid for another home study, one in which I wouldn't be a factor since I was living part-time away from home. Being out hadn't worked so well for us, so we climbed back into the closet. I wasn't thrilled with being erased from the process, but I knew that Sue wanted children more than she wanted anything, so I did what I could to get out of the way. While she met with the lawyer and prospective birth mothers, I signed a lease on a storefront in the Fremont area of Seattle and started building bookshelves.

What started out as a single joint endeavor—making a family and building a life together—morphed into two distinctly parallel ventures. Sue grew increasingly paranoid that someone would find out she was a lesbian and out her to the adoption lawyer. I fretted that being left out of the process would relegate me to second-class parent status. And yet, somehow we managed to support one another while we each pursued our dreams. As I unpacked boxes of books and arranged them on the shelves, Sue sat nearby and sewed a set of brown-skinned Raggedy Ann and Andy dolls. I came home with our little pick-up truck full of baby furniture that my aunt and uncle were no longer using. Sue helped me run the wires for the bookstore's telephone line. Eventually we found a way to weave our separate dreams into something we could both live with.

I opened my bookstore in August of 1989, and over Memorial Day 1990, Sue accompanied me to the annual American Booksellers Association convention in Las Vegas. Before we left, she gave the hotel phone number to her adoption lawyer. In the months that I had focused on opening and running the bookstore, she continued to place ads in the area newspaper classified sections, advertising herself as a potential adoptive parent, exhorting pregnant women to call her lawyer for more information. Her name slowly worked its way up the lawyer's list of parents who waited for babies as those ahead of her were chosen by birth mothers. Her lawyer might call while we were away. So Sue split her time between waiting in the hotel for the phone to ring and wandering the vast aisles of the Las Vegas convention center with me to look at the latest book offerings from publishers.

On the third day of the convention, as we lay exhausted on the hotel bed surrounded by books and trinkets from the trade show floor, the room phone rang. Sue answered while I channel surfed. Sue's voice took on a serious tone at first, and I momentarily hoped that everyone at home was okay and that no one had died or fallen ill and that my bookstore was still standing. I'd left my parents in charge, after all. But after a few moments I figured out she was talking to her adoption lawyer—phrases like birth mother and due date perked me right up. By the time she hung up the phone, I had muted the television and was hanging on her every word.

"We're having a baby girl!" she exclaimed as she hung up the phone. "And she's due next week!"

"Holy shit!" I threw the remote in the air and jumped off

the bed. "We're going to be parents? We're having a baby girl? Just like that?" My ambivalence about becoming a parent evaporated in that moment, replaced by an urge to stock up on baby clothes, receiving blankets, and diapers. "We're going to be mommies next week!"

Relief washed over me as I dared to hope that our huge and seemingly impossible undertaking was nearing an end.

* * *

On the morning of June 13, 1990, I was sitting at my desk in the store's office when Sue called at 8:30 to tell me Anna had been born. "She arrived at 8:08. She's twenty-one inches long and weighs seven pounds, seven ounces."

For the next two days, as Sue stayed at the hospital with the birth mother and baby Anna, I sat alone in the bookstore and waited for her to call me with daily updates. Finally, the seventy-two-hour waiting period ended, and the birth mother signed the adoption paperwork, relinquishing her parental rights, and handed her child over to Sue. My mom joined me at the store and we waited together for Sue and her mother to arrive with the baby. My hopes that a baby would soften my relationship with my parents seemed to be working, at least with my mother.

When they finally arrived and I held that baby in my arms, all uncertainty melted away. I pushed the blanket from her face and unwrapped her so I could see all of her. Anna squeezed her eyes against the bright June sunlight and turned her little red face toward me. I pulled off her hat to find straight black hair. Her perfect little fingers wrapped around my own, and in that moment I was not a lesbian mother, but simply a mother. I pulled her close and breathed her in.

Pamela Helberg is working on her memoir, an intimate look at what happens when the Perfect Lesbian Family falls apart, a story by turns humorous and heartbreaking. Her essays have been published in the anthologies Beyond Belief: The Secret Lives of Women in Extreme Religion *(Seal Press, 2013) and* Untangling the Knot: Queer Voices on Marriage, Relationships, and Identity *(Ooligan Press 2015). She received her MA in Creative Writing from Western Washington University many years ago and is currently working on her master's degree in mental health counseling at Antioch University in Seattle. She enjoys running, kayaking, writing haikus, and hanging out with her writing buddies. She lives in Bellingham, Washington, and blogs somewhat regularly at* pamelahelberg.com.

A Cub is Born

Linda Hirsh

Let the snake wait under
his weed
and the writing
be of words, slow and quick, sharp
to strike, quiet to wait,
sleepless.

William Carlos Williams, *A Sort of Song*

EVEN THOUGH AT AGE FORTY-SEVEN I HAD FAILED AS A SECRETARY AT THE *Hartford Courant* newspaper, I had made enough friends there to keep me from being fired. The alternative? Join cub reporters at the paper's new Enfield bureau. My experience? Writing poetry for small literary publications and art reviews for a local alternative newspaper. I had never in my life written a single news story.

Do bad Girl Fridays make good reporters? I decided to find out. On a steamy August 1, 1987, the newspaper welcomed me to its reporting staff by handing over a beat of three small towns—Willington, Union, and Stafford. It was the first beat in a job that would last a decade.

On day one, I scrambled into the bureau with the other newly hired cubs. The room was dark, desks askew on cigarette- and coffee-stained rugs. The youngsters stumbled over still-packed cartons to get to the typewriters. They sat down and typed. I wondered what they were typing.

The scene was dream-like.

Just as surreal as the setting was the chief. A small, pale man with freckles that lent his face a yellow cast, he was a first-time boss who had not been allowed to pick his own crew. As I got to know him I noted that he simmered quietly. He had mastered the art of lurking. It was as if he wanted to be invisible. Not always, though! Sometimes he stopped haunting and took action. Glistening white incisors sharp as a shiv would appear as he lunged toward a victim. So, rather than a ghost, I thought of him as a vampire. I called him Fang. Although he delivered his instructions in a barely heard whisper, Fang's attitude was deafening. He disagreed with the philosophy of his boss, the man who hired me, to give diamonds-in-the-rough a chance. Now he was faced with one—me.

* * *

Required: a news story a day from each town, even if that meant the headline: *Ant Walks Across The Sidewalk.* Just weeks ago, during my interview for the job, I had informed Harold, the assistant managing editor who had hired me, the painful truth— that news stories were new to me, and that I was a features kind of gal. Looking out his large office window at the poverty of the city below, he assured me that the incoming bureau chief would show me how to put the news I gathered into a story.

"Don't worry, Lin," he said in a soothing tone. "He'll teach you."

Fang blinked his saucer-like eyes with resentment at being pulled in as an instructor. That was Harold's idea, not his. Instead of teaching, this man set a record of sitting at his desk in his stuffy, disheveled, windowless office, throwing visual daggers at me for three days. Then, assessing my readiness, he sent me out to a Willington board of finance meeting.

I am a fan of preparation. When I called the finance board chairman before the meeting, he asked me whether I had ever covered a budget before. I said no, I had never even followed the process in my hometown. The upshot? In appreciation of my honesty, the chairman took it slow and easy. In effect, he was my first journalism teacher.

At the meeting, the members, restless in their creaky chairs, struggled to create a passable town budget in that humid room. Seated in the audience were slouching men in overalls with long johns peeking under denim legs, bringing with them a distinct smell of the fields. The grazing fields, that is. Their attire stood in distinct contrast to the chairman's. His suggested the world of lawyers and accountants.

Afterward, heart pounding, hands clammy, mouth dry, I was happy simply to get the gist down on my portable Radio Shack computer, an archaic technology that showed only three lines of copy at a time and no way to judge the length.

I sent the story. That is, I tried. But the coupler that attached to the phone to send stories to the night editors was undependable. It took three attempts before the line crackled with the story. I could hear the impatience over the phone. It came through with Fang's heavy breathing. I would have guessed it was a pornographic phone call if I didn't know better.

When he finally received it at the other end, he announced that the story was four inches too long. News to me that it should not exceed eight inches. That led to trouble. The next day, he shamed me in front of the other cubs: I was the dummy of the bunch.

"But Harold said you'd teach me how to write news stories," I insisted.

Fang paused for a long beat. His big face turned paler. He blinked his nearly invisible eyelashes in fury.

"You are not an intern," he told me crisply, "and I'm not a teacher."

This was Fang, digging his heels in. Even though he knew my background and was aware of the promise Harold had made, he had dodged his responsibility. He knew he was supposed to give me sensible tips that reporters learned in Journalism 101, but he never gave me a hint of what he thought I was doing wrong—other than to tell me to write shorter stories.

He wasn't finished. I knew because there was another lengthy pause, its silence shrieking in my ear.

"If you mess up once more, I'll fire you," he added.

This was my first strike. And he wasn't going to give me two more. So I told myself to face facts: I was now on probation and would have to learn to hack my own way through the tangled weeds of this jungle. Trial by terror, I knew, could easily become death by machete.

Upon this introduction to my new career, I dubbed myself the world's oldest cub.

* * *

Rost was the business editor. As a secretary, I had overseen his moving arrangements to Connecticut. His kindly countenance overcame the suspicion implicit in his perpetually raised eyebrow. He reminded me of editor Burns in *The Front Page*. When someone called him an old softie, his comeback was, "Yeah, well don't let it get around."

After two weeks on the beat, Rost took me out to lunch to help me solve the problem of finding stories, especially at the time of year I called the dog days: a dearth of news when officials were sunning and swimming in exotic locations with nary a thought about business.

"There's the standard beginning-of-school roundup story," he said.

What a pro! I thought in admiration. I dashed back to the bureau and, after nabbing a school official, produced my story: "Stafford High Updates Curriculum with Five New Course Offerings." I wrote about the coming team-taught art/music, English and world literature, College English, advanced biology and Personal Family Living—a fancy title for health. Rost had joined the ranks of the finance board chairman, becoming my second journalism teacher. Amazing what one can do with some gentle guidance.

That is when the essence of small-town news hit me. College English and Personal Family Living were clichés in my upscale suburb next door to Hartford where many CEOs of the city's insurance companies lived. But in this woodsy corner of north-eastern Connecticut where few went to college, such innovation was not supposed to happen. That's what made it news.

Despite my enlightenment, troubles with Fang did not cease. He took me off probation, but mentioned in detail any trouble that got in my way; for instance, the Radio Shack obstacle. That is why, whenever I tried to send a story, the same questions ran through my head as perspiration dripped off it.

Will the note at the end confirm "story sent"? I remember thinking as I prayed to the beeps going through the phone. *Will it actually get there?* Sometimes, despite its digital assurance, it didn't. And, *Will he like it?*

I remember my relief after reporting on the November primary when I didn't have to resend. I got into my car, turned on a tape of The Beatles on the way home from the late election and felt like I was inside the song. That was when *Help!* and *A Hard Day's Night* turned into *Getting Better.*

But the times the computer link didn't work, I would dictate the story, then head for home, dog-tired and too bummed to even think about music therapy. Fang wrote on my next review that, among other things, "Linda will have to learn to use the Radio Shack."

Much later, after I had moved to another beat, the reporter who followed me had the same trouble sending his stories.

"What do you know!" Fang said. "That happened to Linda, too."

We discovered the cause was telephone lines that were above ground and subject to interference. It never occurred to Fang to remove that minus from my record.

* * *

Finding stories—after Rost's mentoring—was sweet. For instance, one resident proposed a homeless shelter at 51 Main Street in Stafford to serve those who were down-and-out, mostly runaway teens. I figured readers might want to know what the merchants along the street and regular customers thought of sharing their commercial strip with a shelter. Would the ragged occupants chase away their business? Or was that a small price to pay for the good of this unfortunate collection of humanity? There was bound to be reaction.

Fang looked up as I walked into his inner office. His eyes revealed no surprise even though I usually avoided entering his domain. The story I proposed would involve walking down Main Street and asking everyone in and out of view what they thought about the homeless and a shelter in their midst.

Fang beamed.

"Good idea," he said.

I tried to swallow his unexpected praise with aplomb. It rattled me. Then I realized I would have to live up to the proposal.

My first "reaction" story began:

While many residents agree that street people are sleeping on cold stone benches each night, they agree on little else about the homeless. Some question whether the people really lack shelter.

"They are mostly young, fighting with their families, not living within the rules," said Stafford First Selectman Emilio E. Gulliani. (dubbed "Snake" by reporters, and who had a couple of rebellious adolescents at home himself.)

And other officials agreed. But some believe the town's homeless are youngsters evicted from the houses their families own.

Not a word in that story belies the joy I discovered in talking to folks on the street. Even though I gave the first quote to Gulliani in the spirit of the journalist's traditional "officials said," I got better quotes from others. Marvin Galotti, who owned the Station News Room and Coffee Shop at 10 Main Street, said he felt like two people, one who would donate to the cause, the other who does not want to pay the street people's way through life by giving them handouts. He said the businessmen's dilemma is not where the homeless stay at night. It is where they go during the day.

"One of them came in here smelling of marijuana, asked for a free cup of coffee, and when I said there are no free coffees here, he leaned against the guy sitting next to him and asked him for

money," Galotti said. "That guy was my best customer and he never came back."

Galotti said it would be just as difficult to find another location for the shelter.

"It's like a leper colony or a waste dump. No one wants it next door."

Another source, Norm Miles, added his thoughts.

"The Christian community is weak to turn their backs on them. This is the type of thing they should stand up for," said Miles, who had worked in homeless shelters. (An informed opinion that beat "officials said.")

The story went over . . . big! It led to a string of compliments. I knew for certain that Rost and another friend, Erwin, an associate editor and old-timer, were cheering me on down in the main office. Now I strode around the towns upbeat and almost cocky. Fang, never one to give me my due, hinted in a grudging tone that I had improved because friends downtown had promoted me to the publisher and other Big Boys. I couldn't see his logic until Erwin translated Fang's assessment: I had proved myself by surviving Fang's hazing.

"Now they feel like they have made you over in their image," he said, nodding sagely.

* * *

In the culture of the territory I roamed, residents liked to keep to themselves. The newspaper's local news focus made townsfolk suspicious. At first, they were boulders, standing mute after my questions. If called to court, I would not have had to worry about revealing my sources, because I didn't have any.

That changed. To start with, I arrived early for town meetings unlike most reporters who casually slipped into a back seat a half hour after they started—perhaps to appear disinterested or objective. I gossiped with locals and wheedled my way into the heart of what was happening. Soon, I succeeded in training the town hall employees. When they saw me, they knew it was story time.

Like the day I walked into Willington's town hall, once a button factory, and Kay Donin, one of the selectmen's secretaries who was born to be a source, nodded her head toward the one meeting room.

"They're going to be talking about a dispute over the Ashford/Willington town line in there in about fifteen minutes," she said, wiggling her brunette eyebrows like Groucho Marx. "You'll want to attend."

Twenty minutes later, after listening to the pre-conference obligatory hee-hawing, I found myself in the midst of a hot-potato toss between the selectmen of the two towns. They even brought along an aerial photo consultant as referee. Amy Casey, Willington's former assessor, said she thought she knew the shape of the town, but new maps being prepared by the neighboring town of Ashford where she was now the assessor, showed she was wrong. Confused, Casey noticed a shared town line that did not look right and told Madge Brown, now Willington's assessor. The two women then discovered that some homeowners appeared to be residents of both towns!

At the meeting, selectmen, assessors, representatives from a surveying company and the state office of policy and management crowded around maps and exchanged viewpoints—at times heatedly, at times humorously—about the discrepancy. Officials decided that assessors in each town should compile a list of residents caught between the boundaries. When the list was done, the two selectmen would meet with their attorneys, walk the town line together and then schedule a meeting of selectmen from both towns to decide about the land in question. All this was not without jokes about a potential duel between the officials. Several months later, they drew a new town line.

Kay had steered me toward a story bursting with character and characters. I began to believe that I wore magic antennae for drawing them to me. This was one reason for my infatuation with the newspaper business.

In Union, population 550, the residents had a different problem. It involved money the state offered them to rebuild a plank bridge over the creek. The creek had risen so many times that it had frequently drowned the span and waterlogged the planks. So what was the hang-up? Why not take the state money and run?

"Because," said yet another unshaven fellow in baggy overalls that stunk of manure, "we are worried it might be a communist plot."

"Oh," I said, at a loss for a follow-up.

I needed some background facts. That particular town was known for its aloofness. The officials there were so close-mouthed that they even tried to hide public records and documents from reporters. Prying data out of these folks was like looking for diamonds in the gravel outside the former chicken coop that was their town hall. I had to threaten to file a Freedom of Information form. The FOI would nudge the officials in the right direction—to their files—and *presto!* I would have in my eager hands what a source would not give me.

But I continued to ply both officials and residents with charm and compassion. When I finally loosened Union folks up enough to cough up stories, I knew I had ended my first year flush with victory. Despite the locals' reluctance, and Fang's ongoing negativity, I had evolved from cub to veteran reporter. Even better, the search for sources and the writing of stories began to inspire an intense euphoria in me. My job was fun!

I dangled at the end of an innocent time in journalism, before emails replaced face-to-face interviews. Nowadays, I see opinion seeping into news-gathering, and hear that journalists allow their sources a peek at unpublished copy. The cozy relationship between editorial and advertising departments has inevitably resulted in the prevalence of puff pieces. These practices were no-nos of the first order in my time, even after I became a wise old bear.

Born and bred in Philadelphia, Linda Hirsh was trained from toddlerhood on to be an artist. She obediently won prizes throughout high school and a chunky scholarship to Syracuse University School of Art. Linda married upon graduation—in loco parentis to in loco matrimony, i.e. she has never lived alone. This is typical for those brought up in the 1950s. After Tulane University gave her a master's degree, she settled into motherhood. Four children later, her spouse, a college professor, faced their offspring's college tuition and Linda was forced to take a job temping at the Hartford Courant *newspaper. Twelve years and four graduations later, they moved to Bellingham to settle into grandparenthood. Since then, Linda has written two fundraiser books profiling cooks and two chapbooks of poetry along with a memoir from which she abstracted her newspaper years. She plans to make that decade a memoir in itself.*

The Last Date

Frances Howard-Snyder

Sure
love is cruel
and selfish
and totally obtuse—
at least, blinded by the light,
young love is.

William Carlos Williams, *The Ivy Crown*

AFTER A LONG DRIVE ON RUTTED ROADS, THROUGH BARE HILLS, DOTTED
with clusters of mud huts under thatched roofs, and occasional
herders dressed in blankets and pointed hats, herding sheep
or riding donkeys, my father and I approached the small brick
house with its scrappy grass and few dusty geraniums. The
door opened and I saw Ezra, my first love, a twenty-four-year-
old with a scholar's pallor, narrow shoulders, pot belly, and
curved lips. He was living and teaching in this small Lesothan
village as a way of avoiding military service in the South African
army. He didn't want to kill freedom fighters and he didn't want
to spend two years with men who did.

After a brief exchange of pleasantries, my father said that
he'd wait in the car. Ezra and I would need privacy for the awk-
ward conversation I'd traveled 250 miles to have.

"So, you brought your dad," he said over his shoulder as
he led me into the kitchen. There was a hint of irony, even
contempt, in his comment. I was supposed to be embarrassed,
because bringing my dad—in his silver Mercedes—meant that
I was a privileged little girl who couldn't take care of herself.

"Yes," I said.

"For protection?"

This was true, but I didn't want to seem totally pathetic. "Just for the ride."

"You didn't need him when you came before." This was also true. On my previous visits, I had traveled by train and plane and buses crowded with people and chickens.

"He wanted to come," I said.

"In case I changed your mind," he told rather than asked me. He was sophisticated enough to have seen through me and my family. This capacity had impressed me three years ago, as a college freshman, but it irritated me now. His sensual mouth twisted into a sort of grin, his long-lashed eyes narrowed. I remembered how odd I'd thought him when we first met, and how perfect I'd thought him later.

I gave him the coffee beans I'd brought—there was no decent coffee available around here and he had good taste. He started grinding them.

"Your letter came as quite a shock," he said conversationally, as if he'd gotten over the blow.

"Sorry," I said. I had wronged him. And feeling guilty, I'd agreed to come down and discuss the matter face to face instead of leaving it at a letter and a phone call.

"Really?" He paused. "You didn't mean to hurt me?"

"No. I just wanted to be clear." I didn't look him in the eye, but let my gaze wander over the Doors poster and the makeshift bookshelf stuffed with the familiar first editions of Horace, Vergil, Henry Miller, Nabokov, and the glass jars of whole cumin, and cloves, and coriander, conjuring bittersweet memories of learning to appreciate their distinctive flavors.

Ezra filled the kettle. "I'm mostly over it now. But my students took the brunt of it for a couple of days."

He paused and let the message sink in: I'd wronged him.

"I ended up letting one of my female students comfort me," he said.

"Oh?"

"You know the clever one who was always after me?"

"You mean you . . . "

"Fucked her? Yeah." He raised an eyebrow wearily.

"Oh." I said, stupidly. I shouldn't feel betrayed. I was the one who'd broken off the engagement. His encounter with this young black woman didn't count as infidelity to me. If anything, there were ethical issues that had nothing to do with me. But I couldn't help hear it as a slap in my face. I'd thought he'd cajoled me into visiting him "one last time" so that he could win me back. If so, this was a bizarre way of going about it. Or maybe he just wanted to make me jealous, so that I wouldn't pity him, but would come to realize what a prize male specimen I was giving up.

"What do you think about that?" He handed me a mug of black coffee with no sugar. Just the way he liked it and I had pretended to like it.

I tried to hide my distaste about his revelation. I didn't want him to think me priggish or jealous or racist. "Do you and she have a thing now?" I asked casually.

"No. It was just a one-night stand. Probably irrational. I did it only because I was upset."

I'd caused him to break the rules, and possibly hurt a young girl. Another way I'd wronged him.

"Well, be careful." I said and immediately regretted it. That was the sort of remark a fiancée might make. Carry your umbrella, get your flu shot, don't sleep with your students.

He rolled his eyes.

The front door opened and closed with a bang. Ezra's roommate appeared, a Texan Peace Corps worker who'd been very friendly on my previous visits. I greeted him cheerfully. He looked me up and down, glared, and then retreated to his bedroom and slammed the door, angry with me too, apparently.

"He feels my pain," Ezra said with half a laugh. "So, tell me about the new guy."

I wished I hadn't said in the letter that I was in love with someone else. I had toyed with the idea of saying that I couldn't get married because I wanted to go to graduate school in the US, or that I had outgrown Ezra. All three reasons would have been accurate. But graduate school wouldn't have been emphatic enough. He might have reasoned that he could come with me. Saying I'd outgrown him would have been rude and cruel. So, I mentioned the other guy, which was maybe crueler in a different way.

"He's a philosophy student too," I said.

"Great! The two of you can debate the Categorical Imperative in bed," he said.

He was getting in a dig. Something about how Kant didn't approve of promise-breaking. Invoking the great German moralist, like everything else in this conversation, meant that I had wronged him.

I opened my mouth to apologize and then shut it. Ezra was a fine one to talk about morality. I recalled one time, early in our relationship, when I'd tried to pay for a train ticket when the conductor missed me, and he'd laughed at my naiveté. "Why pay when you can get away with not paying?"

Morality was for saps. You know that God is just like Santa Claus for adults, right? Well, when you see through the God delusion, you should be able to see through the moral rules delusion. Steal if you can get away with it. Drink, smoke pot, sleep with whomever you please. He'd dyed my hair pink and persuaded me to steal a bottle of whisky. He'd approved when one of our friends had encouraged his sixteen-year-old girlfriend to leave home and get a job in a shady massage parlor, the one that specialized in "pelvic massages." *Do whatever you feel like and you can get away with.* How would Kant have liked that maxim?

Another time, I'd found him reading *Lolita* and asked him about it. "You should read it," he said and paused provocatively. "It sums up all of Western male sexuality." Halfway through the book I'd pondered this remark. What did that say about him? What did it say about his interest in me? I had hoped he'd been drawn to me because I was smart and well-read. But now I guessed that the attraction had been that I was seventeen and looked even younger. Was I a sort of aging, second-rate nymphet to him? I hadn't questioned him though—not wanting to seem unsophisticated or whiny. This was the pattern of our affair. He would tell me what to think, belittle my attempted objections, and I, intoxicated with love, would believe him.

He was now saying that *I'd* wronged *him*. In breaking my promise to marry him, in telling him so bluntly, in turning up with my father. How dare he? He'd hurt me, humiliated me, tried to control me, told me there was no right or wrong, implying presumably, that nothing he did to me or to anyone else could be wrong. And here he was telling me that I'd wronged him!

I recalled all the discomfort I'd felt over the last two and a half years, at being treated as ordinary, second-rate, easily manipulated. And then suddenly, I laughed. It was over. I had escaped.

His eyes narrowed. "What's so funny?"

I hesitated before answering. Did I really want to explain that I was no longer in thrall to him, that he could no longer manipulate me, that I could see through his hypocrisy? The whole point of this trip had been an attempt to behave graciously after the cowardly way I'd dumped him. And we would never see each other again. Starting a bitter fight would be pointless.

"I'm just thinking about Kant. He was kind of an ass, you know. He said that one should never tell a lie—even to the axe murderer about where his victim is hiding."

Ezra raised his chin in mild acknowledgment. If he didn't know this fact about Kant, he wouldn't let on.

"Are the two of you getting married?" he asked.

I hesitated again, thinking of the list of pros and cons of breaking up that I'd compiled in the university library.

Cons: I'll hurt Ezra. Breaking a promise is wrong. I might never find another husband.

Pros: I won't have to marry someone I don't love. I'll have a chance to go to graduate school. I'll make my parents happy.

The pros had not included "I'll get married to the other guy." It wasn't that the other guy was fictitious. But I knew that he wasn't seriously interested in me. We'd slept together and I'd fallen for him, but he had other plans. He was a sort of emotional stepping stone. My love for him had displaced my love for Ezra. I was now able to see Ezra without the glow of infatuation. And to see him for what he was—insecure, pretentious, ambitious but lazy, sensitive but not particularly empathetic. What a little fool I'd been.

"I don't know," I said, shaking my head. "Too early to tell." I didn't want to tell him the truth, didn't want to give him the satisfaction of knowing that I would be hurt in the way I'd hurt him.

We heard a knock. Ezra opened the door. "Hello, Paul," he said.

"I'm hungry," my father said. "Are the two of you interested in lunch? There must be a decent restaurant in Maseru."

"It's thirty miles away. You sure you don't mind driving both ways."

"Of course not." My father said, and I imagined him thinking, *A small price to pay for my daughter's freedom.*

I sat in front and Ezra sat in the back

My father asked about Lesotho. Ezra was unsurprisingly knowledgeable. In answer to my father's questions, he said: "Around two million." "South Sotho." "Eighty percent of the country is over six thousand feet above sea level." They kept up this exchange of information for most of the drive.

I watched my father as he listened. His regular tennis and field hockey games kept him lean and muscled, and turned his fair skin a brick red; he worked ten hours a day as financial director for a large manufacturing company to provide for his family; his employers valued his intelligence and moral compass.

I wondered what these two men thought of each other. From little hints each had given me, I'd say my father thought of my former lover as lazy, shifty, immoral; while Ezra thought of my dad as successful, but dull and a sellout, possibly someone to take advantage of.

We drove on the rutted road, through bare hills, with clusters of mud huts under thatched roofs, and noted the herders dressed in blankets and pointed hats, herding sheep or riding donkeys.

* * *

Over Kung Pao prawns and Chop Suey in the best Chinese restaurant in Maseru, surrounded by wealthy locals and foreign diplomats and NGOs, Ezra asked about his friends in Cape Town and I told what I knew. When my father left the table, Ezra reached into his pocket.

"You'd better have these." He handed me a set of black-and-white photographs of my naked self. Decent of him, I thought, given what he might do with them, and given how I'd lately given him cause. I gave a quick squinting glance at the photos. Yikes. I looked Rubenesque. Or just plain fat. I wished I hadn't let him take the photographs. Anyway, they would soon be ripped up and dropped in a wastebasket in some gas station bathroom. I pushed aside a worry that he still had the negatives. "Thanks," I said, and felt myself blush. I'd probably never grow out of blushing. I shoved the photographs into my purse.

"I thought of keeping them," he said. A long pause followed and I thought of all the hurtful or humiliating ways he might complete that sentence. But he turned the conversation in a different direction. Perhaps he was growing up too. "You can keep the ring if you like," he added.

"Oh, no!" The ring, a family heirloom, was one of the main reasons I'd agreed to come, to return it in person. I fumbled in my purse and then drew it out.

He slipped it onto his pinkie. Would he give it to another woman, or would this broken engagement make him gun shy?

The conversation on the return journey was similar to the earlier conversation. "Agriculture, diamonds, and remittances from migrant workers in South Africa." "Thunderstorms in summer. Snow in winter," and so on. When we reached the small brick house, we got out of the car and Ezra asked if we'd like to come in for a glass of wine. My father pointed out that we had a long drive back. He shook Ezra's hand.

Then Ezra turned to where I stood waiting uncertainly. Would he shake my hand, hug me, kiss me? "Good luck," he said, and dipped in and gave me a quick peck, "With your new life."

"You too," I murmured. And left out all the other thoughts I could have expressed. *Thank you for all you taught me. Sorry I hurt you. I wish things could have been different.*

As we drove away I watched until he retreated into his small brick house. I had loved him, and my love had transformed his oddness into beauty. From my giddy point of view, his skinny legs had been lean; his contradictions, paradoxes; his lethargy, sophistication. If to love another person is to see the face of God, I had idolized him, seen him with the generous eyes typically reserved for a mother. Perhaps this is the way each of us deserves to be seen and understood. Or perhaps it had all been a massive mistake.

My dad and I drove in silence.

"You all right?" he asked me after half an hour.

"Yes," I said.

He nodded. "You'll do better next time."

Frances Howard-Snyder teaches philosophy at WWU. She has published short stories at Every Day Fiction, Wordhaus, Whatcom Writes, OxMag, *and* Short Fiction Break *(first-place contest winner). When not writing philosophy or fiction, she enjoys spending time with her family, including teenage twin boys, traveling, walking, reading, playing chess, and watching Shakespeare.*

Sunshine and Silence

Peggy Kalpakian Johnson

Go with some show
of inconvenience; sit openly—
To the weather as to grief.
Or do you think you can shut grief in?

William Carlos Williams, *Tract*

GROWING UP IN LOS ANGELES DURING THE 1930S GREAT DEPRESSION, MY great and all-encompassing dream was to go to the University of Southern California. I had always lived in the academic shadow of my older sister, one of those people, Phi Beta Kappa from the day she was born. She was attending UCLA, so USC was the place for me. (As it turned out, of the four Kalpakian daughters, two went to UCLA and two to USC.) All Depression Era children were well aware of the tight economic times, and our family was no exception. My older sister went to UCLA for $29.50 per semester—as opposed to USC's tuition fee of $180 per semester. The exorbitant tuition made this dream impossible. Far too expensive.

After high school, and with my excellent typing skills (sixty-five words a minute on the standard typewriter of that day), I got a job at the Security Pacific National Bank, University and Jefferson Branch located next to the USC campus. I was the bank manager's secretary. I immediately started saving money from my $75 a month salary—not enough for four years at USC, but a start. I told Mr. Paul Cunningham, the bank manager, that I intended to be a USC student soon. Mr. Cunningham was himself a USC alumnus, and he wrote a letter of recommendation for me. As a result I received a Half General

Alumni Scholarship, renewable with B average grades. Tuition for me was now $90 per semester. With help from my parents and working part time, I achieved my impossible dream. In the fall of 1942, I became a USC student.

The country was fully mobilized for war, the entire nation unified in working together. America accepted food and gas rationing, blackout windows, standing in lines when necessary to buy special products. Any man in uniform who hitchhiked was guaranteed to receive a ride. Another sign of America's true heart was the posting of blue stars in their home windows—representing family members in Active Military Service and gold stars for family members Killed in Action. Nearly every home had stars in their windows.

In 1942, when I entered USC, the University announced they were revising their dress code. Women students were no longer required to wear silk stockings, due to the war and the shortage of silk (silk was needed for parachutes). Women students could now wear bobby sox or even paint their legs *as if* they were wearing silk stockings. I never did paint my legs, but I did wear bobby sox often. The University also suggested student ride-sharing to save gas. I paid another student 50 cents for a one-way ride to the USC campus. She drove her father's Packard right past my parents' home on West Olympic Boulevard. I came home on the streetcar and bus for a good deal less.

My first love was history and literature, and I managed to take some of those classes, but I knew that English majors had a hard time finding a job. I majored in Business Administration, Banking, and I hoped for a future in finance. I loved taking classes and learning. I was invited to join Phi Chi Theta, the Business Women's Honorary Sorority, and became an officer.

Part of my scholarship required me to replace the Dean of Business Administration's secretary during her lunch hour, five days a week, from noon to 1:00 PM. The University paid me 50 cents an hour. (The national minimum wage was 40 cents an hour.) This dean, Dean McClung, had his office in the first USC President's office in Old College, built in about 1880.

Old College was located near the big Methodist Church on campus—Victorian at its highest and best. Three stories with turrets and lots of windows. The stairs creaked. Some of the classrooms had elevated tiers for the students; the professor stood at a dais at floor level and looked up as he spoke to the students. Many of my business classes were in Old College and I had a special affection for it. I was sorry to hear years later that it was demolished.

Another scholarship student, Virginia Thomblin, shared the responsibilities with me for the dean's phone calls while his secretary was at lunch. Virginia was a senior, a science major, originally from one of the Dakotas. While we filled in for the dean's secretary, Virginia helped me with algebra, a required course, and I managed to get a B in it.

I was twenty years old and a happy student, still working twenty hours a week at Security Bank, loving my classes and making new friends. I met two other Angelenos from different high schools, Mary Frances Davison and Cecilia Munro. We met in Bovard Auditorium at Dr. Wallbank's Man and Civilization Lecture—a course required for all freshmen. We three were inseparable, and became lifelong friends. At Mary's wedding in 1944, I was her maid of honor and Cecilia was her bridesmaid in a beautiful, wartime all-military wedding. This photograph still sits on my desk as I write this.

In one of President Roosevelt's speeches, he expressed his concern for the young men and women whose love lives had been turned upside down by World War II. When men went to war, everyone knew they might not return. Weekend marriages were common. Some men wanted babies right away. There were many pregnant young widows, and also pregnant fiancées.

The University encouraged current students to write letters to former USC students who were fighting overseas. Names and APO numbers were listed in the Daily Trojan as well as on bulletin boards. I do remember writing at least one such letter. Maybe two. No replies. These were tense, emotional times, for all students, for professors, for all young men and women, for

117

the United States and for the entire world. I remember one student asking a professor if she could skip an exam because she had just got news that her boyfriend had been killed in action in Europe.

In the spring of 1944, all the male students remaining at USC were taken into the US Army. I shall never forget that day; it remains as clear in my mind as if it were yesterday. Long lines of yellow buses parked along University Avenue and the men slowly entered the buses, single file. Every person on campus—student, professor, secretary, custodian, gardener—stood by and watched. We stood in the spring sunshine in absolute deafening silence. Silence as has never occurred at USC before or since, I would guess. There were no brass bands, no patriotic speeches, no flag waving as these young men entered the buses and left for war with no guarantees to return. My boyfriend at the time, a young man I had known since high school, was one of those who boarded the bus for the US Army and the war. He did return and graduated from USC a few years later.

World War II changed the entire world, but on a very personal level it changed the lives of everyone who stood there in the sunshine bidding silent farewell.

Peggy Kalpakian Johnson was born in Constantinople, Turkey, in 1922 and arrived in Los Angeles, California, in 1923, the second child of a vibrant Armenian immigrant family who became proud American citizens. "Sunshine and Silence" is excerpted from a personal memoir that captures the joys and tears, emotions and tensions of that long-ago era. Both of her grandsons, Bear and Brendan McCreary, are graduates of the USC School of Music. Peggy is the mother of four children, including novelist, Laura Kalpakian.

Her Name is Quintana Roo

Linda Q. Lambert

Dissonance
(if you are interested)
leads to discovery

William Carlos Williams, *Paterson*

WHEN JOAN DIDION'S *SLOUCHING TOWARD BETHLEHEM* ENTERED THE LITER-
ary scene in 1968, I devoured it. *Slouching* was a conduit for
understanding the era through which I had lived. As an un-
dergraduate, I spent time on the radical campuses of Berkeley
and San Francisco State. In San Francisco I bought handmade
sandals in North Beach and frequented City Lights Book Store.
I saw *Hair* and witnessed the frontal nudity that had everyone
abuzz. I met Sandra Good, who became a Charles Manson aco-
lyte. I read Huxley's *Doors of Perception*, and, though I was not
otherwise involved in drug use, I ordered peyote from a supplier
in Texas, froze it, dried it, stuffed it into capsules and swallowed
twenty-five one night at the beach, all resulting in no change in
my perception. I heard Ken Kesey speak just before he and his
Merry Band of Pranksters headed across the country in their
Day-Glo-colored drug bus. I had lived these adventures, but I
had no idea of their social significance until *Slouching* conferred
perspective and meaning upon the dissonance of the decade.

In the title essay Didion captured the disjointed lifestyle of
San Francisco hippies specifically, and the atomization, as she
called it, of culture in general. She had a keen understanding of California and of my own territory. She knew the San
Joaquin Valley where I grew up, describing the buildings, the
landscape, the people. She knew the Los Angeles where I was
then living and she dazzled me with her writing about writing.

In "On Keeping a Notebook," my favorite chapter, Didion wrote that her mother had handed her a Big Five tablet with the suggestion that she stop whining and learn to amuse herself by writing down her thoughts. She described notebook keepers as lonely and anxious—a different breed of malcontents. As an early owner of a Big Five tablet myself and with a vague identity as a malcontent, I felt drawn to Joan Didion. I was not alone in my state of dazzle. Dan Wakefield in *The New York Times Book Review* referred to *Slouching* as "a rich display of some of the best prose written in the country."

By 1969, I had graduated with a BA in English, married, lived in Germany for a year, and was back in Los Angeles getting a graduate degree in journalism while my husband finished his film history degree at UCLA. I was a member of Theta Sigma Phi, USC's chapter of the national journalism sorority, now called the Association for Women in Communications. That spring, Theta Sigma Phi met to decide on the recipient of its annual Outstanding Woman in Journalism award. The group was composed of women much younger than I and they all knew each other. Though I was hesitant and felt myself an outsider, I nominated Joan Didion on the strength of my admiration for *Slouching*.

Most students admired, valued, and embraced Didion's style, but a few did not like her gloomy portraits of California and the overlay of pessimism that permeated her essays. Didion herself, in an interview with NPR interviewer Susan Stamberg a few years later, acknowledged that she was "more attracted to the underside of the tapestry," and tended to look at the bleak side of life, an approach that began when she was a child, a penchant that she recognized but couldn't explain.

Some of the group supported the nomination of Jessie Mae Brown Beavers, the editor of *The Sentinel*, an influential African American newspaper in Los Angeles. In the end, Theta Sigma Phi decided that both women should be honored. Several students vied to interview Ms. Beavers. Not wanting to seem pushy, I waited, and then volunteered to interview Joan Didion. I was thrilled to receive the sorority president's nod and the assignment.

It took me a week of picking up, putting down, and picking up the phone before I finally called for an appointment. A woman other than Ms. Didion answered. I explained my assignment. Joan Didion came on the line, her voice young, tentative. Yes, she would meet with me and a student photographer. We agreed on a date and time within the month. I felt a mixture of elation and apprehension.

Like any good journalism student preparing for an interview in the late sixties, I searched the *Readers Guide to Periodicals* and the Doheny Library catalogue for background material on my subject. I neatly typed my questions on three-by-five index cards. How many hours a day do you write? Do you like journalism or fiction writing better? Magazine articles or novels? How did you get Deadeye, Don, and Max, those Haight-Ashbury types, to talk? What kind of writing do you expect to be doing next—fiction or nonfiction? Typical grad student questions, the best I could come up with then.

A month later, I found myself navigating the surface streets between the University of Southern California and Hollywood. I drove slowly, avoiding the freeways so Sharon, the student photographer, and I had more time to prepare, to brace ourselves for our imminent brush with a literary figure. Sharon made sure she had her light meter and extra canisters of film. I mentally refined my questions.

"What if she is too shy to talk?" I asked Sharon. Joan Didion took self-deprecation to new levels, cueing her audience about her own frailties: "I am bad at interviewing people," she wrote in *Slouching*. "I do not like to make telephone calls, and would not like to count the mornings I have sat on some Best Western motel bed somewhere and tried to force myself to put through the call to the assistant district attorney."

"What if she dislikes being interviewed as much as she dislikes interviewing others?" I worried aloud.

"That's your department," Sharon replied. "I'm just going to be inconspicuous and take pictures. Don't worry. It'll be okay."

I had felt instantly connected to Joan Didion when I read

her observations about the San Joaquin Valley. Her comments gave me a sense of being a fellow countryman. The Valley, after all, was a country with a character all its own.

Additional similarities in our backgrounds momentarily brightened the shadow of my worry. She had gone to Berkeley as an English major. So had I. I took "The Modern Novel," a challenging course taught by the legendary Alfred Kazin who later wrote about Joan Didion.

We passed the drab arterials—Washington and Venice boulevards and West Third. Moving across Wilshire Boulevard, the landscape and Didion's Hollywood address on Franklin Avenue suggested prosperity. Finding street parking, we saw a white, two-story house with the blinds drawn. The yard looked casually cared for—the grass was slightly long, the bushes unpruned.

"This isn't what I expected," Sharon said.

"Me either," I replied.

We shrugged, then walked to the front door. I touched the marked-up copy of *Slouching* in my bag. I wanted Joan Didion's signature on it. A woman—perhaps a housekeeper—opened the door. She led us into a living room that I remember as a plain vanilla blur, anxiety having erased my journalist's attention to detail. We eased ourselves onto the sofa and waited for Joan Didion.

A slender woman, dressed in a white top and dark pedal pushers, appeared in the doorway, moving slowly into the room. Didion's presence on the page was large, her presence in person even smaller than I had imagined.

I managed to say, "I'm Linda. This is Sharon. She'll be taking some pictures. Thanks for seeing us." I extended my hand.

Her hello was barely audible, her handshake weightless. She sat down on a small chair, leaned forward, and said—though I hadn't asked— "John is working on a script so we're renting here temporarily."

I thought her reference to her screenwriter husband, John Gregory Dunne, and the rental was an odd opening. Did she establish that John was working so we shouldn't expect an introduction? Why was it important that she communicate that they were renting? Did she think that we two graduate students in our twenties would think less of them because they didn't own their home? I wasn't sure what to say next. I looked to Sharon to supply an answer, but she was concentrating on taking pictures. Didion seemed unconcerned as the camera's clicks continued.

"Will you be able to come to campus for the presentation?" I asked. An uncomfortable silence ensued.

My high-school journalism teacher Delmont Koroch tattooed my psyche with Who-What-When-Where-Why-and-Sometimes-How. Nudged by Mr. Koroch's embedded instruction, I in-filled with basic information. "It's on April thirtieth." Still no response. "A Wednesday."

"No," she said softly without explanation. "No."

Her response was off-putting in its absence of expected etiquette, as in "No, I'm sorry I have another commitment that day." All I could think to do was to change the subject. "Were you sure that you'd be a writer when you were a student at Berkeley?"

"No," she said, "I was so full of self-doubt that they would have had to tell me I was better than Flaubert."

She explained that one of her professors had supplied her name to a publisher who was interested in talented young writers. The publisher—she didn't say which one—contacted her and asked for samples of her writing.

"I was so stunned that I carried the letter around, unanswered in my purse for three years." She hesitated. "It just didn't seem real, and I guess I was afraid I'd be turned down."

"But now," I said, "you've been writing regularly for the *Saturday Evening Post* and other magazines."

"Yes, but I'm working on my second novel. It's an isolating experience. When I'm not reporting, I miss getting into other people's worlds," she said. "I would not like to stop doing nonfiction."

Remembering Didion's affinity for the Central Valley, I said, "I know you're from Sacramento. I grew up in the San Joaquin Valley too, Visalia."

"Were you born there?" She looked at me directly.

"No, I was born in San Francisco. My parents adopted me."

Joan leaned forward. "Tell me about them."

"They were living in Porterville, but when my father was drafted, my mother moved in with her mother in Visalia."

Joan straightened up and smiled. "John and I adopted a little girl. Her name is Quintana Roo. We have always let her know that she is our little *adopted* daughter."

For my generation, there was significant stigma attached to children born out of wedlock and to the women who bore them. My birth mother kept her secret, never divulging my birth, even to the birth father. An adopted child inherently feels that there may be another identity out there—royal parentage perhaps, or trailer trash, a brother or sister in the genetic landscape, unknown cousins, aunts and uncles, and maybe someone who has the same nose.

Parents before the midpoint of the twentieth century generally kept adoption of their children hidden, quite different from Joan Didion and John Dunne's open approach. I had not known about Quintana, and hearing it from her gave me a little chill of recognition, that we shared something besides geographic or educational similarities.

"A 'Q' name . . ." I began. "My maiden name is Quinby. Tell me about her name."

"Quintana Roo is the name of a region in Mexico that John and I liked." She explained that they were in Mexico when Quintana Roo was not yet a state—*terra incognita*. They liked that it meant "unknown region," interpreted as "free of complication."

I thought it was unusual, and a little strange, to name a child after a geopolitical entity, but I liked it. The name carried a sense of hope with it and I said so.

She began to pepper me with questions.

"How do you feel about being adopted? Would you like to know who your biological parents are? When did you find out you were adopted? Do you mind being an only child? Do you know what your name was? Did your parents give you a good life? Are you close to them?"

My adoption had always been my secret. I might have told it to the girls who became my best friends, or to dates with whom I felt "something" might develop. Adoption was the explanation for why I felt different from both my parents. Being adopted was an identity that had permanent residence in my cerebrum and generated endless, unanswerable questions. Why had my mother not kept me? What was she like? Who was my father? Were they still alive? Did I have brothers or sisters? Not until twenty years later did I find the answers when my adoptive father lay dying and I mustered enough courage to ask.

And now Joan Didion was asking *me* about *my* adoption. I told her what I knew in 1969.

I knew the name I was given at birth: Elise. I had a modicum of information about my birth parents: my father was a Marine and my mother was a domestic in San Francisco. The name of the adoption agency was Native Sons and Daughters of California, and my prospective parents drove two hundred miles from Porterville, California, to San Francisco to pick me up when I was eight weeks old. My father was drafted within a few months, and my mother moved in with my grandmother, who was a nurse and more comfortable with babies.

Joan said, "Do you remember when you found out you were adopted?"

I remembered exactly and precisely the moment I learned about my adoption. I was eight years old, sitting on the steps of the stairway from my second-story bedroom that led to the small stage, which hosted a baby grand piano my mother played by ear. With my arm draped over the bannister, I peeked through the slats. From the radio, a large Philco console, I heard a storyteller use the word "adopted."

"Mommy," I said to my mother, who was dusting furniture in the living room, "What does 'adopted' mean?"

She came up the short flight of stairs and put her arm around my shoulder.

"Why, that's what you are, honey. It means that I didn't give birth to you, but Daddy and I chose you."

So there it was, the explanation for why I felt different from both my parents. I *was* different, but it was okay. The truth, my secret, anchored me through my teenage years, and allowed me to grow into the feeling my mother expressed in a card she gave me. "You weren't born under my heart, but you were born in my heart."

Joan's questions were direct and insistent. She listened and observed. As I answered them, I understood how she obtained information from Max, Don, and Deadeye.

Joan looked at the clock, paused, and then said, "Would you like to meet Quintana?"

I was pleased, surprised. I wondered if everyone got to meet her daughter. "Yes," I said, "Very much."

The housekeeper entered the room a few minutes later, holding the hand of a little girl wearing a white dress with blue flowers on it.

"Quintana," said Joan, "this is Linda, and she's adopted just like you."

Quintana smiled with as much enthusiasm as a three-year-old could. I smiled with as much enthusiasm as a young woman, without siblings and who was not interested in having her own children, could.

Joan interviewed me more than I interviewed her that afternoon. She taught a journalism student about interviews by example.

I knew it was time to go. We'd been in the rented house of Joan Didion and John Gregory Dunne for almost two hours. I turned toward Quintana, still close to her mother's side. I interrupted her steady gaze. "Goodbye, Quintana," I said. She recognized my gesture with a little half smile and tilted her face toward me.

Joan moved away from her to shake hands with me, a more substantive exchange this time. Could I call her if I had additional questions about her work? She said yes. She showed me, along with Sharon, to the door.

I remembered the unautographed copy of *Slouching* in my bag, but I did not retrieve it. I was embarrassed that it was underlined, smudged, and dog-eared, as if I had not taken care of her words. I did not want to spoil the moment by asking her for something. She had already given me the gift of personal connection.

As we exited, I glanced over my shoulder and saw Quintana Roo run, arms outstretched, into her mother's embrace.

* * *

Joan did not attend the April ceremony. The sorority mailed the award to her. Theta Sigma Phi decided that the organization's budget could only afford a plaque fashioned of lead, the material used to create newspaper "slugs," spacers between lines of type, resulting in a small, dull gray slab of metal with raised letters. I doubt that it hung next to her Woman of the Year Award from the *Los Angeles Times*. To my great displeasure, the *Daily Trojan* editors relegated my article to the Society page, wrote a nondescript headline, and did not publish any of Sharon's pictures, though I was pleased that the editors retained some good quotes from the Great Writer.

In "On Keeping a Notebook," Joan underlined the importance of keeping in touch with the persons we used to be. The article I wrote as a graduate student over forty years ago is a reminder of the person I once was.

At the time of our interview, Didion had been a mother for three years. Quintana was the daughter to whom Joan had dedicated *Slouching*. Quintana, by virtue of her very name, was the daughter Didion hoped would not experience the tremors of the world described in *Slouching*. Joan's relentless questioning of me reflected concern for the raising of her own child, something I only understood when I had my own children.

Children, whether adopted or not, are terra incognita, unknown regions that good parents explore and understand, all the while modifying their own philosophies of parenting. We venture into maternity hopeful and find that children are rarely "free of complication." I couldn't have known that the assignment of an interview with Joan Didion would be a seed for understanding myself as both an adopted child, and years later, as a mother giving birth to and raising seven children.

Linda Q. Lambert has recently added the Q to her name to honor the Quinbys who adopted her, and to avoid alliterative overkill. In the late '90s, she was LLL the Lesbian Librarian of La Conner. She has completed an MFA from the University of Southern Maine and is spending her retired life doing what she's always wanted: writing. She is the mother of four sons and three daughters, and relies heavily on her wife Amory's editorial advice.

King of the Jungle

Cheryl Stritzel McCarthy

*...the lion flings the woman, taking her
by the throat upon his gullied shoulders...*

William Carlos Williams, *The Lion*

I STOOD RIVETED IN THE OPEN DOORWAY OF THE NEW, CHEAP CRACKER-BOX of a house on the outskirts of Ames, where I would spend this evening babysitting. This home stood in a cluster of houses built the year before, so raw and new I could smell fresh-turned earth in the bare cornfield across the street. The house had no foyer. Its flimsy front door opened directly into a beige-carpeted living room. A lumpy overstuffed couch, single beat-up leather recliner, and TV overfilled the small space. I stared, frozen in fear, at the family pet reclining atop the back of the couch. The young mother, who'd picked me up at home and driven back here, didn't notice.

"Baby Michael is already asleep in his room down the hall." She kicked off her tennies into a pile of detritus in a corner. I didn't move. "Mikey will wake in a few hours." She stepped off carpet onto kitchen linoleum, found her sandals under the kitchen table, thrust one on, and hopped as she pulled on the other, long hair swinging. The kitchen was little more than an alcove off the living room. "You'll hear him cry. When you do, feed him a bottle, change his diaper, and he'll go right back down." She rummaged among mail and dishes on the kitchen counter for her purse.

"Brenda, don't make us late!" her husband roared down the hall and tornadoed into the living room. His handsome young face, framed by a short beard and blond locks that brushed his shoulders, didn't acknowledge me, a thirteen-year-old babysitter in the doorway, clutching a school backpack, wearing a red sweatshirt with a team logo, TIGERLAND, and picture of a tiger printed on the front. His flared jeans swept along grubby synthetic carpet, not quite obscuring Earth shoes. He scanned the windowsill, shifted a heavy black dial phone on a spindly end table, and then dug between recliner cushions. "God! Here they are!" He grabbed keys out of the cushions, shaking off crumbs. "Brenda! We'll be late to our own bar. The shift change is in fifteen minutes, we're on next, and as owners we cannot be late!"

"I'm ready, I'm ready." Brenda spoke calmly, purse hung on her shoulder, her gauzy peasant blouse showing bright embroidery at the round-scooped neck, its white fabric fluttering over jeans. She smiled at me, and I finally stepped into the house, my eyes still riveted on their pet, half-snoozing atop the pilled fuzzy fabric of the couch back.

"Oh!" she glanced from me to the pet and back again. "Right! I get it." Brenda ducked into the kitchen, pushed aside dishes festooned with pizza crusts, located a flyswatter under a crumpled pizza box, and stepped back into the living room. "If he nips you, tap him on the nose with this." She handed me the stick of flimsy plastic. They swirled out the door, legged it up into their pickup, and with a squeal of tires, peeled out of the driveway as the screen door on the house slammed shut behind them.

The pet was a lion. A real, adolescent-aged lion. Uncaged.

* * *

In the early '70s, restrictions against exotic pets were nearly non-existent. The first time I'd babysat for this family was months previously. I'd gone along with my friend Polly on her job. That's when we met the lion. It was a kit then, mewing and unsteady on new legs with big clumsy paws. It had the run of the house, but mostly it dozed on the couch. When the kit wasn't sweetly snoozing, it sucked on my finger with its tiny sandpapery tongue. Polly and I were entranced. We passed the kit from lap to lap, cuddling it, cooing into its darling little big-eyed face, as we ate popcorn and watched Mary Tyler Moore toss her beret on TV.

The job was easy; all we had to do was occasionally check on sleeping baby Michael down the hall, and feed him a bottle if he awoke. The parents would close their bar in downtown Ames at 2:00 AM, do the bookkeeping, clean the joint, go home, and finally drive their babysitter home. The going rate for a thirteen-year-old babysitter was 50 cents per hour, which over a long night like this one added up nicely.

It was one job out of dozens, and I forgot about them until they called months later. Polly was unavailable, so I was going on my own, which was the usual babysitting situation anyway. I assumed their kit had gotten too big for the house, and they'd taken it back to wherever one takes overgrown lions.

They hadn't.

Now, transfixed with terror, my back plastered against the wall, I was eight feet from the king of the jungle. He reclined lazily in alpha position atop the couch back. How could this animal still be here? It was the size of a Labrador. His tawny coat covered smooth muscle that rippled as he stretched and yawned, showing gleaming white incisors, unfurling a river of huge tongue.

It was 7:50 PM on Saturday night. The parents wouldn't be back until 4:00 AM.

Fear rolled off me in waves. The lion smelled it. Idly, as if he couldn't really be bothered, he lifted his head and swung it side to side, sniffing. The great heavy cranium bobbed slowly. As if I were viewing the scene from outside, as if I were standing across the street in a fresh-plowed furrow in the field, I registered that the creature looked like those flocked animal figurines people place on the rear of their cars, with the heads weighted so any motion makes them bob.

Stop! Must focus! I snapped back and assessed the situation. The tiny living room felt like a boxing ring. In one corner stood a human girl, frozen, disbelieving. In the other corner, lolling on his lofty perch, lay the feline combatant, stretched out, relaxed.

The lion had claws and fangs. He had sleek masses of muscle. He had millennia of evolution on his side, evolution that had honed cats into the most efficient hunters ever known.

I had a flyswatter.

His amber eyes rolled over me. His lip curled, showing those incisors again. Watching him, I saw the phone on the leggy little end table, wedged between couch and recliner. The phone! My eyes never leaving his, I exhaled silently and inched out of my corner. The lion's head lolled to one side, but he didn't move. I took a step. He didn't move. I took another step, and another. I sidled along the wall. The lion watched, tongue hanging, panting. He didn't move.

I was nearly to the recliner. On the other side was the phone. I breathed, inched along, breathed, inched. The lion panted. A drop of saliva trembled on the end of his tongue. Slowly, I reached toward the phone. With one hand, I lifted the receiver, my eyes locked on the lion. With the other, I rotary-dialed seven digits, and at her babysitting job across town, Polly picked up on the first ring.

"You'll never believe this!" I screamed in a whisper. On the lion's tongue, the quivering globule of saliva dropped. Quick as a snake, the lion coiled and sprang. I whimpered and dodged as it grabbed the phone cord in its jaw, lassoing the heavy receiver overhead once, twice, three times, building momentum before it slipped out of its saliva-slick jaw and flew into the wall with a solid thwack. The phone base followed, tumbling to the carpet, pulling the spindly end table over with it. I heard the phone go dead.

The lion took one step back toward the couch, turned, and with a single graceful leap reclaimed his perch atop the back. I stood rock-still, assessing the boxing ring, now cut off from the outside world. Minutes ticked by. The lion lolled, head back, eyes baleful under heavy lids.

More minutes ticked by. I couldn't stand in one spot all night. My backpack full of homework was near the front door. Maybe I could get it. I watched, and the lion's eyelids drooped. I sidled along the wall toward my backpack, trying not to breathe. The eyelids hovered half-mast over amber eyeballs, watching me. He didn't move. His lids dropped lower, lower . . . I stretched toward my backpack. His lids drifted lower yet. I hooked a finger through my backpack, lifted it, and inched back toward the cracked faux-leather recliner. I eased into the recliner, and the lion's lids closed.

I exhaled, working on my lap, as the lion dozed and a low hum of chatter emanated from the unwatched TV. I rustled no paper, made no sudden moves. I worked my way through an English assignment on literal versus figurative. Literal meant it actually happened. Figurative meant it was *as if* it had happened. The lion slept. I moved on to another section of English that explored irony in literature. Still the lion snoozed. I did a bit of geology homework that focused on igneous versus sedimentary rock. The lion stirred, slept again. I dug into my backpack for my math book, and was deep into decimals and fractions when the baby wailed from down the hall.

Oh, no. I didn't want to stir, didn't want to upset the fragile peace reigning in our little boxing ring with its pilled upholstery and crumb-ridden cushions, but I had to get up and prepare a bottle. I eased my work off my lap. At my glacial pace, it took a full minute to move from recliner to kitchen. Keeping my head swiveled toward the lion, eyes on him, I rotated my body toward the fridge door, easing it open, extracting a jug of milk. The lion heard the opening door's soft sigh and raised his massive head, knowing that sound meant *food*.

He sprang. This time, going for food instead of the phone, he meant business. By now, I was facing the counter, my back toward the lion. I was pouring milk into the baby's plastic bottle when the missile of the lion's body hit my back with his teeth bared. I screamed and screamed again, arching toward the counter, away from the lion's open jaw, so a nanosecond later when his fangs snapped closed, the lion bit not skin and spine but only my sweatshirt, tearing a chunk out of its red fabric. As I arched forward, I threw the full plastic jug and baby's bottle skyward. Both sprayed milk in wild swooping arcs before crashing to the floor. I snatched up the milk jug just before it *glug, glug, glugged* its way from full to empty all over the floor. I was breathing fast and ragged, adrenaline coursing through me, when I started to cry. I was thirteen, alone in a box of a house with a lion that had ripped into my sweatshirt with its teeth, and responsible for a baby wailing down the hall. A tear or two rolled off my cheek, plopping into the lake of milk at my feet.

Standing in that lake, I thought of my English homework on literal versus figurative, and realized I was literally crying over spilled milk. Not only that, after doing homework on irony in literature, I realized the irony in my present situation: I was wearing a sweatshirt with the sports logo TIGERLAND and a picture of a tiger on the front, even as the back had been torn by a lion's fangs.

But what was this? Could the pool of milk spreading across the linoleum be a blessing? The lion spit out its mouthful of red sweatshirt. Crouching, as if at the shore of an African watering hole, it lapped at the milk. The spill bought me time! As the lion languorously lapped, I quick-prepped the bottle, using the last of the milk in the jug, and tended the baby in his room down the hall, forgetting my own tears as I fed, cleaned, and laid little Mikey back down to sleep.

When I returned, the milk-lake in the kitchen alcove had vanished. The lion lay atop its couch-top back in the living room. He looked livelier, head raised, eyes bright, tail switching. The milk had awakened its appetite, not sated it.

It was midnight. I could not, could not survive another four hours in this room with this beast. Could I somehow corral him? Off the kitchen was a flimsy hollow-core wood door, its veneer chipped at the edges. I opened it and saw a flight of wood-plank stairs, with a rough railing fashioned of a two-by-four length of lumber, down to the basement. Could I lure the lion into the stairwell and latch the door, locking him in the basement?

I needed bait. I could lay a trail of bait leading from the living room couch through the kitchen and down the basement stairs. I flung open one kitchen cupboard, then the other. Where was the Wonder Bread? Every family I knew, except ours, had Wonder Bread. Our Mom, deaf to our entreaties, bought whole-wheat. But oddly, these cupboards were bare. No Wonder Bread. No whole-wheat bread. No box of crackers, no plastic snap-on lidded container of homemade granola, no corn flakes, no Quaker Oats. The fridge was equally dismal: orange juice, crusty jars of condiments, a single head of browning iceberg lettuce. Did this couple survive on frozen pizza? I could start with those two pizza crusts, drying into C-shapes on a crumby plate. But I needed more. Opening the third and last thin plywood cabinet, I saw a dozen Hershey's bars stacked in the far corner.

It did not occur to me that lions likely didn't eat chocolate, but anyway, there was nothing else. I peeled off the wrappers. The smooth chocolate showed a white bloom of age. The lion, relaxed atop the couch back, secure in his place at the top of the food chain, watched with an expression of amused indulgence. He was a predator watching his prey, knowing he could pounce and win with a single paw swipe at the last moment. Why not relax and enjoy the show first?

I laid the chocolate in a Hansel-and-Gretel trail, winding from living room couch to basement stairs. The lion rolled off his perch, and with more curiosity than hunger, began to investigate.

"Here, kitty kitty," I whispered. The lion sniffed and moved. Closer, closer. "Here cat, there's a good boy, there's a good killing machine, come on, you like chocolate, especially old chocolate, come on . . ."

Slowly, lithely, he glided across the kitchen linoleum. He sniffed the chocolate, licked at one piece, pushed it with his tongue, licked the next, moved along, sniffed the next. He wasn't eating them, but he was getting closer to the basement door. I held my breath. I allowed myself to think this might work. I stood rock-still, my back against the kitchen counter, watching the lion's shoulders move in smooth, slow rotation under his sleek coat as he progressed along the trail. A fantasy of the lion locked in the basement blossomed in my mind. He was at the open basement door now, he placed one paw on the top step, then another, he was halfway through the door . . .

Now! I sprang, grabbing the doorknob, slamming the door against the lion's rump, but the lion was quick. Quick and quicker, from its position on the top two stairs, it turned and threw its body against the door, shoving it open as I shoved it closed. Back, forth, back, forth, I nearly got the door closed—I was desperate to hear that solid click—when the lion's heft pushed it open. I planted my sneakers against linoleum and pushed with all my might, moving the door slightly closer to closed. The lion dug its claws into the planks of the top steps and pushed back, moving the door slightly closer to open. Back, forth, back, forth, both of us panting, one of us sweating; it was a wrestling match between girl and lion with a sheet of wood between us, over a trail of aging chocolate pieces. In a fraction of a second, when the lion drew back to coil itself for another try, I saw a sliver of opportunity and flung myself against the door, but too quickly the lion sprang, all four paws off the steps for a moment, blasting the door fully ajar and knocking me to the floor.

I scrambled to my feet. The lion stalked back through the kitchen to its living room territory, eyeing me with contempt, flicking its tail as if asserting superiority over the whole human race. The lion leapt atop his couch-back perch and appeared to doze, but it was watching me. I cleaned up the chocolate, inched back into the living room, turned off the test pattern on the TV, eased into the recliner and sat frozen. Defeat lay over me like a king-sized bedspread. Without claws, hooves, or fangs, I was useless. He didn't get to be king of the jungle by falling for ruses like trails of chocolate leading to basement doors.

Each of us stayed in our corners, in that boxing ring of a living room, through the rest of that long and terrible night. When the parents returned, they didn't notice my exhaustion or tear-streaked face. I forgot to mention the dead phone. It was late and they were beat. "How was your night?" they asked perfunctorily.

It was 4:00 AM. I was thirteen, and had been taught to be polite. "Fine," I squeaked. "Here's your flyswatter."

Cheryl Stritzel McCarthy first saw her name in print in fourth grade, when the Ames Daily Tribune *published her account of her Girl Scout troop's outing to a pumpkin farm. She's been hooked on journalism ever since. She has been published in* The Des Moines Register, The Toledo Blade, The Cleveland Plain Dealer, *and other newspapers. She currently freelances for the* Chicago Tribune *and its sister newspapers across the country, including the* Los Angeles Times, Baltimore Sun, *and* Orlando Sentinel. *On assignment for newspapers and other publications, she has traveled to Turkey, Wales, Hawaii, Scotland, and England. Her book* USA to the UK: The Easy Way, *a lighthearted look at moving to the United Kingdom, was published by British Petroleum's London headquarters. She has written for numerous corporate magazines, including ones with global circulation. She now lives and writes in Bellingham, Washington.*

Our First Fire

Carol McMillan

*Squalor and filth with a sweet cur nestling in the grimy blankets
of your bed and on better roads striplings dreaming of wealth
and happiness. Country life in America!*
    William Carlos Williams, *Kora in Hell: Improvisations*

WIND WHISTLED THROUGH EVERY GAP IN THE POORLY MILLED PLANKS ENCLOS-
ing our cabin. Total darkness vied with blinding light for control
of the night. I huddled with my cat, quaking while simultaneous
lightning and thunder cracked around us. For over half an hour
the stalled storm pounded our tin roof. Unrelenting rain seemed
deafening until earth-rattling thunder eclipsed its sound. My
husband, Bill, offered a blanket, covering us totally. I appreci-
ated the rough wool lessening the lightning's glare, but it did
nothing to dampen the accompanying explosions of thunder.

The summer of 1985 had been so dry that Dan Rather mentioned Okanogan County's drought on national news. With
neither electricity nor running water, Bill and I lived in the
tiny, leaky cabin; the ramshackle little structure had served as
our home for over two years. When snow fell and winds blew
through cracks and crevices, even a barrel stove filled with sea-
soned pine couldn't heat our crooked cabin.

As part of the 1970s back-to-the-land movement, Bill had
left his home in upstate New York to "turn on, tune in, and
drop out" in the highlands of eastern Washington. After picking
apples for a few years, he and his first wife bought forty forest-
ed acres on the side of Mount Hull. When his marriage broke
up, Bill kept the land and Debbie kept their children.

Bill returned to Buffalo where we met two years later. We

married as I was finishing graduate school. In the midst of a recession I found no college eager to employ an anthropologist with a freshly minted PhD. Bill was eager to return to Washington state to be near his children, so we packed up a decommissioned moving van we bought for $500 and headed west to the twelve-by-sixteen-foot cabin on his land. We planned to live there until I found employment somewhere. After arriving on the mountain I found Wenatchee Valley College, thirty-five miles down Highway 97, and joined the staff of that small school. I'd immediately fallen in love with Okanogan County and its pine-covered mountains. We decided to stay.

Somehow Bill convinced me we'd be capable of building a real house on the land. We read books, I drew up plans, and we went to work. After nearly three years of sawing wood, pounding nails, laying pipe, and threading wiring, the house had grown enough to be enclosed and roofed. We had recently installed a new, efficient wood stove. After having learned what it meant to truly be "chilled to the bone," finally I would be warm! Life on the mountain was looking up.

* * *

That night's furious storm was succeeded by a sparkling morning. The air smelled freshly cleansed as Bill and I hiked up the hill to begin our usual day's work on the new house. Five pillars of what was obviously smoke rose across the valley, causing us more than a little concern. Turning on the radio, we listened to the local announcer's urgent words advising county residents to keep an eye out for "sleeper fires." With growing nervousness, I wasn't pleased to learn that fires can smolder for days before growing large enough to create visible smoke. Some fires obviously hadn't waited, but already burned actively across the valley. The rising gray smoke we were watching was distant, however, and the sun on my shoulders soothed the previous night's tension. I picked up some now-familiar tools and hoped to distract my brain from creating unpleasant scenarios. The warm scent of newly sawn pine further eased my concern as I sank nails, locking each board into place, proud of the new skills I'd developed.

Bill heaved up a few more two-by-fours, grunting as he carried them over to me. Looking up, he pointed to the ridge directly above our house.

"That's smoke!"

I was skeptical for a moment. The whiteness billowed like a building thunderstorm, but it did seem an odd color for a cloud. I squinted my eyes and watched a bit longer before finally agreeing.

Smoke!

Grabbing a couple of shovels, we drove the quarter-mile to our nearest neighbors' cabin. Busy stacking next winter's firewood, they hadn't yet noticed the smoke.

"I think that's a fire," Bill called to them, pointing.

It only took one glance before they also grabbed shovels; we ran uphill together. My legs had begun to ache as we approached the fire. Flames from burning sage and bitterbrush flared like torches covering the field. I swallowed my surprise and fear at the intensity, repelled by a wall of heat. Bill bent immediately, attacking the burning fingers licking through the grass. Led by the others, I started scraping soil and flaming debris onto my shovel, then throwing it back into the fire. Working steadily, with no time to pause, we leapfrogged over each other's work. Soon we had created a bare path along the fire's edge, managing to establish a thin barrier. My arms felt like lead. Smoke and ash choked our lungs, but eventually we dammed the flow of red across a small section of the field, clearing fuel from the fire's edge. I could feel blisters forming as I held my shovel too tightly.

"Should I go for help?" My physical reserves were running low and, not knowing how far the fire extended on its other side, I wanted some reinforcements.

"Yeah. Grab the truck." Bill leaned on his shovel as he fished keys from his pocket.

Dust flew when I skidded around the first turn, veering almost immediately to miss a battered green truck, the first of several vehicles racing down the dirt road toward us.

Jumping from my rig I pointed, "Turn left at the next driveway."

People had seen the smoke from where they lived "on top," a cluster of cabins higher up the mountain. Dusty vehicles and battered trucks arrived loaded with hoedads and shovels. Grunts served as greetings while people spread out on both ends of the fire line. One couple hauled tubs of water. They began beating down flames with water-soaked woolen blankets

Several sweaty hours passed while we fought flames beside our neighbors. My throat felt like sandpaper. I coached myself with an internal dialogue, making my arms push the shovel yet one more time. Finally, a loud squeak of brakes behind me brought grateful tears as I saw the Department of Natural Resources truck pull up.

After consuming five acres of sagebrush, the fire had reached a grove of pines; it was now on its way to becoming a serious "crown fire." Quickly untrailering their yellow Cat, firefighters began grading a ring around the flame's perimeter. Singed and smoky, we willingly backed off to let the professionals take control. Our neighbors brought water from their cabin. Swallowing hurt my scratchy throat but my body begged for moisture. I gulped it down, then walked over to find more.

Eventually the fire shrank. We rubbed our aching shoulders; our grimy group waited for flames to consume whatever fuel remained inside the fire line. Gradually we watched the blaze burn itself out. Little conversation passed among us; we all were a bit stunned and shaken by our virginal experience of combating such erratic violence.

After some extended mop-up to put out any remaining hotspots, people began to drift away. Totally exhausted, Bill and I gathered our tools and headed back to the cabin. Dipping water from our hand-dug well, we washed dirt and soot from our bodies, leaving dark smears on the grass. Too tired to eat, we stumbled into bed. Feeling safe for the moment, we slept off our exhaustion, but during that night fires across the valley raged on. Trees exploded; giant flames lit the darkness as we slept.

* * *

The next day we rose a bit stiffly and headed uphill. My rebelling body pounded nails with less energy than it had the previous day. When we stopped for lunch I had a creepy déjà vu feeling. This day had just begun to weirdly mirror the one before. I pointed up the hill.

"That can't be smoke again, can it?"

"No, it's too big. Must be a cloud." Bill looked for a moment, then returned to pounding nails.

But we continued watching the billowing gray form and finally decided it was, indeed, smoke, and lots of it. On the noon news, the radio mentioned a huge fire currently burning on Barker Mountain, southeast of us, very near the homes of our closest friends. Five thousand acres had already burned and the fire was heading north, toward our land. Sniffing the air, I could already detect the faint smell of smoke. The odor of burning ponderosa pine and sagebrush might be considered pleasant if it weren't signaling the possible destruction of our home. At that moment it smelled to me like brimstone.

Grabbing shovels again, we jumped into our old red farm truck and raced the fifteen miles to our local Co-op. In the town of Tonasket, the Okanogan River Co-op serves as the center for local information. There we found our friends Sandy and Raina slumped onto a bench. Along with their husbands, these were our best friends in the Okanogan.

"They're gone," Sandy said fairly matter-of-factly. "Our houses have burned."

Raina looked up at us. "All the men are up there. They're fighting the fire. Trying to save the other houses." Her tone was flat.

Only one road led up Siwash Creek and the fire had moved across it, blocking any escape route. We huddled together, feeling helpless. Someone came running into the Co-op, reassuring us that all the people up the mountain were okay, but that the road was, indeed, surrounded by flames. No one could get up or down. Knowing there were several large plowed fields and that the men were pretty fire savvy, I had to believe they'd be okay. Weighed down by a feeling of impotence, there was little we could do.

We helped for a while with the refugees, then started home to attempt making our own land more fire-resistant; the inferno was headed our way. My pulse raced and my throat felt too dry to swallow as we watched in amazement the giant flames paralleling eight miles of road between Tonasket and Havillah. I felt like escaping prey running before a furious dragon. By that time the radio told us the fire had burned over 20,000 acres, quadrupling in size in less than a day; fanned by twenty-mile-per-hour winds, it was out of control.

We stayed up most of the night, clearing building scraps, brush, wood, and grass from around the house. We packed the rusty old moving van with most of our worldly goods, preparing to evacuate if necessary.

As sunset tinted the mountain peaks, my love for this land felt like a pillow inside my chest, soft and downy and huge. I sat on our unfinished deck, looking across the valley to the Cascade Range. How lucky I was to live here, but how vulnerable I felt. The term "fire ecology" no longer existed as mere words in an environmental textbook; it now held a place in my body's visceral memory, complete with too-vivid sensory details. Mourning the losses of our friends' homes I feared that our own might turn to charcoal before we could even move in. Night came as I watched an increasingly red, smoke-filled sky; I needn't fall asleep to be inside a nightmare.

The next morning found shifting winds blowing the fire away toward the northeast; the situation had become more hopeful for our land. We climbed into the truck once more and returned to Tonasket, hoping to help friends.

"Everyone's gone back up Siwash. You can get through on the road now."

Barely pausing, we headed east from the Co-op, bumping our way up the rutted road, conscious of the drop-off that ended on rocks a hundred feet below. Reaching the wide Siwash Valley, we pulled into Treebeard and Raina's driveway.

"Oh my god; it didn't burn!"

We were greeted by the welcome shock of finding their home still standing. Rumors fly during fires and people report seeing things they are certain have happened, but they're often wrong.

Unfortunately, what we'd heard about Sandy and Danny's home was confirmed; Sandy and Danny's, and our other friends' Robbie and Melanie's homes had both been totally destroyed. As I later witnessed, the conflagration had been so intense that canning jars had melted completely in their underground root cellars.

* * *

For the next three days we fought the fire. Being stronger and more experienced than I, Bill joined others on the active front, while I patrolled for hot spots in previously burned areas. If you've ever thrown water on a campfire to douse the flames, and if you can multiply by a factor of hundreds the odor that arises, you then would have an idea of the smell that engulfed me. Black and crunchy with bits of charcoal crumbled underfoot, I walked the edges of the burn, trying to avoid stepping onto glowing coals or, much worse, falling into holes left where fire had followed the roots of a tree into the ground. Small corpses were twisted into odd shapes—animals not quick enough to have fled. Surprised and slightly horrified, I watched surviving robins pick through the charred remains of luckless others. I might have expected that from the normal scavengers, crows and ravens, but in robins the sight rested as a bit of nausea in my gut. I wanted to yell at them, chasing them away. An understanding that they merely sought a meal as traumatized survivors did little to help.

Fires can flare up again and again if winds increase, so shoveling combustible material away from hot spots lessened the chances of a recurrence. There were ten miles of burn line perimeter around the Siwash area to be monitored. Again, I worked past the pain as new blisters formed across my palms.

We all gathered that evening in Treebeard and Raina's still-standing house. During dinner Danny recounted the loss of his and Sandy's home. It had been the end of the first day; they'd been fighting flames far across the Siwash valley when fire rounded the back side of a ridge and exploded through the trees, coming toward them. Realizing their home could be in danger, he and Sandy jumped into their truck and took off across the fields. Danny said he had looked at the speedometer and seen they were going thirty miles per hour while barely winning the race with the flames. Having reached the trees' crowns, the firestorm roared, sending burning materials far ahead of itself. Danny said it became so deafening that it shook the earth. At their house he'd dropped Sandy off to grab what she could, while Danny used the truck to herd their horse down to the spring where everything was still wet. With all four wheels leaving the ground over the bumps, he was literally flying down the hill. He had only moments to return and grab a few items from the barn and toolshed before he and Sandy had to flee for their lives.

When I saw their home's remains a few days later it felt as if I were looking at a dear friend's mutilated corpse; so many warm and loving times had been spent there. Even days later stumps still burned around the remains. A twisted metal roof alone rose above the ashes.

No person lost his or her life in the Barker Mountain fire, but numerous injuries occurred. Unfortunately, animals fared worse. Sandy and Danny's horse and cat survived, but their neighbor's horse was killed, and several cats and chickens also died, while others suffered burns, ranging from singed paws to third degree. Fire is not a gentle cleanser; it is brutal and indiscriminate, leaving devastation that must be experienced to be understood. Eastern Washington state, contrary to the rest of the country's generalized image of Seattle's wetness, is classified as desert "fire ecology." Those of us choosing to live there are forced to become fire savvy. In the Okanogan Valley "trial by fire" is not a metaphor.

In the wake of the fire, Robbie and Melanie abandoned the hills and moved into town, but Sandy and Danny rebuilt a home on a different section of their land. Before the next winter set in, Bill and I had moved into our new house.

* * *

Wide picture windows framed snow-covered peaks of the Pasayten Wilderness. Snug inside my airy home, I admired our view across the Okanogan Valley. Outside, behind the house, a woodshed held six cords of carefully stacked tamarack. Stoking the stove's crackling blaze, I honored the fire that heated our home. I wondered how our friends were faring. Years of efforts creating their homes had vanished in less than a day. Sorrow for their loss had become a familiar ache by now. Our human efforts seemed negligible beside the force of flames last summer, but we hadn't surrendered. Now I warmed my hands beside the iron box created to tame such power. Destroyer and preserver, like a Hindu deity, fire demanded respect from our lesser human lives. I carried guilt and gratitude in equal measures: guilt, for still having a home, and gratitude for the same. I picked up my cat, snuggling my nose into her warm, purring body. Carrying her across the room, we nestled together in a corner of the couch. Bill and I had chosen the unconquered magnitude of these mountains. Wrapping Gretchen in my arms, I marveled at the fragile line of survival here, a necessary give and take between Nature and human endeavors. In several months, I knew, we would face another summer.

Carol McMillan, PhD, is a poet/painter/anthropologist whose writing is often inspired by her adventures. Her book White Water, Red Walls *is the story of a two-week raft trip through the Grand Canyon. Carol's poetry has been published in several anthologies. A 2013 recipient of the Sue C. Boynton Poetry Merit Award, Carol currently is gratefully living in Bellingham where she participates in writing groups and reads at many local open mics.*

Leaving the Roman Lands

Kenneth W. Meyer

Gagarin says... he could have gone on forever
William Carlos Williams, *Heel & Toe to the End*

IN MAY 1976 AFTER SPENDING A SEMESTER IN EGYPT, JAMIE AND I WERE bound for India. We hadn't been friends during study in Alexandria and we were never going to be friends, but we were on this expedition to India together, as sometimes happens in travel, where you wind up trekking to the oracle in Delphi with Lars who sat next to you for three hours on the bus, etc. After spending two weeks in Greece—the second week hiking around the monasteries on Mount Athos—by June 11 we had hitchhiked into Istanbul, where thirty-six hours later we were now deciding what means of transportation to use on the next leg of the trip. This discussion was critical since I had a mere five hundred dollars to spend over the next three months (I know, I know, but in 1976 this sounded perfectly reasonable).

Within a javelin-throw of Saint Sophia, the fourth-largest cathedral in the world, was a hangout for the students called "The Pudding Shop" where everyone went and left messages for each other on the bulletin board: *Angie, waited for four days for you, going on to Ephesus; Lowell, you still owe me 75 dollars and you're going to pay it; Stella from Manhattan, your mother called, inquire at the register; Eliot was sick here (several times);* and so on. After a day at the Blue Mosque or Saint Sophia you would stroll into The Pudding Shop and see who was doing what. Our second day in town Jamie reported he had seen a notice there: *Driver wanted to go to Pakistan, call this number 3766-2588.* Maybe we should check this out. I called the number and was informed a group of four Pakistani college students were driving four new automobiles to Pakistan from Germany, perhaps for their parents or who knew what the arrangement was. However, these youths didn't actually want to drive the cars. That was beneath their dignity. To us young guys from New York, this made no sense (we would have asked, how much do I have to pay you to drive a new car from Istanbul to Pakistan—which sounded like a grand adventure), but I wasn't there to judge. We arranged an interview and met with two young men in their twenties in a café where small glasses or *istikan* of tea arrived on a brass tray—someone had informed me a Turkish office worker could go through twenty-five such glasses of tea in a day, which I suspected was one reason for the abundance of wars in the Middle East. The two young fellows were Idris and Maqbul, engineering students in West Germany who were certain (perhaps with reason) that nothing would ever go wrong in their lives. Their English was excellent. We were advised that in the convoy were two Peugeot 504s, one diesel Mercedes 230SL, and one BMW sedan. They expected to reach Tehran in three days, and Lahore in five days. I had no international driver's license and we were just two guys who walked in off the street, but this didn't seem to alarm the Pakistanis.

"Is he a good driver?" asked Maqbul, pointing at me.

"Oh, he's a very good driver," Jamie was quick to respond. We didn't volunteer that I had just totaled a VW bug last December back in the States. Why remain chained to the past? The cars were all standard shift, which Jamie was quick to admit he couldn't drive, so if we did this, it would be me doing the actual work.

"We will call you tonight," Maqbul informed us.

We retraced our steps to the Daily Inn, where five dollars a night bought you a bed in a room accommodating four. Peering into the squat toilet there I had seen a rat swim by, but as long as each resident kept to their assigned domain, why be anxious? Jamie and I reviewed the meeting as I cozied up to Attila's nearby roadside counter for a Styrofoam plate of rice and kebabs.

"Are these guys crazy or what? They don't know us from Adam," I asked.

"And you should actually get paid for this," observed Jamie. He ran a hand through his thinning hair and another two strands fell to the pavement.

However, when all was said and done, I said why not. Foreign travel was like walking in space: you detached from the capsule, fed out your line, and enjoyed the spectacular view. There was no Time and you felt there were no limits. Just keep going. And hey, the chances of being hit by space debris or of accidentally unhooking your line were miniscule, right? At age twenty you felt you were invincible.

The call came at 7:30 PM: "You have the job. Come to the Bezoglu Hotel at 6:00 AM."

* * *

Before retiring that night I walked down what had been the *Mese* or main artery of Constantinople and saw Sara through the window of the Wagons-Lits Agency. She was a British woman in her late twenties working on her own in Turkey. I had bounced some ideas off her earlier that day (meaning: wishing I had some) and had found her helpful and admirable. My theory was that there were many admirable souls in this world, but some of them were simply modest and retiring—which was also admirable. Having just come from Egypt I knew it wasn't easy for a western woman to make her way alone in the Muslim world, and my suspicion was most western women would pass on the opportunity to try. She did have the advantage of not being blonde, which seemed to double all jeopardy for women east of Greece.

I entered and told her of our impending departure. She suggested, "You're not worried about it being a drug thing?"

The cold hand of fear reached for my heart, but I slapped it away. "Wouldn't drugs be going the other way?"

She admitted that was usually the case. "East of Ankara the roads are bad," she advised. "Use the horn a lot. Be careful."

"You know, when I think of Istanbul I'll always think of you."

"What did I do?"

"I don't know, you're just part of the scene. I'll come see if you're still here on the way back."

"I'll be here."

* * *

We rose at 5:00 AM the next day, blearily threw our meager possessions (in my case a change of clothes, journal, two extra pair of underwear) into our shoulder bags (mine was a leather item from Egypt with a scene of the pyramids on the front) and found someplace to have a couple of eggs. I remember nothing about the taxi ride to the Pakistanis' hotel, which I may have slept through while Jamie haggled with the taxi driver. I'm not a morning person.

The Bezoglu Hotel was a three-story establishment constructed against the inner course of the forty-foot-high Theodosian Walls, the battlements of the eastern Caesars, most of which are still in place today. Looking at what remained of these walls you understood why the city had fallen only twice in 1100 years. Constantinople had been a tough nut to crack. The old *polis* was surrounded on three sides by water and vulnerable to a land siege only from the west. The French, German, and Spanish so-called crusaders had attacked along the seaward walls in 1204 and had a lucky day, breaking through, but only the invention of the cannon had enabled the besiegers of 1453 to pulverize a segment of the western walls. From 320 to 1204 no one had gotten in at all, quite a record. In comparison to the old battlements, the hotel looked like a shack propped up against the Taj Mahal. The scene had a depressing effect on me, as if the city had fallen a few months ago and not 523 years earlier. I think Maqbul and his cohorts had to give me a Turkish coffee to get my brain moving, and that helped.

I was going to drive the Mercedes 230SL, but it didn't seem foreign. I came from a family with a long tradition of owning obscure German cars. My father favored small, fuel-efficient models with strange gearshift patterns. In some of these cases I believe my father had one of the few such autos in North America. (You don't believe me? Ever hear of something called a "DKW"? I rest my case.) Regarding more than one of them we joked there was no need to worry about it being stolen, because who could drive it? I found the 230SL was built like a tank, and on this excursion it needed to be.

In forty minutes we were driving to Asia over the Bosphorus Bridge, which had only been completed three years earlier. Later in the morning we were in fir-clad mountains, proceeding toward Ankara. Driving in Turkey was not for the faint-hearted. Once you got in from the coast most of the roads were two-laned. Everyone wanted to pass and the only way to stop the oncoming cars from doing so was to flash your lights at them, meaning "Don't do it!" The car horn was more important than the brakes. Trucks were to be overtaken at the earliest opportunity. There was no guardrail on the mountain roads, so there was no margin for error, there was only "I passed him!" or Your Last Flight.

The need for light-flashing was brought home as soon as we were climbing through the firs east of the bridge. The road had of course become a two-laner, and all the oncoming traffic was determined to pass trucks. No amount of hand waving, honking, or cursing seemed to deter them. There was only a limited shoulder between the Mercedes and a yawning precipice, and after the closest of several close calls, I skidded to a halt in the pine needles and soil. A spray of pebbles sailed into Infinity and we all disembarked and mopped the dust from our faces.

"Mr. Ken, you must use the lights to tell the other cars not to pass. You must do this," said Maqbul.

"Okay." Thereafter I did so.

* * *

It was during this trip that I had ample opportunity to try what my father called the "heel and toe" method. He had done a few amateur road rallies in his youth and was referring to keeping the toes of your right foot on the accelerator and your heel on the brake, alternating the pressure on the gas or brake in tight turns and so forth. I think when he mentioned this I snickered to myself as children do and asked when one would ever have use for such an exotic method—for which you also had to keep your right leg lifted in the air. Suddenly it wasn't just a story any more.

Ankara, the capital of Turkey, was an hour-long blur of coal-begrimed buildings and one just wanted to get out of that valley. I think I spied the tomb of Ataturk on one hill in the distance. We slept the first night in Sivas, after having driven 548 miles. My only memory of this city is that the locals refused to accept crumpled or soiled banknotes, which seemed to be their way of testing the patience of visitors, or maybe was a local joke (surely Sivas inhabitants don't have a reputation for fastidiousness?). But in general the Turks were hospitable. The Pakistanis had a low opinion of Turkey (Maqbul: "Let me tell you: every Turk is a thief.") but in fact, as our odyssey progressed, my opinion of the Turks rose day by day. In the west everything is filtered through the lens of the longstanding Greek-Turkish enmity, with all sympathy usually given to Greece, "the mother of western civilization," poor things, we must stand by them. There were fewer visitors to Turkey but once you were there you found there was a strong tradition of being hospitable to guests. Here's an example: on the return trip through Turkey in September, thirty of us westerners were in a bus that broke down in between Sivas and Erzurum. We all disembarked and were standing around the wheat fields, the Italians sharing their precious last jar of Nutella, when we saw a group of rural folk approaching. "Oh no, they're coming to cut our heads off!" Decapitation figuring prominently in stories about Turkish brigands. But it turned out the villagers had seen our vehicle was disabled and were bringing us watermelons to eat on that hot September day. Shame.

Whenever there was a difficulty or a policeman approached,

Maqbul and the Pakistanis played the Islamic card, usually successfully. By this I mean one of them would lean out the window: "Oh officer, peace be with you. Did we make an illegal turn? We are lost, I'm so sorry. Be a Muslim brother and forgive us. . ." Or later, at the Iranian border: "Is it illegal to bring in more than 10,000 rials? Oh, we didn't know. Be a Muslim brother. . ." And so on. As an infidel brother, of course I couldn't use that gambit. And Jamie was a Jewish brother, a fact not volunteered.

Sara was wrong about the roads east of Ankara being bad: there were no paved roads east of Ankara. What there were were arteries of tamped earth, many segments of which had a surprising amount of traffic, mostly eighteen-wheelers bound to and from Tehran. The joke regarding the road was that the Shah of Iran had given Turkey hundreds of millions of dollars to improve infrastructure, but the Turks had used it to invade Cyprus. I supposed it was a matter of priorities. . . .

After several hours on our highway of red earth, we stopped in Erzurum, 272 miles east of Sivas, for a late lunch. We would sleep in Makou, Iran, that night, after passing south of Mount Ararat. The name Erzurum pre-dated even the arrival of the Seljuk and Ottoman Turks, as it was the Arabic *Ard el-Rum,* Land of the Romans. This sounds strange to westerners but in other words, prior to the battle of Manzikert in 1071, if you were charging west on your horses, if you reached this point, you were entering the territory of the eastern Roman Empire. Conversely, if you continued east from here, you were entering Armenia or lands controlled by the Arab Caliph.

For lunch that day I was having *corba*, a kind of lentil soup, accompanied by a flat loaf of *yekmek,* bread, and was gazing wistfully at a sign over the door advertising Tekel Biere. Since I had several more hours to drive over who knew what kind of terrain (pretty awful terrain, it turned out), it didn't seem like the time for a beer. It was interesting to note in this connection that our Pakistani hosts—though boasting of their familiarity with alcohol—refrained altogether from inebriants during our drive through Turkey and Iran. They were probably playing it safe. You never knew what the reaction of the locals might be.

Just as I was thinking this, I was interrupted by the screech of metal on metal, and the roar of a vehicle taking off. I turned in time to see a brown sedan speed away from our truck stop and disappear around a city corner.

"He just backed into that white station wagon and tore off!" Jamie informed me. My companion's conversation during the last thirty-six hours had mostly been limited to cries of "Look out!" Though last night he had offered that I was "doing great."

Our four Pakistani hosts at the next table were indignant and speaking in what I supposed was Punjabi. The station wagon had been parked next to the 230SL. The offending driver might have hit dad's new wheels!

"So much for exchanging insurance info. . . ." I remarked.

Still in Erzurum, a post-prandial review of status of the vehicles yielded the following: one of the Peugeot 504s was in fair condition, but the Pakistani driver (one of our hosts had to drive after all) had nearly burned out the clutch on the second and driving it was a trial. The right front wheel of the BMW was wobbling and looked like it was going to come off at any minute. The 230SL however was doing the best of all: it had lurched through any pothole and although I had stalled it out a few times, its idle was steady and unperturbed. What an advertisement for Mercedes.

"Mr. Ken." The Pakistanis pronounced it "Cain." "Are you ready?"

Travel is like space-walking: you reel out a little more of the space-tether, breathe in, breathe out, carefully, keeping your heart-rate down. The sun is already descending toward the walls of Constantinople, mission control all systems are go. You're facing east, leaving the land of the Romans.

"Ready."

Kenneth W. Meyer from an early age has had an interest in non-western cultures and spent most of his adult life abroad in and around China and the Muslim world. His short fiction, letters, and poems have appeared in London Magazine, London Review of Books, *and elsewhere. He also lived for some years in Greece and Cyprus, and is currently working on a novel set in Renaissance Italy.*

Elemental

Kate A. Miller

In the night
his eyes carry him
to unknown places.
He is your friend.

William Carlos Williams, *The Turtle*

AT THE AGE OF TEN I WANTED A CHEMISTRY SET MORE THAN ANYTHING ELSE. I was an avid reader and spent many afternoons stretched out on the rug in the narrow hallway of our house in Providence, Rhode Island, working my way letter by letter through all twenty-six volumes of the World Book Children's Encyclopedia my parents had purchased from one of those smooth-talking door-to-door salesmen. Browsing through the C's I must have come across cathode rays, carbon dioxide, and Marie Curie, discovering chemistry as well as California Condors and the Caribbean. In my daydreams I began to imagine myself donning a crisp white lab coat, pushing open the door to a room full of bright light and clean shiny surfaces. Maybe it was the lure of unexplored territory that made me crave my own chemistry set, the mystery of something I had only read about: all those powders and potions, beakers and vials.

When my parents handed me a large rectangular box at the breakfast table on the morning of my eleventh birthday, heavy and cool and fire-engine red when I tore through the brightly colored paper, I was ecstatic. Here it was, the chemistry set I had been dreaming of! Having badgered and pleaded for months, I was still surprised they had actually gotten the set for me. It sure looked expensive, and I knew our family didn't have as much money as many of my classmates did.

My father and I spent the rest of the day clearing out a space for me on *his* side of the basement, next to the utility sink, where I could perform my experiments; my very own chemistry laboratory. I don't know if dad moved me into his workshop to protect my younger siblings from potentially hazardous spills or if he was acknowledging how grown up I was now that I had my very own chemistry set. After all, the kids' side of the cellar was for playing but Dad's side was for real work, not kids' stuff.

Though the rest of the house on Rhode Island Avenue belonged to my mother, the basement belonged to my father and us kids. The left side of the basement was my father's wood-working shop: hammers, saws, pliers, and screwdrivers with plastic yellow handles hung from the pegboard above his workbench in neat rows, arranged in descending order, like the keys on my mother's piano upstairs. Sounds of ice clinking against glass always preceded my father as he came downstairs after a day at the office, drink in hand, prepared to putter on one of his many projects, refinishing the coffee table or building another bird house, content until my mother called us all up to dinner. We were not allowed in my father's side of the basement.

The right side of the basement belonged to us kids. The walls were made of brown pressed cardboard smudged with pencil marks and crayon scribbles—secret messages left by the previous owners, the Reeds. In some places the walls had been punched right through, leaving ragged holes, revealing the dark recesses of the unfinished basement beyond. The Reeds had had three children, just like our family, until the oldest boy fell to his death out of a second-floor window while roughhousing with his brothers. Our parents never told us which window, but we kids spent hours circling the house, staring up at the blank gaze of the upstairs windows and searching the ground below for grisly clues: stains that looked like dried blood or spidery cracks in the sidewalk. Though I played in the basement quite happily during the daytime, I avoided the back room where the biggest holes gaped, and never ventured down to the kids' side of the cellar at night.

Receiving the chemistry set and being promoted to Dad's side of the basement made me swell with pride. With that pride came a sense of responsibility. I remember holding the magical box and marveling at all the possibilities it contained, like stars that remain invisible to the naked eye yet wait to be glimpsed through the polished glass of a telescope. Before I even peeked inside my new chemistry set, I spent a lot of time organizing my lab, pestering my mother for the various household items the setup sheet on the front of the box recommended: plastic straws, an old set of measuring spoons, common household ingredients like salt and food coloring, paper towels, plastic film containers. Dad helped me build a small shelf above the counter, letting me screw in the brackets myself. I pounded in a few nails, hung up the measuring cups and spoons, and soon my lab looked as trim and tidy as my father's adjoining workspace.

After assembling all my materials, I placed the chemistry set on the counter and climbed up on my stool, dizzy with excitement. The red metal case opened like a book, revealing its ordered, labeled contents, a language not yet deciphered. I flipped open the instruction book to the first page, fingers trembling with anticipation. WARNING: CONTENTS ARE POISONOUS. I glanced back at the kit, spread before me on the wooden countertop, noticing many of the bottles had poison warnings on their labels. I shifted nervously but read on. DO NOT USE WITHOUT PARENTAL PERMISSION. NEVER INGEST. DO NOT COMBINE CHEMICALS UNLESS SPECIFICALLY INSTRUCTED. NEVER LEAVE CHEMICALS UNATTENDED AROUND SMALL CHILDREN.

Needless to say, the chemistry set's litany of cautions admonishing me from the pages of the instruction booklet made me uneasy. I was a nervous child; what I lacked in boldness I made up for with a vivid imagination. I hadn't thought that these experiments might be dangerous. I wanted the wonder of discovery, knowledge, and adventure from the safety of my own home, not the possibility of accidental death. What if I forgot and licked my finger? What if I spilled two chemicals that weren't supposed to mix? Would there be a fire or an explosion? What if I dropped a little piece of contaminated paper on the floor by mistake and our bowlegged beagle, Connie, came downstairs and ate the paper and got sick and died? I put the booklet down and closed the box, making sure the latch snapped firmly shut, then spent the rest of the afternoon outside, joining the favorite neighborhood game, kickball, already in progress in the street. I ran and shouted and walloped the ball around with the rest of the kids until dusk, leaving the fearsome responsibilities of the chemist back in the basement.

Ashamed by my aborted attempt at chemistry, I forced myself to venture into the basement again the next day and try a few beginning experiments, quickly paging past the bold warnings in the book and carefully avoiding any bottles stamped with skull and crossbone. I was too nervous to really enjoy these experiments and too guilty—having begged and pleaded for this set for months—to give up so easily. Taking out the litmus paper I tested the pH of several substances: red for an acidic solution (lemon juice had a pH of 2.3), blue for alkaline solutions, like salt water. No adventure here. Then I cautiously combined some of the less toxic compounds, following the booklet's instructions on how to make liquids change color or produce smoke. Over the next few weeks I attempted to create a variety of noxious odors. Caught between my curiosity and my fears, I made a bad chemist, jumpy and inattentive, and most experiments failed to produce the promised smelly results. After a few half-hearted tries I would escape to the park, which relinquished its ominous nighttime atmosphere in the bright sunlit days.

Whenever my younger siblings and their friends clattered down the steps to play on the kids' side of the basement while I was working in my lab, I would stop mid-experiment, quickly stowing my equipment and slamming the case shut. Once my eight-year-old sister, Betsy, lingered on the landing.

"Let me try an experiment, please? Just one?" she wheedled, shaking her Shirley Temple blond curls as she surveyed my lab.

"No," I yelled, "You're not old enough, go away!" I turned

and began scrubbing the counter vigorously, making sure to remove any residue of potentially lethal powder or liquid.

One night, a couple of months after my birthday, I woke from a particularly vivid dream. I had been standing in a doorway to a huge room filled with aunts and uncles, cousins and grandparents, all gathered around a small wooden box, weeping. I couldn't see into the box so I pushed through the crowd of wailing women and stiff-shouldered men until I could peer over the sides and view the contents. My heart stopped cold. There I saw Douglas, my baby brother, with his square head and blond cowlick, pale and still in his Mickey Mouse nightshirt, eyes closed behind the thick lenses of his glasses. He looked like he had just fallen asleep but I knew better; he was dead and it was my fault.

I slept fitfully the rest of the night; the sheets tangled around me like ropes. At dawn I crept past my brother's bedroom, where he slept peacefully in his crib, and snuck downstairs to the basement. Opening the chemistry set one more time, I gazed longingly at the brightly colored bottles, touching each beaker and vial; finally I shut the case tight, tying a piece of string around it for good measure. I shredded the instruction booklet—with its bold red-and-black warnings and predictions of doom—into tiny pieces of colored confetti and tossed them into the trash barrel, then looked around the basement for the highest shelf, dragging my father's stepladder over and climbing up, clutching the chemistry set tightly in my arms. Heaving the box onto the shelf, I pushed it as far back as I could reach, then shoved some crumpled-up paper and rags in front to hide the shiny red of the metallic case. I climbed back down and stowed the ladder, then ran up the stairs, leaving the cool quiet of the basement for the blue sky and my waiting bike.

My parents never inquired about the set or about my progress as a budding scientist. For months I made periodic loudly announced forays into the murky basement, straightening the shelf, rearranging the measuring cups and spoons, and dusting the counter, though gradually I relinquished even this ruse.

I did manage to memorize one experiment from my brief stint as a chemist. Every once in a while, when a friend was visiting, we'd descend to the basement armed with half a dozen empty prescription bottles or plastic film containers, a bottle of vinegar, and a box of baking soda. Combine the ingredients with tap water, firmly cap, shake, and *pow!* A baking soda and vinegar explosion! It was chemistry, it was exciting, and it was non-toxic.

When my parents sold the house years later, prospective buyers invariably inquired about the pattern of circular impressions that dotted the plasterboard ceiling of the basement over the utility sink. "Our daughter in her chemistry phase," my parents would explain sheepishly, though not without a trace of pride in their voices.

I was into my thirties before I was finally diagnosed with panic disorder, the physiological explanation for all the anxious years I labeled myself neurotic: the elevators I couldn't ride, the trips I didn't take (cars and planes frightened me equally, though for some reason I loved the subway), and the times I couldn't even make it out my front door. I sat stunned in the young psychologist's office as he commented on my "textbook case," detailing the subtle interaction of serotonin balance and synapses firing in the brain, rationalizing away years of paralyzing attacks: pounding heart, shortness of breath, sweaty palms, the surge of dread that breaks over me like a wave, leaving me wrung out and drained in its wake.

I have my own house now, with neither a basement nor an attic; my bedroom is on the second floor, under the eaves. The waves still ebb and flow like tides but there are pills I can take when a big storm brews. I still startle awake every once in a while, gasping in the thick air as I reach for the light, but the window is open to the smell of cedars and the rattle of rain. Before long the wind has lulled me back to sleep. Of all the houses I lived in growing up, the only place that appears regularly in my dreams is the basement of 24 Rhode Island Avenue. In one of these recurring dreams I descend the creaky wooden stairs in the darkness, groping my way along the pocked walls until

I see, through one of the yawning holes, a flash of blue light—marsh gas or the hot flare of a Bunsen burner. Caught between fear and fascination, I wiggle through the hole, trailing along as the light bobs ahead of me like the dancing ball above song lyrics, trying to glimpse what it illuminates before the flame flickers out.

Kate A. Miller has lived in Bellingham since 1997 and teaches at Western Washington University. She is an avid reader and has written all of her life in multiple genres including poetry, creative nonfiction, and fiction. She loves nature, birds, dogs, and writing, though not necessarily in that order. She recently had a poem, "Solar Storm," published in the Summer Solstice 2013 issue of Cirque. *She is (still) working on a memoir in a group with other fantastic Northwest writers. The lines in William Carlos Williams' poem "The Turtle," inspire her to explore the hard places in her past, not knowing exactly where her writing will take her, only that it will be new. Turtles carry their homes with them, the world on their backs, and can survive great calamity.*

One Man, One Vote:
How My Son Voted for a
Loser but Ended up a Winner

Linda Morrow

I think I have never been so exalted
As I am now by you

William Carlos Williams, *Aux Imagistes*

ON A FRIDAY EVENING, SHORTLY AFTER HIS EIGHTEENTH BIRTHDAY, STEVE shuffled into the kitchen and made his way to our wooden trestle-top dining table where the rest of the family had already gathered.

"Steve, Dad's home from Albany, and I called you several times to come for dinner. We've been waiting for you," I said sternly.

"Hi, Pops," Steve smiled at Roger, and turned toward me. "I sorry," he replied, slumping down in his seat, a hangdog expression on his face. Steve loved drama and with the entire family as an audience he was playing this one to the hilt. "Stupid 'peech," he muttered, elbows on the table, chin cradled in his hands.

His dad looked at him clueless. "What?" Roger asked.

"President Reagan is giving a speech tonight, Dad," offered Steve's youngest brother, Josh, a fourteen-year-old freshman. "Steve's probably going to miss one of his favorite shows."

With the 1984 Presidential election looming and long before the days of cable TV, the political campaigning caused frequent interruptions in Steve's carefully planned viewing schedule. "You got that right, Shrimpo," grumbled Steve. "No Mr. T." Then his face brightened and he turned toward Mike, his middle brother and a senior in high school. "Who you vote for, Mikey-Boy?"

Mike looked up from his steaming plate of spaghetti and meatballs. "I can't vote, Steve. I'm not old enough. You have to be eighteen to vote."

Steve said nothing, but I could see the wheels turning as he pondered Mike's response. Then a grin split his face. "I eighteen," he exclaimed. "I can vote! I wanna vote!"

My mind raced back to that bleak day in 1966, eight weeks after Steve's birth, when my husband and I sat in our pediatrician's office. "I'm sorry to have to tell you this," he said, peering through his thick-lensed horn-rimmed glasses, "but your son is a little Mongoloid Idiot. He is unlikely to outlive his teens." But here was Steve, eighteen and old enough to vote. Down syndrome had not stopped him. He was happy, relatively healthy, and blessed with a sense of humor that drew people toward him. Many people in our community of Hanover, New Hampshire, knew Steve and loved him.

However, I wondered if Steve might face some difficulty registering to vote, some requirement he couldn't meet because he had Down syndrome. I didn't want Steve to be disappointed so I decided to check out the situation first.

Jeanette Hall, the town clerk, greeted me warmly as I walked into her office. With her bubbly personality and flaming red hair, she was a presence in the small town of Hanover and seemed to know everyone. I explained Steve had expressed an interest in voting in the upcoming presidential election and I wondered what the eligibility requirements were.

"Oh that Stevie! He is such a sweetheart! How is he doing?"

Inwardly I cringed at Jeanette's use of the diminutive, which made Steve sound like a little boy. And I wondered how many other eighteen-year-old males she referred to as sweethearts; but I knew she meant well. "He's doing great, Jeanette. He wants to participate in the upcoming election. Is there anything in New Hampshire's regulations that would keep him from registering to vote?"

Jeanette assured me Steve met all of the qualifications: a US citizen, eighteen years of age, and a resident of the state. "You just bring Stevie right in here, and we'll get him all set up. Make sure to bring his birth certificate and if you have something addressed to him as proof of residence that would be helpful."

The following day, after school, Steve and I drove to City Hall and Jeanette's office. Steve headed straight for her desk brandishing his birth certificate. "I born," he exclaimed. "I eighteen. I wanna vote!"

Within minutes Steve was a registered voter. As soon as he got home he drew a circle around Tuesday, November 6—Election Day—on all five of the calendars he kept on his desk. Steve left nothing to chance.

Steve now took an intense interest in the election and the candidates. While much of the country was agog over Walter Mondale's choice of Geraldine Ferraro as his running mate, Steve focused only on Reagan vs. Mondale. In his own way, Steve followed the campaign on radio and television. He listened to the two presidential debates held in October, and only grumbled a bit about the missed TV shows. Daily he combed the papers for pictures of the two candidates. These he carefully cut out and took to school to share with his teacher and classmates.

Sima Paskowitz taught a self-contained class of eight special needs teenagers. She stood barely five feet tall and many of her students towered over her. Full of boundless energy and determination, she believed strongly in her students' abilities and their right to be participating members of their community. Sima saw Steve's interest in the Presidential race as a learning opportunity for all her students. She developed a unit around the upcoming election. She encouraged Steve's classmates who were eighteen and older to become registered voters. She provided sample ballots for the class and together the students studied how to recognize the names of the candidates and mark the ballots. Sima also helped her students understand that voting was both a privilege and a private act. The choice to support a particular candidate was theirs and theirs alone. For Steve and his friends, having a true choice in any matter was something they seldom experienced. The opportunity to decide on his candidate filled Steve with pride and self-importance. I fully expected Steve to announce he was going to vote for Ronald Reagan. As the incumbent, the President had received plenty of press over the past four years and was certainly better known to Steve. However, my son surprised me.

One evening at dinner Steve tapped his fork against his glass of milk. "Attention, please! I have announcement!" Assured he had everyone's full attention, he stood up. "Ladies and gentlemen. I vote for Mondale. Mondale for President!" Then he took a bow and sat down.

"Steve," Mike asked, "how did you decide to vote for Mr. Mondale?"

We were all curious. His dad and I were firmly in the Mondale camp, but we'd been careful not to voice our opinions within earshot of our son. Steve had told us many times, "Voting private. Paskowitz say so."

As Steve began his explanation, we all listened carefully. When excited, the pace of his speech accelerated and became difficult to understand, even for us—his family. With the campaign drawing to a close, both candidates had been buying time on TV for ads and speeches. However, Steve's decision wasn't based on any of the hot issues of the campaign: proposals for economic recovery from a recent recession, tax cuts, or an increase in defense spending.

Instead Steve described the system he had devised for tracking which candidate more frequently caused the cancelation of his favorite TV shows, especially *The A-Team* and Mr. T. Holding one of his calendars where he religiously X'd out each passing day, Steve pointed to a series of crudely drawn squares and circles. "See," he said earnestly. "Square is Reagan. Circle is Mondale."

"Huh? I don't get it," replied Josh.

"You silly! Can't you count, Shrimpo?" teased Steve. "Reagan, 1-2-3-4-5-6 squares. I miss TV show. Mondale, 1-2 circles. I miss TV show. I vote for Mondale!"

After a moment of silence, Mike nodded his head. "Oh, I know, Steve! The squares and circles show when you missed a TV show because either President Reagan or Mr. Mondale was making a speech."

"You got that right Mikey-Boy," chortled Steve. Undoubtedly Walter Mondale had far less money to spend for TV time than Ronald Reagan. Thus, Steve had thrown his support to the less intrusive candidate!

None of us laughed. Then Mike added what I had been thinking. "Well Steve, sounds like you've made your decision, and your reason makes as much sense as anything else I've heard."

Steve beamed.

The following Friday, when Roger arrived home from his work week in Albany, he had a present for Steve, a Mondale campaign button. Above the image of the smiling candidate, white block letters on a blue background spelled out W-A-L-T-E-R M-O-N-D-A-L-E. Below, the words "for PRESIDENT 1984" stood out against a red background. Steve wondered about the two donkeys (which he called horses), which stood on either side of Mondale's portrait, but he was delighted with his gift. Each morning, he carefully pinned the button on whatever shirt he'd picked out to wear that day.

Monday evening, November 5, Steve had a hard time winding down. He reminded his brothers several times, "Tomorrow is voting day. Tomorrow I vote." He was keenly aware that the next day he would be doing something neither one of them could do. He loved that the family's attention was focused on him and his big day.

Late the following afternoon, Steve sat beside me as I backed our Ford wagon down the driveway and headed for Hanover High School's gymnasium, the town's official polling place. Dusk was rapidly approaching and a biting wind created mini-tornados of dead, brown leaves as I searched for a parking spot. Townspeople streamed in and out of the double doors that marked the entrance of the gym. Steve stared out at the glut of supporters of various national, state, and local candidates who had gathered in a cordoned-off area one hundred feet from the entrance to the gym, as required by New Hampshire law. They walked back and forth carrying signs and posters. He looked overwhelmed.

"Look, a parade," he observed.

Although I had tried to prepare Steve for what the gym would look like as a polling place, he still did a double-take as we entered the brightly lit space. Parka-clad voters navigated slowly through a maze defined by sections of rope looped through stanchions. Placards labeled "A-F," "G-M," and "N-Z" directed folks to the three checklist tables. Pairs of serious-looking officials, all women, sat behind each of the tables equipped with rulers to help them scan down the checklist for each voter's name, and pencils to cross off the name once it was located. A bank of individual voting booths lined one wall, each one adorned with a red-white-and-blue-striped curtain that hung halfway down the enclosure.

"Hey, just like the flag," offered Steve, pointing to the curtains.

A second maze led from the voting booths to the exit checklist station; beyond that stood a gray metal ballot box flanked by two uniformed members of Hanover's finest—both male.

Mike, who'd been waiting for us by the gym's entrance, draped a reassuring arm over his older brother's shoulders. "Are you ready, big brother?! Today's your day. You get to vote for the President of the United States!"

Just then, Brendon, one of Mike's classmates and captain of the soccer team strode up to the brothers. "Mike, Steve!" he exclaimed. "Are you guys here to vote?"

"Just me," answered Steve. "Mikey-Boy too young. He not old enough." Steve looked up at Brendon, a strapping six-footer, clad in his Hanover High letterman's jacket, festooned with a pin for ice hockey as well as soccer. "You vote, Brendon?"

"Yup," replied Brendon. "I'm eighteen!"

Steve stood a little straighter and threw back his shoulders. "Just like me," he crowed. "You vote now?"

"Naw, I gotta wait for my mom. It's my first time voting, just like you and she wants to watch me. Who are you voting for?"

"I not tell," replied Steve. "Private choice."

As I gently nudged Steve in the direction of the maze, I threw a grateful smile over my shoulder at Brendan. Mike's and Josh's friends always treated their brother with dignity and respect. When we reached the first checklist table, Steve stopped and announced, "I Steve Cohen. I here to vote."

If the gray-haired official behind the table noticed anything different about the five-foot-tall young man, bundled into a navy blue parka with a New England Patriots watch cap sitting atop his dark brown hair, she kept her face neutral. Steve peered at her closely through his black-rimmed glasses as she moved her ruler down the list of names. "Cohen . . . Cohen . . . Cohen, Steve." She muttered. "Okay, here you are." She drew a line through Steve's name. The woman next to her handed Steve his ballot.

Steve stared with wonder at the folded paper in his hand. "Now, I vote," he declared.

I pointed to an empty booth. "Do you want me to go with you, Steve?"

"No way! I a man. I do it myself."

I stood back as Steve headed for the nearest empty booth and slid the curtain closed. I hardly noticed the other voters who moved around me. I didn't hear the muted voices in the crowded gymnasium. Instead I focused on the curtain of the booth where Steve was voting, on the pair of slightly bowed, jean-clad legs with the rolled-up cuffs. My heart swelled and I swallowed hard. I thought about obstacles faced and opportunities denied over the last eighteen years. Steve's vote was only one among millions, but it was a vote of an eager, proud and plucky participant with a huge heart. I realized I had just witnessed my son take his first step toward adulthood.

Steve's sneakered feet shifted from their pigeon-toed stance and pivoted. The curtain swayed and Steve emerged beaming. "I done, Mom. Your turn now."

"I hope Mondale win," said Steve as he, Mike, and I drove home. I couldn't tell him then what I, and just about everyone else in America, knew—not a chance!

During dinner, Roger called to talk with Steve about his first voting experience. Steve bounced up and down on the balls of his feet as he gave his dad a blow-by-blow account. After clearing their places, the three brothers headed down to the basement family room to watch the election returns while I loaded the dishwasher.

Within minutes Josh came back upstairs to get me. "Mom, we need you. Steve's really upset."

Steve sat cross-legged on the carpet in front of the TV. He held his glasses in one hand and wiped his eyes with the other. His nose ran. His precious Mondale button lay forlornly on the rug beside him.

"Steve, what's wrong?" I asked. Steve rarely cried and I couldn't imagine what had brought him to tears.

"I sad, Mom," he sniffled. "Mondale lose."

Although the polls were still open in the western part of the country, the TV announcers confirmed that Reagan had indeed been reelected—by a landslide.

"I wanna vote again," announced Steve.

"What do you mean?" I replied. "You already voted. You can only vote once, Steve."

"We told him that," offered Josh.

"No! Not fair! I wanna vote again. I wanna vote for Reagan."

I wrapped my arms around my son. "Steve, you're sad because the person you voted for didn't win. That's okay. I voted for Mondale, too, and so did Dad. Sometimes you win and sometimes you lose."

"I still sad," repeated Steve stubbornly.

"You know what, Steve? The important thing is you voted. You made a private choice. You voted for President. That makes *you* a winner. Now, I think it's time for some ice cream."

Steve's face brightened. "Okay, can I have 'nilla with chocolate sauce?"

"You bet," I laughed. And the two of us headed up the stairs and into the kitchen.

* * *

During his lifetime, Steve had the opportunity to vote in seven more presidential elections. I don't know if he always exercised his right to vote, because by the time the next election occurred he no longer lived at home. I do know Steve was an enthusiastic supporter of Barack Obama. During his 2008 campaign, Steve used colored pencils to render his impression of the candidate standing behind a podium giving a campaign speech. Today that framed sketch hangs on a hallway wall in my home.

Steve died unexpectedly on November 6, 2015 at the age of forty-nine. A week later his Celebration of Life took place in Burlington, Vermont, where he'd lived for over twenty years. Outside the picture window of the cavernous rented room overlooking Lake Champlain, leaden storm clouds scudded by and stone-colored waves burst along the shoreline. Well before the scheduled start time, folks began filing in. Soon all the tables and chairs were filled and people started lining the walls. Those paying tribute to Steve included employees of Howard Center, the agency that supported my son and enabled him to live as independently as possible; fellow workers from the grocery store where Steve (aka "the Mayor") held the title of longest-tenured employee; in-home caregivers past and present who shared his condo; peers from the developmental disability community; former teachers; current friends; and those from the distant past.

Photos documenting Steve's life—including one of him, ballot in hand, triumphantly emerging from behind the election booth's red-white-and-blue curtain—flashed by on a large overhead screen. In a corner a young woman shouldered her guitar. She struck the opening chords and her rich alto voice wrapped around us as she began to sing the plaintive song popularized by Frank Sinatra: *I Did It My Way.* Tears rolled down my face as I listened to the lyrics and recalled the harsh words spoken by the pediatrician when Steve was just a baby in my arms. Oh, Steve, I whispered to myself. Not only did you prove the doctor wrong and live your life your way, but you were a winner—in every way, every day.

Linda Morrow moved to the big city of Bellingham after living for twenty-five years on a dirt road in Vermont's "Northeast Kingdom." She is grateful for the warm welcome she's received from the area's writing community. A special shout-out to the Talespinners, whose unflinching support has carried her through the long process of her still-in-revision memoir about raising her son, born with Down syndrome in 1966. "One Man, One Vote" is an excerpt from that memoir.

The Mountain We Climbed

Marla Morrow

. . . the mountain we climbed

William Carlos Williams, *A Unison*

THE VENETIAN BLIND IN MY FATHER'S ROOM HAS BEEN LOWERED TO HALF-mast. The bird feeder that hangs below it is intentionally de-void of seed. The resident rats have burgeoned from birds' care-less castings and are unafraid. I watch them squat on their haunches and hiss at the wheelchair-bound infirm who are folded at the belly over their seatbelts and nod outside in the sunlit courtyard, unaware. The crumpled patients are has-tened into the nursing home's muted hallway of artificial light and hard, red plastic flowers. The broad, double-locked door seals behind them, slowly then absolute. I watch the aluminum wheel rims of their mobility arc to round a corner and disap-pear. My father's wheelchair waits at his bedside. The frame is skeletal with spindly spokes and rackety wheels that wrench us to the left during transport. The fluorescent lights have been dimmed and whine an incessant dirge. The walls of his room, once painted yellow, have darkened to an ebbing of hope hue. He lives immediately adjacent to the nursing home's commer-cial kitchen, and his accommodations have absorbed the odors of sustenance prepared for those who can only ingest their food with ill-fitting false teeth or spongy pale gums. I smell bulk canned green peas and carrots boiled to mush, mashed ba-nanas, pureed meat, whipped potatoes rehydrated from dried flakes, and Postum for a beverage. Dinner. I open the hall door for fresh air. The stench of human waste and wasting overpow-ers the combative assault of ammonia.

My father sleeps. We occupy this space of gloom. His subsistence comprises a hospital bed, an Ichiro bobblehead doll, an illuminated wristwatch that flashes lime green, and attendants that come to him in quiet, thick-soled shoes. Magazines litter the floor: *The Bugle*, a large print *Reader's Digest*, *Field and Stream*, *The Western Horseman*, and a limp, stapled newsletter published by vestigial members of the Civilian Conservation Corps. The text has been inked by a manual typewriter. The issue has been hand-addressed with nearly illegible scrawls. I gather all of them and place them on my father's nightstand. I smooth their wrinkled pages, close them so the slick glossy covers are topside up and stack them according to size, edges even. Straight. Ordered. I have empowered myself with control of something. I stand back, arms crossed, to study my delusion. Then I hurl the stack of magazines across the room. I have nothing else to do but retrieve.

My father and I are alone, but I know Mr. Death patrols these hallways. He listens. He smells. He pauses outside doors. I know he will soon enter this room. I don't like him much. We've passed shoulders twenty years before this time and circumstance.

* * *

In the upper elevations well above Walla Walla, we had trailered our horses for a weeklong trail ride to the established campsite of my father and his elk-hunting buddies. Base camp was their fabled territorial Mecca, and I was privileged to tread the sacred ground inside the boundaries they marked every autumn with ritualistic pissing. On our first waking morn in mid-July, we rode through ice-tipped, dark evergreens that surrounded us, past the infamous landmark Nellie's Tit (an anatomically implausible apex), to our idyllic destination, Old Man's Ridge. We dismounted our tractable steeds, replaced bitted bridles with halters, and slip-knotted the horses to the puzzle-patterned bark boles of ponderosa pines. I rubbed the poll between my chestnut mare's white-rimmed ears. "You'll be fine," I toned to her. I loosened her saddle's front cinch by a two-finger measurement. My fingers slid easily between the cinch and the beginning of her barrel. I tried to assuage the angst I felt leaving my mare as improbable but perhaps prey. There was a reputed overpopulation of ravenous mountain lions in "The Blues." My mare had sledgehammered crescent moons into the metal walls of our barn with her hind hooves. I convinced myself she possessed reliable defenses. My father and I began our descent to Old Man's Ridge. That was the last time when my father and I were together that I had discerned Mr. Death's foreboding presence.

Mr. Death lurked there at the icy ridge of the Blue Mountains waiting to trip us, waiting to shove. I chose to traverse the ridge by a crawl. My father chose to crimp his body down low. He riveted his weight to his boot heels and drove them into the dried tufts of yellowing moss and russet pine needles shed from a hunched uprooted tree. The canyon on the far side was only half lit by crepuscular illumination. The canyon side we zigzagged was a dark shade of blue that hadn't yet turned toward the morning. Gravity jerked a misfit shiny rock airborne. We watched it ricochet down, down, farther and farther down. The rock's percussive crashing became a mere ping and still it fell. Like the rock, I too was somewhat of a misfit on Old Man's Ridge, neither old at thirty-three years of age nor a man. Unlike the rock, I knew that if I slipped and fell, my fleshed body of 206 bones would plummet and cleave from life to death. The distant evergreens appeared to be readied skewers. My boot slipped in a pocket of loose rocks. My leg stretched behind me and my body elongated flat. Frozen leaves and twisted twigs pressed into me. I was sliding down toward the maw of the canyon. Mr. Death was ice and pitch. I grabbed a small bush. The dried roots held. I shoved my boot toe into solid ground and scrabbled upward.

"For Christ's sake, honey! Be careful! Don't look down!" my father hollered. "Watch my boots." I hardened my muscles to attenuate their shakes, and followed his footsteps with a tunneled intensity on my gloved hands and wool-panted knees.

The steep icy slope we descended was powdered with glistening drifts of soil, grit, and scrub. Second-growth lodgepole pine, fir, and spruce were scattered in prickly clusters. My father paused to stand and yank up his pants. They never fit after he'd broken his hip as a volunteer firefighter by falling through the roof of a house in flames. After that, his right hip rode higher than the left giving him a permanent hitch in his giddy up. He leveled himself on a slab of basalt and jutted up the brim of his worn cowboy hat with his thick thumb revealing brush-cut hairs silvered by his sixty-plus years. A drop of sweat dangled on the end of his brown hook nose like a crystalline bead of decoration.

"Are you sure you aren't part Indian?" I asked. My fear of falling to a fatal angle of repose had been overcome by his confidence to stand and my prevailing curiosity. "You were born in Northern Cheyenne territory of Montana and you look Indian. Mom said Indian men don't have hair on their chests. I don't know if that's true, but you've only got three." (They had been tallied and reported by my mother.) Three hairs! They were an improbable but hopeful segue to my father's true ethnicity that could be confided in me where the disclosure would only be echoed by the Blue Mountain canyons, then fall away. I could wait for the revelation. I picked up a knot of dry moss and began to ravel the contorted fibers.

My father struggled to lift the layers of his traditional hunters' red-and-black plaid wool jacket, flannel shirt, and thick-weave long underwear to bare his paunch. "This white belly belongs to the offspring of an Englishman," he said. "My relations 'across the pond' wore thunder bags and knickers to cover their white arses. I wear boxers and wool trousers to cover mine. No, honey, I'm not part Indian and neither are you."

The dangling drop of sweat swung off his nose when he twisted toward the surprise sound of brittle brush crackling nearby. We weren't alone. My father slid a Woodsman pistol from his hip holster and cocked the firearm without aim. He crept forward. A sudden wind rattled hollow branches. He stood expectant and poised, the Woodsman lifted, but still without aim. I thought of his targets from the shooting range. Dead centers every one. Something moved. My breathing was shallow and quick. My mouth puckered from an acrid taste. Was the sound made by a stalking mountain lion? What if the beast was ravaged with hunger, slavering in anticipation of soft flesh and blood that pulsed? Ours. The wind stilled and our world became silent and tethered to the unknown. My father's grip clamped tighter around the Woodsman. He crept toward the shield of a mountain larch. Another step. Steady. I imagined the lion's strategy. The bunched muscles. The push off. The yowl! I expected my father's pistol to fire. I muffled my ears. I held my breath and my faith in my father's expert marksmanship, but he clicked the pistol's safety on and holstered the Woodsman against his thigh. "There's nothing there," he said. His voice was vitriolic.

"What do you mean there's nothing there?" I quavered. "What do you mean?"

"Come on over and look, but be careful of your footing, honey. You don't want to fall."

I stood on the basalt slab and could see the rack and bones of a two-point buck stripped of flesh and hide. His skull was contorted skyward and I could see the emptied orbits that once cradled his eyes and the gentle life glow within them.

"A damn cougar killed him," my father said. "That's what those mountain lions do, sink their claws into the jaw and snap the neck sideways. There's too many of them here killing all our elk." He slid his gloved hands underneath the buck's rib cage, lifted the skeleton and rested the rattling bones on the ground in proper alignment. They lay still in their continuum of decay. My father's gesture seemed like a wordless eulogium and a sacred burial above ground.

"Well, that's their dinner," I said, suddenly the devil's advocate. "Better them than us!" From my perspective, Mr. Death had been judicious. "You know how much I love elk roast for dinner, but the cougars can't go to the grocery store like we can to buy a pound of burger and a can of beans." My father had taken off his cowboy hat and was shaking his head from side to side, but I just kept on with my admonition like a black robe at the pulpit. "Cougars are the elk's natural predator. They keep their population in check. Too many elk and their forage is razed," I said. My father was swinging his hat with gathering momentum in elliptical loops on the tip of his index finger. I knew I'd better finish my unwelcome sermon before his hat rocketed sky bound and hitched on a lofty pine. "There's not enough nutrition to support the herd, so the weak ones are the easiest prey which actually strengthens the genetic tenacity. You've always told me about survival of the fittest." I stopped blabbering. My "congregation" was silent but the whirring of my father's hat was not. Why did I always preach to a deaf stone? We'd had this discourse before. I could tell my father was silently grousing to himself, but his belly was growling hunger. My own stomach felt a little bit hollow. I picked up an elbowed twig and tossed the tip of umber-colored pine needles toward him. I tempered my zealotry and squelched the fervor in my voice. "Hey," I said. "Are you hungry?"

He just grunted and pulled wax papered bundles from his orange canvas backpack. My father was clearly annoyed with me, but his steadfast role as my paternal provider prevailed. "Do you want a sourdough?" he asked.

"Sure," I said. "I'd love one."

My father had been crowned the venerable Sourdough Pancake King by our family. His infamous sourdough starter that was kept refrigerated in a small brown crock had accompanied us to The Blues. That morning, too early for sunrise, one kerosene lantern suspended in the cook tent had stenciled our shadows upon the well-staked canvas walls. A potbelly stove snapped heat into the chill and the thick ooze of pitch smelled of the forest fragrance we would pass on horseback toward Old Man's Ridge. My father had fried sourdough pancake batter in a cast-iron skillet until the cakes were primed to flip, bubbling on the top side and golden brown underneath. He had rolled up the leftover flapjacks from breakfast with slabs of peanut butter and dollops of his fragrant strawberry jam for our ride.

Swallowing sourdough roll-ups swathed with peanut butter predictably required a slide of java. My father reached for his dented thermos that insulated what we regarded as our multiple daily vitamins. We shared a round metal cup that was ridged on the inside and filled with steaming coffee. The cup's ridges harbored drops of the brew for the very last tip up and swallow. All discord and cougars be gone, the "peace pipe" had been passed.

I seated myself on a bench rock and rooted my boots into a scrap of soil holed into the steep slope. I fit with my father on Old Man's Ridge. By invitation, he'd carved a place for me. A slant of light illuminated a distant wedge of evergreen forest to blue. The deep canyons seemed to have no end. They had jostled and punched and roared and slammed into each other with a godly might that was so powerful it could only be fearfully imagined and yet, there it was before us.

* * *

I am jolted from my reverie by a slam into the exterior wall of my father's room. A tetchy voice bellows, "God dammit!" I hear an electric wheelchair back up and slam into the same wall a short distance farther down the carpeted corridor. I reach for a plastic cup of water. A papered straw is stuck to the side of the cup and offers no source of entertainment. I find another paper-wrapped straw, assiduously remove the end paper and blow off the remnant into the plastic garbage can beside me. My father moans something unintelligible. "What did you say?" I wait for an answer that will never come. His lips are parted and dry. I moisten them with a cotton swab that I've dipped into petroleum jelly. I watch my father's earthly time tick by faster than the flashing hour of his lime green wristwatch.

Mr. Death nears the nursing home's double-locked front door purposed to keep the infirm inside and keep out the unwelcome. My father doesn't wait for Mr. Death to enter. He hollers as loud as he can for a dying man, "Come on in! What the hell's the holdup?" My father has already ripped the oxygen tube from his nose and has refused to eat or drink for two days now. His skin has yellowed waxen. No matter how hard I grip his hand, he is slipping away from me, this hallowed man. Mr. Death waits patiently at my father's bedside until my father's last heartbeat, until his last life wish for death has been accorded. Mr. Death cradles my father's soul and silently departs while I sleep.

Now in memory, my father is still alive there in The Blues. We're there this very moment as I write and we're there this very moment as you read. We are together on Old Man's Ridge skirted by that deep drop of canyon, still jawing back and forth to one another.

"How're you doing, honey?" he asks.

"I'm wondering how the horses are," I say. "You've got me worried about them being slip-knot tied to the pines, just sitting ducks for a hungry big cat. That fat ass Russian guy at the grocery store told me horse meat has a delectable flavor of venison and beef, sweet but gamey. He rubbed his big fat belly and he licked his big fat lips. I was wearing my cowgirl hat and he thought he was being real funny. I told him I don't eat my friends. Let's go back." I say. "We know a mountain lion was here eating elk and we're in its territorial hunting grounds." I tug on my father's sleeve. "Come on."

"Right here," he says, jabbing his crooked finger at a narrow deer trail. "Coyote scat. You can use dried scat for fuel. Remember to always keep a pad of steel wool dry for fire starter and waterproof matches in a 35-millimeter film canister. They fit just right."

"I want to know everything you know about these Blue Mountains," I say, a nascent voyager of the majestic. "Are we looking at the Wenaha watershed?"

"That's part of it, honey. I've been elk hunting here for thirty years and I've only got an elk tag for the watershed twice."

"Where's Slick Ear from where we're at?" I ask.

"Never shoot an elk at the bottom of a canyon," my father says. "Some clam digger did and he spent two days packing out the meat." My father looks at me and grins. "He should've stayed on the beach with his clam gun. Never aim until you're sure there's something you want to shoot," he says. "Remember honey, you only get one shot."

* * *

Now I know Mr. Death can be a welcome companion when the time is right and that he can't ever steal everything away from us. We choose the memories we cache, and our hearts remain a burial ground for keeping our departed loved ones warm-blooded. We all are eternal. There is no darkness. My father and I are on the mountain we climbed in unison pondering the glory.

Marla Morrow is a lifelong learner and responds to the traditional autumnal call for furthering education. She's honored and grateful to have received tutelage from prestigious resident professors and to reside in a vibrant community that highly values the literary, visual, and performing arts. Her poetry and prose have been published in Clover: A Literary Rag, The Kumquat Challenge (Honorable Mention), and The Bellingham Herald. One of her poems will soon be published in SpeakEasy an anthology of selected Whatcom County poets. Her flash fiction has been awarded Honorable Mention online. Marla Morrow is a Ferndale Arts Commissioner who coordinates countywide poetry events and competitions during April National Poetry Month. She chairs the Ferndale Cherry Blossom Festival.

For The Love of Goat

Jennifer Mueller

When I was younger
It was plain to me
I must make something of myself.

William Carlos Williams, *Pastoral*

AS PEACE CORPS VOLUNTEERS IN KENYA, WE DIDN'T HAVE MUCH TO OUR names, just a small bag that would fit on our laps as we rode the packed Nissan vans that crisscrossed Kenya's brilliant red roads. My fiancé, Craig, lived in the next village over and it was Christmas. Most Kenyans traveled back to their home areas for the month of December—even the post office would all but shut down—so there was almost nothing for us to do.

Craig and I had been invited by some missionaries that in a small-world moment knew Craig's parents. With little money, traveling took on a mix of crashing on other people's floors, finding hidden gems of places for next to nothing and splurging when a bathtub was just mandatory. There was little else that would get out the ground-in red dirt from my heels, even a pumice stone hardly helped.

After Christmas at our new friends', it was hard to leave the luxurious confines of the missionary family's home, so different from the little concrete boxes that we lived in. They'd had the first oven we had seen in nearly a year and a half; a TV with a VCR, on which we'd watched kids' cartoons with their children; and a cheese ball at a feast we could never recreate with my local kerosene stove and no running water. My own house, while plumbed, tempted me with toilet, sink, and shower, but never a single drop of water ran through my pipes.

Taking advantage of leaving our towns, we decided to do a little sightseeing before returning home. From Nakuru where the missionaries lived, located in the famous Rift Valley, we headed north where the Kenyan president was from, an area that had received much benefit from all the aid coming in to the Kenyan treasury. There we saw something that we had not seen since we left home, a watermelon for sale at a roadside stall. We carried one the size of a small baby in our laps the rest of the way to Lake Baringo, another Rift Valley lake that dotted the huge gash that cut its way through Kenya. Acacia trees spread out along the way where the Kipsigis and Pokot peoples lived.

That night we found lodging in a quaint rest house with half-log walls and a thatch roof. We sat under a wide porch that overlooked the lake and the Njemps who paddled by using their hands as oars in their curious reed half-canoes. The cutest white baby goat wandered around close enough to let us pet it as we relaxed in the shade. Our own little villages were not touristy, so sitting outside, even though we knew many people, became an invitation to wholesale staring events. It was glorious to feast on Pringles we were given as a Christmas gift in Nakuru and watermelon with no one watching us.

Later we ate a delicious meal of fish from the lake, cooked whole with the head on. I had a little issue with it staring at me as we ate, but once Craig gallantly removed its offending stare, we ate well. Fish was not a common food in my village since there was no water close by. At least for the moment the evening was perfect.

Rain started to fall as we settled down to sleep. It settled the dust that got into everything, and as we were just about to sleep, there was a knock on the door.

"Would you like another room? It is raining," the manager asked.

We were puzzled by his question. "Thanks, but we're fine."

Baringo got very few rainstorms coming through. Just our luck to be there on one of those rare occasions. I'd swear almost as soon as the manager got far enough away that he couldn't hear us, the rain picked up. Not a problem, we thought at first, because we had already been in the country during El Niño when it hadn't stopped raining for five months. We just rolled over and *tried* to sleep.

I didn't fall asleep as quickly as my fiancé, never had. So I was the first to hear it. *Drip. Drip. Drip.* I thought what I was hearing was from the overhang, but then it got louder and nearer my head. *Drip. Drip. Drip.*

"Hey, I'm turning on the light," I said to Craig to prepare him for the brightness.

By the light of a single bulb hanging from the ceiling, I could see a literal torrent of water running down the picturesque log-and-cement walls. The roof needed a bit of work, to say the least. In defense of the property manager, there was no need for good roof; it didn't rain much.

We packed our small bags quickly. It was raining in sheets by the time we dashed up to the main building.

"Now we need another room," Craig said.

The manager smiled and led us to a concrete box a lot like the ones we had to live in every day. As soon as we sat down on the bed we could hear that there was a party going on in the adjacent room.

Standing on the bed, we looked through a vent in the wall and saw the local revelers at a table. There were about twenty people spread out around a large table, probably one of the few large meeting rooms in town. Beer and fish all around. And the music.

There was no way to sleep with all the noise. For us that was no problem; we were engaged after all, and we usually only saw each other on weekends. We couldn't even call the other up during the week since neither of us had a phone, let alone running water. We could find plenty to do in a dry room. The bed was too squeaky, but there was always the floor.

Later, for the third time that night we tried to go to sleep. The party next door had cleared off finally, and the building was in darkness, but the roof over our heads was metal and in the rain sounded like a drum concert. Even so, we were exhausted and finally tuned out the sound.

We were almost asleep when the goat, the same cute little white kid that my fiancé had petted as we lounged on the porch of our original room, started bleating. The manager had put him inside out of the rain because he was only a kid. This wouldn't have been a problem, except his mother was on the other side of us in the courtyard.

Concrete rooms echo. (We had once put a chicken in the shower room back at Craig's house to keep it overnight until we had it for dinner, and the entire building vibrated as that cock crowed at the full moon.) Moreover, the manager had gone home, so he wasn't there to hear the poor kid's crying.

"You awake?" Craig asked. It was probably three in the morning by now.

"Like I can sleep," I moaned.

"How much do you think they would charge us for that goat if they found him missing in the morning?"

I smiled. "Oh probably not more than eight hundred shillings." I could almost taste the recipe as I prepared it in my head.

We never did climb out of bed, but I was surely cooking that goat in my dreams.

Goat Stew courtesy of Lucy Njoki
    1 kilo goat meat
    1 onion
    1 tomato
    1 small bunch dania (cilantro)
    1 spicy pepper, English name unknown
    salt to taste.

Fry onion and tomato, add dania and pepper when onions are well melted. Fry goat in the flavored oil, then add water and cook until tender and soup is tasty. Serve with Ugali.

As a Peace Corps volunteer in Kenya a few years back, Jennifer Mueller traveled quite a bit. She's been to a lot of the places she's written about. Her scrapbook is filled with stories of rafting on the Nile in Uganda, living in a Montana ghost town, going on African safaris, and visiting Puerto Rican beaches, Mayan ruins, European youth hostels, and forts on the Ghana coast. Jennifer still travels in her head every time she writes even if she doesn't get out as much as she wishes. She lives in the Pacific Northwest and looks forward to filling many more pages.

Welcome to St. Anthony's 1965

Joe Nolting

It's a strange courage
you give me ancient star.

William Carlos Williams, *El Hombre*

I PEERED AT THE CLASSROOM CLOCK AS THE HANDS CREPT TOWARD THREE. Just below the timepiece was a picture of the Blessed Virgin that had yellowed with age. I whispered a thank you to Mary's jaundiced face. In five minutes I would have survived my first day as the New Kid in Sister Agnes's seventh-grade class at St. Anthony's. I did okay. A girl was nice to me at lunch, at least she talked to me, telling me about the other students, kids with weird names—Six Fingers and Needle and Pepin, who was on his third try to pass seventh grade. Guess I wouldn't be making good friends like I had in Cleveland, after all. I dug in my pants' pocket and felt a dime trapped in a nest of lint. Maybe I'd stop for candy on the walk home. Ten cents could buy a roll of Necco Wafers and a Mars Bar. A hallway buzzer signaled three o'clock—time to head out—and I breathed a sigh of relief.

"Joseph, please remain after class for a few moments," Sister Agnes ordered. "I don't know what the rules were at your former school, but boys at St. Anthony's, especially those in seventh grade, are expected to wear ties." She gazed at me over the top of her steel-rimmed spectacles. "It's disrespectful to do otherwise."

"I'm sorry, Sister." I tried not to stare at her thin, dark mustache. "I won't let it happen again."

"I can assure you that you won't," Sister Agnes said and turned away.

I exited the school and crossed St. Anthony's version of a playground—a half-acre of cracked blacktop backing up to the crumbling red-bricked building. The school reflected everything about this section of town, once a textile-manufacturing center bustling with immigrants from neighboring Quebec. Now the place looked as tired as a late-round fighter.

"Hey, *New Kid*," shouted David Provost, a guy from my class. "We wanna show you something." He waved me toward him and four other seventh-grade boys. The group stood by a tree on the street corner.

I walked slowly and couldn't see anything special about the old beech tree whose bark was scarred with carved initials. "My name's not New Kid," I said. "It's Joe."

"I thought your name was *fucking douchebag*." Provost's smile showed a blackened stub of a front tooth. The other boys laughed.

My left hand curled tightly around my notebook. "What do you wanna show me?" I felt my heart jitterbug inside my chest and my face redden.

"Oh-h-h, he's blushing like a girl." Pepin, who was big and muscular and needed a shave, stepped away from the pack and walked up to me. The ape-like man-child grunted and grabbed my right arm. I tried to shake him off but Needle Menieur, a short, fat kid who sat behind me in class, lunged for my left arm and my notebook fell to the ground. The other boys, Lumbra—a wiry guy with a glass eye—and Six Fingers with his huge hands, jumped in to help their buddies. They pulled my arms behind me, pinning my back to the tree. Every time I squirmed, they reefed on my arms harder.

Provost, the pack's ringleader, hawked and spat through the gap in his teeth and a wad of yellow snot landed on one of my new sneakers. "We're gonna give you a nice welcome from St. Anthony's and see if you're tough like us guys who live down on Flynn." He drew back his right hand and punched me solidly in the stomach. I doubled over, gasping for air.

"Hey, my turn," Needle swapped places with Provost. "*New Kid*, I heard you moved from Cleveland over by Lake Queerie.

That makes you fuckin' queer bait." He drove his fist into my face splitting my upper lip. I spat out a mouthful of blood and my eyes filled with tears.

Needle moved aside and Six Fingers stepped forward. I wondered if the extra finger would make his fist hurt more. His punch flattened my nose and I heard something crunch inside it. Blood flowed from both nostrils joining the steady stream from my mouth. "Hey, *New Kid*, are you cryin'? You fuckin' pussy. Looks like you had your fuckin' period." Six Fingers chuckled.

Lumbra stepped in close. I saw my battered face reflected in his glass eye. He smacked me in the cheek just below my left eye.

Pepin finished with a wicked roundhouse to my chest. It felt as though everything inside me was broken and my heart had taken on a new, troubled rhythm.

Each of the boys then spat on my notebook, covering its surface with green and brown loogies as they walked away in single file like an evil centipede. They didn't bother to look back at me. "Welcome to St. Anthony's," the boys shouted in a wicked-sounding chorus that echoed against the wall of the school.

I leaned against the tree staring at my spoiled notebook. That morning I had purchased it from Sister Agnes for 25 cents—my entire weekly allowance. Like ties for boys, it was a required item at St. Anthony's.

Numbness spread through my body for the first half-mile of the walk home. I focused on my feet, willing them to move, until I reached Ralph's Esso service station. Slipping inside the men's room, I peered into the greasy, cracked mirror at the disaster I had become: swollen upper lip, a growing crescent of purple beneath the left eye, and a dried sea of blood on my neck and new button-down shirt. I sat on the toilet, covered my face with my hands, and cried. I cried so hard I could barely breathe. I cried because my face and chest hurt, because my notebook was ruined, because I missed my Cleveland friends, and because I didn't know how I would handle another day at St. Anthony's.

After a few minutes I swallowed the last hiccupping sob.

Grabbing a handful of paper towels from the dispenser, I wet them in the sink and wiped off my face, neck, and shirt. I swung the bathroom door open and eased outside.

"Hey there, young fellah, these restrooms are for paying customers," a trim man with slicked-back hair blocked my path. He wore a blue service station uniform with RALPH embossed over his shirt pocket.

"Sorry," I mumbled. "I fell off my bike and just wanted to get cleaned up."

"I don't see no bike," he eyed me suspiciously. "Looks like you've been in trouble and I don't want no trouble around my business. Now get outta here. If I see you again, I'll call the police."

I edged around him in silence with my head down and continued toward home. When I neared Twitchells, our corner grocery, I thought about the dime in my pocket and the rich array of sweets at the store's candy counter, but it would hurt too much to chew; besides, I needed the money to buy a notebook. I wanted to scream at this ugly place and its ugly school and ugly rules about ties and the ugly kids with broken teeth and glass eyes and six fingers who jumped you and beat the hell out of you until you looked and felt uglier than the worst stretch of broken sidewalk.

When I got home I pushed the kitchen screen door open. My mother stood over the sink peeling potatoes. She looked at me and kept unraveling spuds for our family of nine. "How was your first day?" A mountain of potato shavings grew higher as her fingers guided the peeler.

"Okay, I guess." My swollen lip slurred my words.

Mom wiped her hands on her apron and examined me more carefully. "My Lord, what happened to you?"

"I, um, stopped to play football with some guys and a kid accidentally kneed me in the face."

"You boys need to be more careful," Mom sighed. "But I'm glad you're making new friends at school."

"Mom, I need fifteen cents for a notebook."

She laid down the potato peeler and put her hands on her narrow hips. "I just gave you your allowance this morning to buy a notebook."

"I lost it on my way home." I looked at the floor. My gaze followed a crack in the lime-green linoleum. I wanted to shrink down and hide within that tiny gap.

"Joe, you've got to be more responsible." Fatigue washed over her brown eyes. "You're the oldest boy in the family." She shook her head and I saw strands of gray in her raven-black hair. "Your father and I are working hard to make sure you and your brothers and sisters have food, clothes, and go to a good Catholic school. If you start losing your notebooks and ruining your new clothes, I don't know what we're going to do."

"I'm sorry, Mom." And I was sorry, but mostly for myself.

"If I have to give you another allowance, you can at least help out by keeping an eye on Tom." My little brother had just turned two. "He's watching cartoons. Why don't you take him outside to play?"

My brother liked spending time with me so it didn't require any persuading to get him to turn off *The Flintstones*. We headed out to the front yard where I found a soccer ball and we kicked it back and forth. Tom stopped kicking the ball and stared up at me, his pudgy face filled with concern, "Why you have owies? Why you sad?"

"Hey, buddy, I got my owies from playing football." I picked up the soccer ball and pretended to study it. "But I'm okay now."

"But why you sad?"

"You are a smart little guy." I lifted him up and held him close. "How can I be sad when I get to hang out with you?" I wished I had bought him candy with my dime.

"Tell me a story." He hopped up and down. "Tell me a story."

"Okay, let's sit by the tree." My brother enjoyed the short tales I invented for him. "Hmmm . . . let's see. Once upon a time there was a boy named Jon. One day he was swept away from his home by a terrible storm."

"Did he get hurt?" Tom's little face was full of worry.

"Just listen. You'll find out." I patted his head. "Jon woke up in a new place—Bullyland—where a lot of mean bully-beings lived. Each day when he walked to the village to look for food, the bully-beings would be hiding behind trees. As Jon got near they would jump out and push him down onto the ground and kick dirt at him."

"Now I'm getting mad." My little brother balled his hands into tiny fists.

"It's okay, Tom, it's just a story." I wrapped an arm around his shoulder. "That night when Jon went home he asked his neighbor—a wizard—for help. The wizard gave him a bag of magic powder. The next morning when Jon went to the village, the band of bully-beings jumped out from behind the trees. Just when they were about to knock him down, he reached into the bag, grabbed a handful of the special powder, and threw it on them. They coughed and sputtered and sneezed and rubbed their eyes. Then they went back behind their trees and fell asleep and never gave Jon trouble again."

"Yay, he beat the bad guys," Tom said.

"Yes, he did," I took my little brother by the hand. "C'mon, I think it's almost time for supper." I led Tom inside to the bathroom and helped him wash his hands and face. I glanced into the mirror. My lip had stopped swelling but the dark bruise beneath my eye had grown rings of green and yellow like a disfigured planet.

"Supper time," my mother called. I lifted Tom into his chair at the dining room table and a moment later my five other siblings wandered in. When my parents took their places we folded our hands and Dad gave the blessing: "Bless us, O Lord, and these thy gifts which we are about to receive from thy bounty through Christ, our Lord."

"Amen," we added.

Dad began scooping mashed potatoes onto his plate, but paused and peered at me through tired eyes. "What in the world happened to you?"

"I, um, got banged up in a football game after school."

For a moment everyone at the table stared at me, perhaps deciding about the accuracy of my football injury story.

"Well, I sure hope you hit the other guys back just as hard." Dad said and gestured to my older sister Laura. "Pass that pork roast over here, please."

I ate without saying anything else. My school-aged siblings seemed too caught up in the excitement of their first day to pay me much attention.

That night I lay awake a long time wondering what I was going to do in the morning. My nose throbbed, jolts of pain—like electrical shocks—pulsed through the side of my face, and my chest hurt whenever I took a deep breath. I knew my mother wouldn't let me stay home and if I left the house but skipped school, Sister Agnes would alert my parents and I'd be in deep trouble. I would have to face the gang of boys from St. Anthony's. And without a wizard or magic powder, I'd have to figure this out by myself.

The guys who beat me up wouldn't expect me to show up at school. But I'd be there even if it killed me. A blurry, half-formed plan crept dream-like into my mind.

I awoke the next morning feeling stiff and sore and with a sour memory of the beating I had taken. After carefully putting on pants and a shirt, I fished a clip-on tie from my closet, scribbled a note for my mom, and left early for school. I took a longer route to St. Anthony's, one that went down Flynn Avenue—the area where tough guys lived in old homes that used to house clothing mill workers.

The name on the battered mailbox told me I had the right place. It was not much bigger than a shack. Tarpaper blanketed its sagging roof, the siding had no paint, and cardboard filled many of the windowpanes. Provost opened his front door and walked across a yard littered with rusted car parts. Somehow he seemed smaller than he had yesterday.

"Hey, Dave," I yelled in as powerful a voice as I could find inside me.

Provost looked up, startled. He glanced nervously up and

down the street as if to see if I had brought others with me, or perhaps hoping that his posse of bullies would show up. "What do you want?" His eyes were two dark slits.

"Nothing." My heart pounded furiously as I walked a few steps closer. "Just headed to school."

"Kinda early for school." He took a step backward.

"Gotta get there early to buy a notebook. I dropped my other one in a puddle on my way home yesterday."

"That's too bad." Provost gave a nervous grin showing his blackened stub. "I bet it was a nasty puddle."

"Real nasty." I edged nearer to him. A different, braver version of me was guiding my actions while my scared self watched from afar.

"Maybe you better get going if you gotta get to school early," Provost said.

"Maybe I need to finish my story," I said. "It was a tough walk home. After I dropped my notebook, I tripped and must have hit my head." I shrugged. "Guess I don't remember much."

"Maybe that's a good thing," Provost offered, "the not remembering part."

"Yeah," I stared at him and he looked away. "Maybe it is a good thing."

Provost cleared his throat. "Hey, um, me and some guys are going to play football after school." He looked at me sideways as though I were a strange dog who might bite. "We could use another guy to even up the teams."

"I'll think about it." I started to leave, then stopped and turned to face Provost again. "Oh, and by the way, my name is Joe. Just in case you forgot."

He nodded but said nothing.

When I walked away, I felt my scared self and my brave self come together as one.

Joe Nolting taught middle school in Alaska for thirty years. He enjoys Bellingham's rich literary community and all things outdoors. Currently he's working on a young adult novel about the persecution of a gay high-school student by a fundamentalist religious sect.

Bluey and the Great Betrayal

Janet Oakley

. . . beside the white
chickens.

William Carlos Williams, *The Red Wheelbarrow*

GLITTERING GOWNS AND POLISHED SUITS. COCKTAIL AND CHAMPAGNE GLASSes full and shimmering while Bach's *Brandenburg Concerto* played by the Cambridge Brass Ensemble drifted up from the open courtyard two stories below. Standing in the middle of the crowd of French, English, and Japanese scientists, Nobel Prize-winner Americans, and Russians accompanied by their KGB handlers, I took in the scene as a dozen languages and clinking glass surrounded me. A guest at an international soiree hosted by an American physics society conference at Isabella Stewart Gardner's 15th-century Venetian-style palace in Boston, I was as close as I would ever get to high society in my lifetime. Attending the soiree were some of the greatest minds in physics and magnetism at the height of the Cold War.

"Do you know anyone?" I asked my mom as I nibbled on a cracker. I certainly didn't. I was a little girl when we moved from Washington, DC, to Pittsburgh where Dad started his post-war job with Westinghouse. Now he was here in one of the crowded galleries visiting with old friends from there and his Naval Ordnance days, leaving us on our own. I felt a bit self-conscious in the beautiful dress Mom had made for me.

"There's Doctor and Mrs. Bozarth over there and I see several old friends from our days in DC. What a wonderful gathering." I sensed that, like me, she was feeling a bit left out, but Mom, a bona fide trooper and forever optimist, wasn't going to let that spoil the evening. As the crowd milled around us, she pointed out the paintings on the wall. John Singer Sargent, James McNeill Whistler, Manet, Degas, and Michelangelo were just part of the Gardner collection spread throughout three floors. Watching my mom was magical. She wore a cocktail dress she made herself that showed off her stunning auburn hair. Mom was a non-drinker, yet she did not look out of place.

A man dressed to the nines holding a martini and hors d'oeuvres plate loaded with artichoke spread and figs approached us. "How are you, Marty?" he asked my mother. Mom quickly introduced me to him, explaining that he was a fellow scientist and co-worker of my dad's. She hadn't seen him since my family left DC. They chatted about old times and talked about the gathering. After a bit, he turned to me. "A college grad now. Congratulations. I haven't seen you since you were this high." He patted the air to show my first-grade height. He paused and then asked me, "How was Bluey?"

"Bluey?"

"Yes," the stranger said. "That old rooster."

Indeed, how was Bluey? I hadn't thought about him in years.

Bluey was one of the chicks my brothers and I got for Easter in 1953. I remember discovering them when we came downstairs to look for our Easter baskets. Next to the dining room table decorated with Easter grass and chocolate Easter eggs was a small wood crate. In it were three downy chicks, one yellow, one blue, and the third a peachy pink. A crookneck lamp kept them warm. Back in the 1950s, it was legal to inject dye into a fertilized egg. When the chick hatched, its down was not the normal sunshine yellow of a Leghorn (the most common breed of Easter chicks back then), but whatever dye with which the embryo was infused. Around Easter time it was very common to see a small flock of rainbow colors in the window of a pet store. We quickly named our chicks Whitey, Peachy, and Bluey. Peachy was mine.

As a child, I didn't understand that having chicks in a WWII-era triplex might have its challenges. My brothers and I lived with our parents on E Street in the Anacostia neighborhood of Washington, DC, a typical post-war community of young families making their way after the Great Depression and the costly world war. Like many families, fathers had come to work for the various federal agencies involved in defense and the home front during the war. Mothers took care of the ration shopping and raising children, but many also worked in secretarial pools or volunteered with the USO like my mom.

I remember E Street being a steep hill with apartments at the crest and woods and a stream at the bottom. In between were sets of triplexes on both sides of the street: three independent, two-story family units attached side by side. Each home had its own entrance and front and back yards. My home was on the end of one of these flat-roofed brick structures. A small metal awning over the front door's stoop greeted visitors, but it was a good place for sitting or playing jacks. Past the grassy front where I played tag with my neighborhood friends, a long sidewalk ran up and down the hill. It was our venue for riding on books set on metal roller skates with leather ties. The streets in winter for sledding. The alleyways in the back created passageways to other adventures.

It was in our backyard framed by a chain-link fence that we let the chicks out to explore on the first warm day. There they pecked around the swing set, the sandbox, and an umbrella clothesline where my mother hung the laundry. Mom also had a raised box for vegetables, but until the seeds were planted, the chicks could scratch there. During the first couple of weeks, the chicks came into the house at night. Later when they were older, they roosted outside in a chicken-wire cage under the back steps. Sweet Easter innocents from a pet store.

Peachy was my chick and sadly, the first to die not long after the chicks were put outside. Some illness or something it pecked up. When I found it dead in the garden, I was heartbroken. It was still in its peach-colored fuzz, just a baby. With Mom's help, my brothers and I staged a solemn burial in the back, and afterward we watched Whitey and Bluey closely as they grew from fluff into youngsters with long legs and pinfeathers.

Whitey, my baby brother's chick, was next, having somehow squeezed through the chain-link fence and down into the next triplex yard where the neighbor's dog caught and killed it. I didn't go look. Only Bluey remained.

As spring shifted into a muggy hot summer, our attention shifted to catching fireflies and other distractions, like the "lightning rocks" we loved to bang together to create sparks. One neighbor had a television, so four or five of us often watched *Howdy Doody* en masse. On the Fourth of July we gathered up at the top of E Street to watch the fireworks a few miles away at the Washington Monument. Once we went up there to watch a historic home burn down. The wood frame building had survived the Civil War, the Spanish-American War, and two world wars, but not the wickedness of errant boys. It could not be saved.

Bluey became part of that summer as he sprouted the fine feathers and a tail that any hen would admire. Shades of blue lingered around his head. He lived outside for good, following us around when we came out to play. Sometimes we would stop and dig up worms in the garden for him. He'd bob his head and scratch beside us. As he grew into a full-fledged rooster, he also took to pecking my mom's feet between her open-toed shoes when she put up the laundry. When someone came into the yard, he would flap his wings and crow and would sometimes charge. All summer long he was the cock of the yard.

Fall came and with the turning of leaves in our community woods and on the Capitol Mall, there was a nip to the air as well. School started and we spent less time with Bluey. Looking back, I think Mom got tired of Bluey pecking on her toes or scaring my baby brother. He was a fowl who was becoming fouler by the day.

One day, Mom announced that Bluey needed a new home for winter. He would be happier on a farm with other chickens. At first I was sad. I thought it funny the way he rushed toward me to say hello when I came into the backyard. I never felt threatened by him. But with winter coming and no place to keep him, it seemed a good solution.

The day we took Bluey down to the farmer's market somewhere in the market district of DC, I didn't get out of our 1940 Plymouth as Dad handed him over to the farmer. Instead, I watched from the backseat. "Goodbye, Bluey," I called from the window. I was very happy to know that he would have a good life.

All those years.

* * *

So there I was in my beautiful burgundy voile sheath Mom had made for me for this grand, grand soiree at the Gardner Museum. Mom at my side. Live classical music, wine, and gourmet food.

"So how was Bluey?" the stranger asked.

Instantly, as this interloper, this destroyer of childhood-safe memories, asked the question, a long-forgotten image of Mom leaning over a broiler pan flashed through my mind. I remembered a scrawny roast chicken too tough to eat. I gasped as I watched my mom's face fill with shame at this deeply held secret. Bluey had never gone to the farm. He had ended up in our oven. Mom looked so exposed and hurt that this man had betrayed her. She mentioned later that she had never liked him.

Years later when I became a parent, I understood how sacred this trust of truth is with a child as well as the secrets a mother carries to protect that child. But at this instant, I could only laugh over the absurdity of the revelation amid such an elegant event. I nearly dropped my plate and giggled the rest of the evening.

Of course, I forgave her, my beautiful, loving mother.

Janet Oakley, writing as J.L. Oakley, is an award-winning author of historical fiction and memoir essays. Her writings appear in various literary publications, including Clover: A Literary Rag. Timber Rose, *set in the North Cascades at the turn of century, is a 2015 WILLA award silver finalist and first-place 2014 Chaucer Award winner.* Tree Soldier *won the 2012 EPIC ebook Award, 2013 Chanticleer Grand Prize, and was the selection for the 2013 Everybody Reads program in Whatcom County. In the spring of 2015, Oakley published her first mystery novella,* Saddle Road, *for the launch of the Lei Crime Kindle World series. A second novella,* Coconut Island, *debuted at the end of October 2015. When not writing, she enjoys gardening and demonstrating 19th century life.*

The Thing I Didn't Do

Laura Rink

This that I have struggled against is the very thing I should have chosen—but all's right now.
William Carlos Williams, *Kora in Hell: Improvisations XVII*

WITH MY HUSBAND, I STROLL DOWN ONE OF THE TREE-LINED STREETS OF SAN Luis Obispo where we attended college together thirty years ago. This is an unplanned stop near the end of a five-week springtime road trip—a stop I didn't want to make as I was eager to get home to Washington. Bill's wishes prevailed and here we are, on this sidewalk in our old college town, headed to the local brewery. The sun warms my face and a breeze tugs at the hem of my sundress—it is a typical balmy day in SLO town. What is not typical is the tingling on the skin of my forearms, the weighted flutters in my chest, and the unsettled nature of my gut. This physical unrest increases as we progress down the sidewalk, and I don't understand why. Bill speaks but I don't hear his words. My mind is trying to figure out what my body is trying to tell me. This anxiety roiling through me has no apparent cause. A few more blocks, and then I realize my feet are taking me toward the thing I didn't do three decades ago.

In 1985, I was studying at Cal Poly, San Luis Obispo to be an elementary school teacher, though I had always, since the third grade, wanted to be a writer. And I was a writer, of sorts, though I was too embarrassed to say so out loud. I had Ideas. I started a lot of pieces, finished very few, my mind unable to settle anywhere for long. Besides, to embark on a writing career was impractical, was to embrace poverty, and I had neither the courage nor the confidence to do so. Much safer to be an elementary school teacher.

We continue down the sidewalk and this thing I didn't do in college bubbles to the surface. Haltingly I tell my husband about Linnaea's Café, the poetry place, the place I had associated with writers and literary endeavors. As an aspiring writer I had been drawn to Linnaea's, had sought out the event posters hanging on campus, had seen the doorway as I passed along the street. But my desire to go there, to be among people who felt as I did about putting words on the page, was a desire I thwarted time and again—in the two years I lived here, I never crossed Linnaea's threshold.

Bill doesn't remember Linnaea's. A poetry reading wasn't something he would have chosen to go to, though he would have gone with me if I had asked. But I didn't ask. I verbalized this longing to no one, and my own anxiety prevented me from going alone. Instead I stood on the sidewalk across the street, paralyzed, immobile, rooted—unable to walk into the café.

Over the years, as I struggled to take myself seriously as a writer, I've wondered What If . . . I had gone to Linnaea's Café? What If . . . I had allowed myself to be part of a literary community? What If . . . I had committed to a writing life, pursued my MFA degree, been a Writer? Would I now have the writing career that I have been hesitant to pursue? If Only . . . but my feet never led me into Linnaea's.

And thirty years later, my feet aren't supposed to be leading me there either—we are bound for SLO Brewery.

I finish relating all of this to Bill, in fits and starts, emotions I can't catalog interfering with my thoughts. We turn the corner to the brewery, and there, right in front of us is Linnaea's Café, still in business, the door propped open. I go numb. Bill says let's go in. No, I say, no, it's over, it's past, I didn't do it then, the moment is gone, no, no, no. I don't know why I am so adamant. Perhaps I don't want to face those What Ifs. At the same time I want it to be thirty years ago—I want another chance.

Bill's phone rings and he takes the call, wandering down the sidewalk a bit. I'm thankful to have his attention diverted as I strive to understand the distress flowing through me. I start to follow him, then retrace my steps to Linnaea's and look at the posters in the window. I see music, but no poetry. I don't know how I feel about that. I move away, and Bill finishes his call. We cross the street to the brewery, enjoy a flight of beer and some wings while sitting upstairs looking down at the street, Linnaea's doorway in my peripheral vision. I feel sort of out of body, here and not here. How much better would my writing be now if I had gone into the café then? Would I still be reluctant to tell people I'm a writer? And why at age fifty am I so full of doubt?

We leave the brewery and Bill says, "Dessert," and guides me across the street to Linnaea's. The beer has relaxed my resistance—I say nothing but am grateful for his hand on my back. I cross the threshold. "Feels like home," he says, and I nod. The café does have that Bellingham vibe—casual, fair-trade coffee, gluten-free vegan desserts. College-aged men and women intent on their laptops sit alone at small wood tables. The aromas of brewing coffee and baking cookies drift behind us as we pass the counter, glance at the watercolors for sale on the yellow walls, and venture out the back door into an oasis. I am struck—I did not know this garden patio existed and perhaps thirty years ago it didn't, yet this is the kind of place I seek out in towns and cities, a piece of soothing nature in a concrete world, a refuge: koi pond, small waterfall, wood arbor, trailing vines, plants in pots, secluded nooks with benches and small tables.

"Let's get dessert," Bill says, "and sit out here."

I nod. Tears fill my eyes. This place could have been my place. I can picture myself sitting back here, writing. I find it hard to breathe with the pressure of all those What Ifs bearing down. We go back to the counter to select dessert, and I can barely compose myself. I can't speak. I blink back tears. Bill asks if the café still does poetry readings. Yes, but nothing tonight, is the reply. I am glad there is still poetry but none tonight—whether to be here for that is not a decision I want to make. We pick out desserts, pay, and return to the back patio.

My tears keep coming, my voice breaks as I try to verbalize to Bill what I'm feeling but I don't know. I listen to the water gurgle into the pond, watch the koi swim under the lily pads, wonder again: if I had come here thirty years ago, how would that experience have influenced my writing? My tears won't stop—I don't understand.

And then I think I do. This is grief. I am mourning. I am mourning never coming here, but also the whole alternate life I might have had, had I pursued writing as a career. Some part of me has continued to believe that had I embraced the writing life all those years ago, had I entered Linnaea's, listened to writers read their words, read my own words, something magical would have happened. I would have become a writer, a real one, and for thirty years I have hung onto this delusion.

I didn't cross that threshold then because I wouldn't claim writing for myself. It was not a dream deferred but a dream discounted—I thought my writing wasn't good enough, that I wasn't good enough. And I've clung to that belief all these years. Not going to Linnaea's has become the scapegoat of all my writing failures, or, more accurately, failures to write. No wonder sitting in this peaceful oasis all I can do is weep.

My college years were marked by indecision and discontent. I didn't really want to be a teacher, but what to be? I flipped through the school catalog, scanning the list of majors, and reading class descriptions. Only one subject brought every cell of my body to attention. I transferred to a college that had a creative writing program. I got my BA in English but did not continue on for an MFA. Then I kept my part-time job at an insurance agency and wrote sporadically, sharing my work sparingly and with great fear, my writing like a diversion, not the vocation it is.

Now, hunched over the low table to shield the other patrons from my dismay, I manage to take a bite of my raspberry bar, sweet, and have a taste of Bill's lemon crumb cake, sour. A breeze lifts the ivy, swirls my hair into my mouth, ruffles our napkins. Sitting here in the urban garden, I fluctuate between getting a grip and being depressed. I feel fifty years old and twenty years old, trapped by the same indecision: what to be?

I have no answers.

We leave. Trudging down the sidewalk dappled with light and shadow under the overgrown trees, the pleasant weather at odds with the jagged bits of emotions swirling inside of me, I feel Linnaea's behind me, and the burden of a past I cannot undo. My grief is constricting, wrapped tight around me, making it hard to move. I'm relieved Bill is content to be silent and lead the way through town, since I still don't know what to do or say or ask for.

We cross to the next block and I recognize another doorway, this one housing a hair salon, which doesn't seem correct to me. I stare at the recent paint and the old wood door and then remember—this is where the bookstore used to be. This threshold I did cross thirty years ago, many times with no hesitation—I have always been comfortable in bookstores. Remembering that bookstore reminds me of my current one, which leads me to reflect on my current life.

A few years ago, I was struggling to write and feeling isolated—none of my friends were writers—and discouraged—I was writing very little. Time was clattering by, and I feared I might never get around to writing all the stories residing within me. This fear was becoming greater than the anxiety that kept me from doing anything about it. When I read that the local bookstore was offering an afternoon of free mini-workshops for writers, I told myself I needed to go, my writing needed me to go, and I felt apprehension building inside me. I was going to feel anxious whether I thought about going or actually went, so I made myself attend, trying to dampen my trepidation by pretending it was only another visit to the bookstore.

The readings gallery was packed. Uncomfortable, I scrunched by strangers and huddled in a chair next to the wall. I recognized one woman—we had a prior, though slight, acquaintance from Boy Scouts—who later spoke on a panel about being a self-published author. During that panel, another woman told of her experience in starting her first novel. Her enthusiasm and her being older than me were inspirational—perhaps it wasn't too late to embark on a writing career, which at this time meant committing to writing full-time and finishing pieces worthy of being read by others. A man introduced write-outs, bimonthly events where a group of writers go to a restaurant, coffee shop, or library, and spend the day writing. A vibrant woman talked about a large writing group that gathered once a month for a happy hour, and I signed up for their email newsletter. I left slightly overwhelmed, yet mostly proud of myself for going there, for owning up in a small way to being a writer.

Though I thought I was ready to meet other writers, a combination of social anxiety and self-doubt kept me from the monthly writer happy hours for almost a year. In order to get through that doorway, I needed to know that when I walked in, I would see some familiar faces. What I did first was go on several write-outs—the small group setting with minimal personal interaction appealed to me, as well as the structure and implied permission to write for several hours. At the write-outs, sitting with the other writers, I felt like a writer in my core and I was a writer, in a way I hadn't been sitting at home alone.

At one of the write-outs, I saw the woman, the self-published author, I had recognized at the workshop a few months ago. We spoke briefly about our writing projects. The week following the write-out, this woman I had a thin connection to, this author, sent me an email inviting me to join her critique group. I read her email three times, fear and desire twining in my chest. I would have to present a piece of writing every week, and receive their criticism. I wanted their criticism. Though I was also scared to expose myself, to expose my writing. But mostly, I was tired of denying myself writing opportunities, of accruing regret, of repressing the words that belonged on the page. Approaching my fifties, I felt the urgency to get done whatever needed doing, and for me that meant writing. My desire to be the writer I had always longed to be was finally greater than my fear of failing, of embarrassment, greater even than the paralyzing anxiety I'd dealt with most of my life. To the author's email, I replied yes.

Each week I felt the positive pressure of needing to have something decent to read to my critique group, which made me write or revise most days. That external structure helped with the actual writing but my mental state still needed bolstering. Before each meeting, I would tell myself you *can* do this, you *will* do this. Bit by bit I started to believe in myself. Hearing these three other women read their stuff—they are accomplished writers—and having them see merit in my own writing was the kind of encouragement that had been lacking in my life. Our weekly time together balanced the natural isolation of writing.

My confidence increased—in a two-steps forward, one-step back kind of trajectory—and my writing improved, and I readied myself to face the next challenge: read my writing at the monthly Open Mic night. Public speaking is not one of my strengths; it is a particular fear. But this is what writers do; they read their work aloud. In the same readings gallery at the local bookstore, I sat internally trembling until my name was called. And then a lovely thing happened—everybody clapped. Their applause got me out of my seat and behind the lectern. I stared at my pages and read, while my heart flung itself against my ribcage and sweat oozed out of every pore. When I finished, I looked up and everybody clapped again, and what's more they smiled—they had enjoyed hearing my words.

Afterward, nothing magical happened. I didn't write the Great American Novel. A prestigious literary journal didn't accept my well-crafted short story. My struggles with writing and self-defeating behaviors didn't vanish. However, the supportive atmosphere brought me back the next month, and the month after that, and every month for almost a year. Reading aloud got a little easier, my heart steadier, though I still sweated quite a bit.

While my mind has been tracing my writing journey, I have been following Bill, my body on autopilot. He glances over his shoulder to make sure I am still with him. I nod, and then continue to trail behind him on the tree-shadowed sidewalk. All of this writerly stuff I have done over the last few years was not enough to prevent despair and regret from overwhelming me when I went into Linnaea's today. Some part of me has been holding back its approval, its consent, still determined to prevent me from fully embracing being a writer because I didn't embrace it thirty years ago. The doubt-filled voice of my insecure twenty-year-old self has played on a continuous loop in my mind, and my habit of listening to her gave her credibility. But now I realize that I have been listening to a voice that no longer speaks the truth, that I am more familiar with who I've been, than who I am. How do I know this? Because the support of other writers has kept me writing in spite of that doubting voice, and has, at times, hushed it.

Now it's my turn to hush that voice, and replace it with a new one, a stronger one. I take a full breath of the warm air and the heavy tightness in my body loosens. My chest expands and my shoulders drop. I quicken my step, and slip my hand into Bill's. He gives me a squeeze. A part of me will always regret not going to Linnaea's, but this unexpected visit to our college town has given me a gift. Attending those mini-workshops, going on write-outs, joining a critique group, and reading at Open Mic are all me finally crossing the threshold into the writing life. I am fifty years old. I have found my literary place, and I am a writer, a real one.

Laura Rink writes most days—dreaming up stories keeps her grounded in everyday life. She is currently working on a collection of linked short stories, writing with authentic curiosity to find out who the characters are and what they want. Her website LauraRink.com features an occasional blog and a picture of her calico cat.

Life Abides

Betty Scott

Past that, past the image:
a voice!
out of the mist
above the waves and
the sound of waves, a
voice   .   speaking!

William Carlos Williams, *The Sound of Waves*

ONCE AT THE DINNER TABLE, I SAID TO MY YOUNG CHILDREN: "IT TAKES GREAT eyes to see great things. Greatness surrounds us all the time. Most people don't perceive what is always present." That night I was referring to a mother's love and a teacher's duty. Someday they'd understand the power of obligation, learned from daily homework, the practice of reading and writing, even yard work. They groaned and said, "Daddy, make her stop." He was quick to oblige and said, "Shut up."

It takes great eyes to see great things. Greatness surrounds us all the time. Most people don't perceive what is always present.

For years since the first United Nations Earth Summit I've wondered: What will be humanity's story? Our legacy. Insatiable greed? Unmet needs of refugees? Misguided power? Humans "fracking" and poisoning Mother Earth and each other? Or will we be soldiers of compassion and rebirth, fostering hope and wisdom?

Will my children and grandchildren find beauty in a dry creek bed, devotion in the squawks of geese, grace in the ancient cedars with their knotted roots in the woods beyond our yards? If some day grief opens their hearts and minds, will their roots travel deep enough to protect each other and the earth?

For most of us, love and grief abide: those grim weeper twins, overshadowed, of course, by the grim reaper itself. While grief and love wax and wane, they lodge in our cells and in the folds of our brains. At unexpected moments, the twin weepers will open us up and set us down on ancient pathways of bitterness, greed, and war, or compassion, generosity, and kindness. Sometimes to flourish emotionally, a family's vision must mimic the optimism and courage of blades of grass sprouting energetically in spring above a canopy of snow.

Eventually, my husband and I divorced. As a single mother, in grief and in love, I had few moments alone to think or weep. One October day, I finished teaching, rushed from college to the store and home. The night before, my fourteen-year-old son, nicknamed Cosmo by his peers, had a 102 fever, a sore throat, the shivers, and a cough that sounded like car wheels spitting gravel. I unloaded the groceries, tended to my son, and said to Shelley, my daughter: "Honey, I have a headache. Please bring me two aspirin and water, cold water from the refrigerator." A junior in high school, she was practicing her flute and resented the interruption "Honey," I repeated, my head in my hands, "bring the water and aspirin to me lovingly. Otherwise the aspirin won't work well, and my headache will linger."

My children shared viruses as if they were chocolate-covered peanuts. Rarely a week went by when someone in the house wasn't contagious. I didn't have time to be sick; when a virus hit me, I worked anyway. No substitutes for part-time college instructors or full-time single moms.

For dinner that night, we ate canned chicken soup and a tossed salad, with the emphasis on tossed. "I have to leave." I sighed. "I encouraged my students to attend a reading at Village Books tonight. I told them how important it was. How can I not show up?"

My son drooped and asked me not to go. My daughter complained too. I felt guilty leaving them. But a college instructor's job doesn't end when the bell rings, even though adjuncts are paid only for the hours in the classroom.

That night in the bookstore, I sat on a metal chair beside a lady wearing maroon sweats. A pencil-space away from each other, we waited for author Barry Lopez to read from his new book *Field Notes,* a collection of his stories published by Knopf. It was an unusually hot and humid October night. Crammed into the room, our body heat increased the temperature. Damp with sweat, I imagined us strangers revolving in a large dryer drum. I thought of the world "evolve," which sounded good to me. I was thirsty and would have loved to purchase a soda. But in my wallet were five $1 bills, needed for school lunches.

I looked behind me: not a single student from class had come to the reading. No one. My students and my children would not hear Barry Lopez, who could guide them through the woods, reminding them of the significance of redwood trees and the spirit of birds nesting within them. I sighed. I couldn't inspire the young in my life to follow my lead, to value reading and writing, and Mother Earth. The thought churned my stomach. What kind of mother and teacher was I? I swallowed grief and shame. I marginalized myself.

The stakes are high in moments of twin-weeper reckonings. Harder to shun the destructive, too-often present power of blame. I was in no condition to see greatness, or to create order out of the chaos of my disappointments. Into the cauldron of thoughts, I threw my students' education, my children's well-being, the planet's survival, and my self-worth: *What do I know?! I travel by car, from home to work and home again. When day is nearly done and the kids are in bed, I grade student papers, leaving pencil marks in the margins. Every day, I climb a mountain of course work and technology glitches.* As I write this remembrance now, two decades later, love and loss still live close to my bones, in my children's lives, and most likely in yours, Dear Readers, with grim-weeper moments of your own. Or should I say, Dear Congregants, for readers congregate around words to see and feel their power.

When Barry Lopez walked up to the podium, energy surged through the room. It lasted beyond applause. He looked great in blue jeans, and a leather belt with a silver buckle, a blue, buttoned-down shirt, a green tie, and turquoise rings. When he spoke, his hands moved. When he smiled, his eyes softened. I fell in love with the grace of his language, his precision of thought, his embrace of loss and love. His voice rang out like a canyon wren singing and soaring above the depths of the Grand Canyon. Truth be told, which I could not admit to myself back then, I envied his freedom from parenting.

The reading was over. I drove home under a full moon and a swollen heart, to my kids and to those papers in my school bag that traveled with me, in the car and home again.

My daughter was awake. She rushed toward me before I had time to shut the door. "What took you so long? Shhh . . . be quiet. Cosmo finally went to sleep. He's been a brat. I have a headache."

Under the influence of Barry Lopez's elegant reading, I grabbed a chair, climbed up to the cabinet above our refrigerator and took down a pair of wine glasses that belonged to my grandmother, dusty with disuse. That's when I rediscovered a white box, the size of a ring box, tied with a silver ribbon. Inside were hand-decorated sugar cubes. On each rectangle, a flower of pink icing with a yellow dot in its center and green leaves. I washed the glasses, took out a clean dishtowel and wiped them until they sparkled. I went to the refrigerator and brought out the pitcher of cold water. I filled the glasses gracefully, like a high mountain stream cascading into a creek. Water bubbles surged to the surface and ringed the edges.

"Hey, Honey, look at this." I opened the lid of the ring box. "From my wedding reception. The day your dad and I were married."

"Gross, Mom. They look like the fossilized feces of an endangered species."

We burst out laughing. But our laughter soon turned to tears. My daughter's tears into sobs.

"I know you miss your dad," I said.

"Mom," she waved her hand to tell me to stop. "I have something to tell you. You know my friend Casey . . . since grade

school . . . missed a lot of school lately . . . she returned yesterday . . . she's so thin and pale . . ." Shelley gasped for air.
"She's been in the hospital . . . no one told me. . . . Mom, I said
to her, *where have you been? You look like death* . . . why did
I say that? I didn't know . . . how could this be . . . she's only
sixteen . . . I can't take it back . . . it's cancer. . . ."

I sighed. Was this day ever going to end? "I'm glad you told
me," I said. I grabbed a box of tissues. Ran to the medicine cabinet for the aspirin. My hands were shaking when I refilled our
wine glasses, water drops puddling onto the table. I left them
there. "Life's not fair," I said. I put two tablets into her hand
and gently folded my hand around hers.

That October night when Barry Lopez came through town,
my daughter and I shared the twin weepers beneath the grim
reaper. When I tucked her into bed, I put the box of sugar
cubes on her nightstand.

"What do you want me to do with them?" she complained.

"They're a keepsake, honey. It's what we've got."

"Dad says life sucks and then you die."

"Well I say greatness surrounds us all the time. It takes great
eyes to see great things. Some days, it's hard to see what's always present."

"Mom, you're lying. And that's lame."

"Give me a break, Shelley. I am so damn tired."

As I went to bed angry, smothered beneath blankets of my
own insignificance, I imagined the story she would tell to some
future therapist:

*Ever hear of a fish flopping itself into a boat? Well, that's my
mom. Mom leaves me to babysit my sick brother so she can sit
inside a bookstore, missing a real sunset, hooked to other flopping flounders, some even wearing maroon sweats.*

I finally fell asleep, and I woke perturbed.

The next morning, the kids stayed home from school, my
son with his fever, my grieving daughter with her disappointments and a headache. Shelley handed me the ring box with
the decorative sugar cubes. "Throw them away," she said.

I put the box in my pocket, and rushed off to work, slamming the door behind me, feeling endangered and beleaguered, a single mother at a college funded to expand its buildings, while eighty percent of its faculty were low-paid part-timers, with our on-again, off-again health insurance policies.

When I returned home that afternoon, a doe and fawn were grazing in my yard, the doe with patchy fur and a foreleg limp, the spotted fawn beneath her mother's back legs, their necks outstretched, nibbling on blades of grass. Compassion waved through me, and under my breath I whispered to myself: "Greatness limps around us all the time. It takes great eyes to see great things."

When I opened the front door, music was blaring from Cosmo's bedroom and Shelley in her room was practicing her flute as loud as she possibly could. I felt a headache coming on. I dragged the wooden chair to the refrigerator, climbed up, and put the sugar cubes back in the cupboard. Keepsakes are for safekeeping.

As I write to you, Dear Congregants, about those days and nights, I'm glad that the ring box still sits above the refrigerator. Objects honor memories; some are twin-weeper days, shadowed by the grim reaper. The sugar cubes remind me of optimistic spring flowers sprouting above a canopy of snow.

One year after Barry Lopez came through town, Shelley graduated from high school and put away her flute. Eighteen years later, after a fall that left her temporarily housebound, she began writing her stories. Much to my surprise and delight. I've been her first reader and the editor of her young adult novels. How great it is, to be a writing duo: a mother and daughter, not always in sync, yet abiding in one another. On grim days, I imagine her discovering the sugar cubes, as I did, beside her great grandmother's wine glasses. She'll remember her limp toward greatness; she'll sit tall, bend forward, pencil in hand, and as grace and life abide, she'll revise her story of grief, laughter, and love, her voice singing like a canyon wren.

In the 1980s, Betty Scott wrote a bimonthly column for the Wenatchee World titled "Musings by Betty Scott." In 1992 she earned an MA in English, with a writing emphasis from Western Washington University. Her poetry and essays have won awards and been published online and in many Northwest and British Columbia publications. As an editor and writer, she loves to explore the interplay of sounds and sense, experimenting with poetic and essay structures until new relationships emerge. Her daughter's writing interests follow the women in Scott's family, kindled most certainly by Laura Kalpakian. For several years Laura's family shared with her their creative insights. On prom nights, they even wrapped her with loving attention in Laura's shawl and clutch purse!

Before the Storm

Jessica H. Stone

Time is a storm in which we are all lost.

William Carlos Williams, *Selected Essays*

EXCEPT FOR THE SUNSCREEN WE WERE NAKED. GEORGE, ALL BRONZY AND blond, shielding his eyes from the sun. Me, freckled and tourist pale, my auburn hair already turning to strawberry.

I shifted slightly, felt the deck's rough surface beneath my bare bottom. "Non-skid," George explained. "Helps you get a grip on deck." Non-skid. Another new term for me to learn.

He watched the sails, two frayed wings, fringed with loose threads, stained and faded. Like most of this old boat, the triangle sheets of canvas had seen better days. Still, *Rêve*, with her white fiberglass hull and tomato-red stripe, was a proud and feisty girl. She plunged deep into the rolling swells then slipped easily up and over the crests. She'd found a rhythm and we were along for the ride.

I glanced past George to my puppy, Kip. He rolled around the deck with his snout firmly wedged into a plastic peanut butter jar—his tail in a constant twirl.

Leaving Kip and Kitty, my elderly Siamese, behind on the island had not been an option. When we'd heard about the tropical storm roaring toward St. Thomas, George grabbed my hand.

"Come on babes, let's outrun that bad boy. We can make Puerto Rico before sundown. You can leave your critters with Debi—her house is solid concrete—they'll be fine."

But I wouldn't abandon my pets. After all, they'd come this far with me. We were family.

George must have decided that he wanted female companionship more than he wanted a fur-free living space, because now, while Kip played on deck, Kitty snoozed below, snug behind my duffel bag in the forward berth.

"Wing on wing," George said. He stretched his arms wide to mirror the shape of the sails. "We're flying now." He grinned and gave me a quick kiss. Then he stretched out beside me, one arm slung over his eyes, one hand touching my thigh.

I smiled at him then turned my face toward the sun. I breathed in clean, salt-splashed wind tinged with a faint scent of mildew—probably from the sails, maybe from a tangled pile of line George kept in a bucket lashed to the mast.

I made a mental note to wash those ropes, to clean the green slime from them, to make them fresh again. Already my to-do list filled pages and I'd only been onboard, what? A week? Two?

"George." I leaned over and brushed a curl from his forehead. "What day is it?"

"Um, twenty-second, I think." He gave my thigh a light squeeze.

"No, I mean, what *day* is it?"

George rose up on one elbow and turned to look at me. I sucked in my stomach. He grinned.

"Babes, you haven't even been here long enough to get a good tan and already you're on island time." He slid one finger down the length of my body—neck to navel. "Tuesday," he said. "It's Tuesday afternoon." He leaned closer and kissed my throat. "You're gonna be one hot chick when you get that tan." He nuzzled my ear and gave my lobe a little bite. Then he sat up straight and yawned. "But right now, what this Tuesday afternoon needs is rum and Coke. And the bar is open." He stood and stretched. "Want diet or regular?"

I pressed my belly with one hand. "Diet—always diet."

"Okay, got it." He turned away, then paused and turned back to me. "Ah, by the way, just so you know. . ." He shielded his eyes with both hands and smiled wide. "What I said about the tan? Well, you're already a hot chick—white skin, freckles, and all."

I shook my head and couldn't help but smile as I watched him move across the deck to the cockpit. Strong, toned, sure of his footing despite the lift and fall of the hull. George, I thought, was my knight. True, he'd ridden in on a battered old boat instead of a prancing white horse, but still a knight to my rescue. When he disappeared below, I leaned back again and closed my eyes.

* * *

Tuesday afternoon. My former colleagues would be well into the second or even third hour of their weekly faculty meeting. I'd spent every Tuesday afternoon for the past six years in a windowless room with those academics—debating issues that were always deemed of great importance but that now, under this blazing Caribbean sun, I could barely remember.

I'd lived those six years hunkered down in a hermetically sealed, air-conditioned office typing papers that I hoped would be important enough to bump me up the university ladder and grant me a job for life. I'd ignored the California beaches and the healthy glow of fresh air and Vitamin D, and I'd ignored my young husband and his need for bonding. My life was all about publish or perish.

My priorities were misplaced. I should have paid attention to the sunlight, to the fresh air, and to the romance. The week my divorce finalized, my colleagues informed me that I had, in fact, perished. Apparently I had typed enough papers, but it had been nineteen years since the department had granted tenure to a woman and I was not the game changer.

When the letter arrived, the one that ended my career at San Diego State, I'd done the only sane thing I could think of. I bought a gallon tub of Ben and Jerry's ice cream, packed up the puppy and headed to my best friend's house for consolation.

I sat cross-legged on Gwen's living room floor scooping Cherry Garcia directly from the tub to my mouth. The puppy licked at drops that melted down my hand and dripped to the floor.

Gwen tried comforting me by citing all the people we both

knew who'd failed to obtain tenure. That made things worse. I ate faster. Then she tried logic.

"You can easily get another position. They have to give you a good recommendation. You did a good job." But logic didn't work either. Finally, in exasperation, she grabbed the spoon and snatched the tub of ice cream from me. "Enough!" she said. "This is going in the trash."

When she returned from the kitchen, she held a globe—the kind you see in grade school classrooms—the kind with raised land masses and a grid to show latitudes and longitudes. She set it on the floor and kneeled down next to me.

"Look," she said, "I know this sounds like a cliché, but here's what you're going to do. You're gonna close your eyes and I'm gonna spin this globe and you're gonna stick out one finger and wherever it lands, you are going to move there. Spend a full year there. Get your act together."

Maybe I should have rejected her plan as absurd or just plain foolish. But at the time, when my options seemed limited to weeping and gaining weight, her idea seemed, well . . . reasonable.

I closed my eyes, she spun. My finger landed on a lumpy ridge of islands curving around the Caribbean Sea. I leaned in to look. Gwen beamed.

"Perfect," she said.

* * *

Once I'd made the decision, things moved quickly. Before long I found myself, along with my two pets, settling into a rented room on the island of St. Thomas in the US Virgin Islands. At thirty-nine, my landlady, Debi, was only a couple of years older than me and within days we were pals. She showed me where to shop, introduced me to her hair stylist, and pointed out the best clubs for meeting guys. On Wednesday, she asked me if I wanted to go yachting on Sunday. She couldn't make it but she knew the captain. He'd welcome me.

Yachting. I had visions of a gleaming white mega-yacht with polished teak decks, uniformed crew holding trays of champagne, and a sophisticated silver-haired captain. I went shopping and bought the full outfit—a yachting outfit—complete with pleated white slacks, a striped boat-necked shirt, and a navy blazer. I even found a pair of white deck shoes. For three nights I dreamed of yachting.

On Sunday the dream shattered. My mega-yacht had turned into a blistered and battered old boat held together with duct tape and twine. My silver-haired captain had morphed into a forty-year-old handsome, but unemployed divorced man, George, who'd arrived on the island two years earlier without enough funds to leave. And the crew? One dreadlocked Rasta sleepy from ganja, a couple of college kids on holiday, and the local pot dealer. Clearly, I was overdressed.

We headed out from St. Thomas to the British island of St. John. Beer flowed freely, joints were passed, and a super-sized bag of Cheetos floated from hand to hand. I'd never been on a sailboat before so I declined all the refreshments and sat by myself, on deck, with my back pressed against the mast. I was planning a few choice words for Debi.

About halfway through a rough passage, George and I were the only ones not suffering from seasickness.

"Hey," he yelled to me. "Come in the cockpit and steer. I need to keep these guys from puking on my deck."

He told me to grab the helm, hold the course steady, and to look at the horizon so that I wouldn't get sick. Then he sprinted up to the bow to spin a heaving college girl toward the railing.

I had no idea what holding the course steady meant, and I didn't feel at all sick, but I took hold of the boat's steering wheel. A bolt of electricity shot up both arms—arrowed straight to my heart. At the exact second when my hands touched the helm, my life changed forever. In that flash, I felt a freedom I'd never known before. For the first time in my life I felt at home— truly at home. In that moment, I knew I was more than a divorced woman, more than a failed academic. And even though

I'd never set foot on a deck before that morning, I knew, right down to my bones, I was a sailor.

By the time George returned his motley crew to St. Thomas, I'd developed a plan. We could use the money I'd slated for my year of travel—the money I'd pulled from my retirement fund—to fix up *Rêve*. In exchange for my footing repair bills, George would take Kip, Kitty, and me sailing. We'd spend twelve months exploring the Caribbean island chain. It didn't take much convincing to get George to agree to my plan. He bragged to anyone who would listen about "his smokin' deal."

I didn't have any idea how much boat work would cost but it probably wouldn't have mattered. I had enough money to travel for one year and I was willing to spend every cent of it just to be on that little boat, at sea.

* * *

Rêve lurched up and smacked down hard, sending a cool spray of seawater across the deck. Pulled from my memories I glanced over at Kip again. He was still working hard for that last lick of peanut butter. He was one happy little dog. And my old cat? From what I could tell from the snoozing and the purring, he was okay with our move, too.

I took a deep breath and surveyed my world. We skimmed over the surface of the sea propelled by the breath of God. A strong new lover by my side, my critters close and safe, and the storm now behind us. At least one storm, now behind us.

The hull shushed through the waves, the plastic jar sounded *tap, tap, tap* as Kip shook his head, and through the stereo, Bob Marley sang of freedom. *Redemption songs . . . these songs of freedom.* A song of freedom, how apt.

* * *

If I'd spun a crystal ball the way Gwen had spun that globe, I might have seen a cloudy warning of the storms that would come, the terror, and the grief. But if I'd seen those warnings, heeded their wisdom, used better judgement, I would have missed the glitter of sunlight on an indigo ocean. Wouldn't have seen turtles dancing with their garlands of kelp. I would have missed the moments now tattooed on my heart. Walking away from that great and dangerous love might have been the prudent choice, but back then, on the bow of a little white boat with a tomato-red stripe, all I knew was freedom.

Jessica H. Stone enjoys all boats, all dogs, most cats, and Bellingham. As an avid blue water sailor, she and her Border collie, Kip McSnip, cruised the Caribbean, navigated Puget Sound, sailed the Mexican coast, wandered the Sea of Cortez, and crossed the South Pacific Ocean. Jes is the author of the best-selling book, Doggy on Deck: Life at Sea with a Salty Dog. *Her recent release,* How to Retire on a Boat, *helps others to fall in love, as she has, with the sea and with life aboard. Her novel,* The Last Outrageous Woman, *won First Place in Women's Literature, the Somerset Award, 2014 Chanticleer Reviews. Published by Coffeetown Press, it will be available Fall 2017. Jessica is currently working on the first of five novels in the* Sheaffer Blue Mystery Series. *She can be found on the Web at www.jessicahstone.com.*

The Errand

Jean Waight

This also
I place in your hands . . .

William Carlos Williams, *Russia*

AFTER BUSES, AIRPORTS, LONG LINES, AND A CRAMPED FLIGHT FROM SEATTLE to Mesa, the entry garden in front of Sunrise Towers Assisted Living should have been a treat. But all I could see was the irony in the attention to safety, the garden loop railings so fat and smooth, nothing to hurt a grabbing hand or catch a handbag strap, no way to fall into the pond. If the placid residents in this attractive high-rise had known the errand I was on, they'd have looked for pitchforks.

On my flight, I'd had time to stew. After all of the demands my father had made on me, after all my efforts to maintain his dignity and keep him out of trouble. Years of it. The pride I used to feel with each of my successes in extricating Dad from one problem or another, practical or fanciful, now sat like indigestion. This time he'd really torn it, gone too far with his imperial act. He now courted eviction. But there was more to my tight, trapped feeling. He and I had become parodies of ourselves: a weak despot and his cartoonish, long-suffering assistant. Is this what our relationship comes to in these years of decline? Where is the daughter, his once-cherished firstborn? I'd lost her somewhere. And lost the father I'd known, too.

Now inside the broad tiled foyer of Sunrise Towers, I ignored the living room on the right, which threw open its French doors invitingly, and proceeded to the receptionist's safety-glassed station for my appointment with Gary, the director.

My stomach was jumpy. We have a situation, Gary had termed it, in his first-ever phone call to my Northwest home. He had been professional and calm, but then again, maybe because he needed my help to get a straight answer from Ed, my father. The straight answer, when I got it, only made the picture worse. What would Gary *do*, now that I was here? He hadn't tipped his hand.

The exchange ahead of us had more import to me and Dad than to Sunrise Towers. Gary sat in the power position. His was the unappealable decision. Dad could stay, or Dad must go. And aside from the difficulty I'd face finding another placement, if he were to be evicted, how could his pride absorb the blow?

The receptionist said Gary was ready for me.

He asked after my travels as he ushered me to a seat in front of his desk. His starched long-sleeved shirt rested on muscular arms. The strength I could see seemed a bulwark against having to prove anything. He reminded me, in a good way, of middle managers I'd worked with in insurance companies. Practical. Competent. Fair.

"I want to thank you for keeping the gun until I could get here. I appreciate the way you handled the incident. You got the police to leave without making my father answer their question!"

"I was sure you and I could resolve it privately," he said.

I sat unable to take the next step even though we both knew I was there to pick up the gun; fear of the gun now topped my fear about eviction.

He took the lead. "Shall we?"

"Um, first, Gary, did you check . . . was it . . . I'm wondering if could it be loaded?"

"It was. I unloaded it."

Miserable news, though I still was sure Dad wouldn't hurt anyone. I waited for Gary to editorialize about what poor judgment my father had shown moving in to this secure, gracious place concealing a gun against his rental agreement and against all common sense. Would he also bring up other sins such as my father's refusal to be served by a waiter he'd taken a dislike to? But Gary sat silent, still waiting on me. Could it be that getting rid of the gun was his only concern? Maybe he wasn't going to evict Dad. A faint snippet of the Hallelujah Chorus came into my head, up through my woozy tension. But I wouldn't ask if he'd evict Dad—it felt like talking might make it happen. Instead I now rushed to finish up.

"I'm sure sorry, Gary. Thank you again."

"I was happy to take care of it, Jean."

"I'm certainly not going to take a gun home with me. My thought is to sell it here in Mesa. Can you suggest a decent pawnshop I can take it to?"

"Sure. There's one about two miles due east that is okay. Here, I'll write the name down for you." He rocked forward in his executive chair. A pad and pen came into easy reach. I leaned forward in turn to take the slip of paper from him. I took a deep breath, and nodded all okay.

He got up and stepped behind to a squat safe, unobtrusive under a leafy plant, and brought out the offending handgun. Some sort of Saturday Night Special, I supposed, in its original glossy paperboard carton. He handed it to me. I didn't want to look, and I didn't want to be seen with it, the color artwork advertising to the world the shiny barrel and crisp precision of some 1970s Clint Eastwood fantasy. He went back to the safe. He placed three small but weighty cartons of ammunition on the edge of his desk in front of me.

I quailed.

"Do you have . . . can you help me find another box for all this?"

He understood, and beckoned the receptionist. A box appeared, labeled Del Monte Pineapple. I thanked Gary, rose, steadied myself on the edge of his desk, took the box, and left his office.

My cab arrived. I found the door handle in spite of blinding sunlight and settled myself into the backseat, the box in tight control on my lap. We turned onto the arterial and I looked out

at the dry urban landscape that the Towers garden had temporarily kept at bay. A window was open. The outside air smelled
clean enough, though greenery was in short supply among concrete and red dirt and hills. I wished that either of my sisters
could be with me. I wanted a companion, a partner today, to
ease a sense of constriction.

How did I end up in such a pinched role with my father?
Rosemary certainly hadn't. Before she fell ill, my youngest sister had taken part in elder care. The polar opposite of me, she'd
not censored herself, rendering flip judgments on his gambits,
putting her foot down, defending her boundaries. And she
wouldn't begin to engage him on his invention project, the last
of his impractical schemes for building a legacy. On the one visit we did together, she and I clashed right there in Dad's small,
overheated apartment, in front of him, when she flatly and
abruptly countermanded him. He protested vigorously, and I
didn't understand how his evident warmth toward Rosemary
could flourish like it did, if she was used to talking to him that
way. I also worried she'd make my work on his list of problems
all the harder. My other sister, Julie, was farther away by geog-
raphy, schedule, and history with Dad—their early tests of will
left us all shaken—and now that I'd had three years of near-so-
lo responsibility after Rosemary died, I couldn't any longer feel
that my way had been so much smarter.

I marveled that Julie and Dad had lately repaired the
long-unspoken past when she flew to Arizona from Ohio for
a visit. Maybe it was not such a marvel. He recovered from
Rosemary's death, but it seemed to soften him. Unbidden, he
opened up to Julie and apologized for his harsh treatment of
her childhood defiance. Some things are more important than
the To-Do list, and I was thrilled for Dad and Julie. But the To-
Do list still felt too long and too much on me.

The cab moved smoothly along the thoroughfare. I looked
down at my hands, resting as casually as I could manage on
the box. A couple of finger joints showed arthritic swellings,
much milder than Dad's. Wrinkles crossed the knuckles, and

veins rode high on the backs of my hands, like Mom's. Still, to me, nice hands even as they reminded me I'm too old for this shit.

Something shifted in me. Sure, I was being dumped on. But with growing hope that Dad wouldn't be evicted, and now well on my way to ridding us of the gun, I could begin to see the humor in the incident that brought me to this cab with its faint odor of air freshener. It certainly hadn't started out one bit funny. Gary's call had sent me pacing the hall for several minutes. Then I'd called Dad through clenched jaw about the two policemen who had paid him a visit.

"That, yes," he'd said to me, clearing his throat, delaying. "Apparently . . . apparently I called 9-1-1 *in error*," he said in singsong fashion, magnanimous in his willingness to explain himself, if really necessary. "I was *trying* to get *4-1-1* because I'd been looking all *over* for the phone number to find out about the *eyeglasses* that I ordered a long *time* ago. I was getting mad my new glasses hadn't *arrived.*"

But Dad's precise words to the 9-1-1 operator were, "I'm so mad I could shoot someone!" A Kodak moment.

"It was just an expression," he'd told me. "I told the policemen everything was fine."

So I'd had to ask, point blank: "Dad, *do* you have a gun?" I'd waited, wrapping and unwrapping the curly phone cord around a finger. In the end he told me the truth—he'd had the pistol for twenty years, far longer than he'd lived at Sunrise. It's never even been out of the box, I remembered him saying. Yeah. Like it came *loaded.* To think I'd been proud of his capabilities: he'd been able to choose and arrange his own move to Sunrise Towers, in his eighties, no help asked. The sly one. I must have chuckled aloud, because the cab driver looked back inquiringly through his mirror.

Still Dad had thought he could keep it secret. I suppose I could have simply told him I must tell Gary the truth: my father does have a gun. Instead I found myself playing the thought-guide like he had done in my upbringing, going through the unallayed suspicions, the rental agreement. Click. Dad thought of another way forward. Perhaps Bill, my husband, might like to have it, "for fifty bucks. It's a nice pistol."

Bill, home from work early that day, was of course listening to me speak with Dad, and he evidently even heard what was coming through the earpiece. He grinned and I covered the mouthpiece while he cracked what a great idea this was, how understanding the TSA will be about the gun in my luggage, and how kindly they will see me to a phone so I can call home about my arrest. No, Bill didn't want the pistol. But a face-saving plan was hatched—Dad would give up the gun to Gary, and I would sell it.

The thoroughfare had narrowed, the buildings now plainer, flatter. The cab pulled into a dusty parking lot where a small building crouched. I asked the driver to wait, and, finding the entrance amid the black iron armor, pushed on it, one arm wrapped tightly around the pineapple box. I stepped inside a room that felt no bigger than fourteen feet square.

The pawnshop had two other customers, men in their thirties, peering into the glass cases that formed an L firmly segregating the customer area from the manager's runway and office behind. In this small space there would be no completely private transaction. The men appraised me with the politeness of scant attention as I stood hesitating for a moment. To me an alien place, but probably nothing to fear here.

I turned to find a narrow elbow-high counter. The manager, so nondescript in his dress and appearance that it had to be intentional, soundlessly glided up to see what I may have brought in.

"So, I have a handgun to sell, bought twenty years ago and never used." I reached into the brown box and lifted out the pistol's illustrated carton.

A flicker of surprise. Maybe he hadn't believed me, or maybe he saw something unexpected to admire. He opened the lid and picked up the pistol, turned it over in his hand. "What are you wanting to get for it?" he asked.

I shook off some of my anxious torpor and kicked myself into action. "I don't know, fifty dollars?"

The cowboy-thin customer nearest me looked sideways to catch my eye, keeping his head down and forward, pretending uninterrupted absorption in the items in the case, but I noticed and glanced sideways as well, to see him subtly shake his head. I followed his lead, pretending not to have received any message, any help. "Well, of course," I added quickly, "it is in new condition, and I have this ammunition, too. It is probably worth more than that. What would you give me for it?"

"Just a moment," the manager said, and turned into his adjoining office and stood at a computer positioned to allow him to keep an eye on the main door. Security and vigilance always. Soon he was back.

"I could probably do one-fifty."

"Okay," I said, and he presented the paperwork, explaining the need to document ownership. I filled in Dad's information. Cash was counted into my hand and we were done. My silent confederate had gone, but outside, there he was. He told me the pawnshop would probably get five or even six hundred dollars for the pistol I'd just sold. I nodded that I believed him, and then thanked him sincerely for his kindness. There really are a lot of nice people in the world.

I got into the waiting cab for the ride back to Dad's hothouse apartment and our reunion. On arriving, I paid the driver and watched him pull away. This time I passed through the garden more slowly. I stopped to look down at koi in a pond artfully rimmed by succulents like unfurled fans. Overhead, tropical palm fronds sheltered me from the glare, lacing the light, their leaf-scar-textured pillars mingling with a desert-native palo verde. The oasis, though an artificial combination, created a harmonious effect. How did the designer know that tropical palms would give Dad, in his now-small world, old friends from a happy year spent in Southeast Asia?

Inside the lobby, I signed for a visitor's badge and took the elevator to the ninth floor to Dad's apartment. Dad's rangy six-foot frame slumped in his chair facing the TV. He lifted his head. He'd been expecting me, and greeted me warmly. After bending to hug him about the shoulders, I told him about my pawnshop adventure, and I pressed the $150 into his hand. He didn't get that a trip to a pawnshop could be a big deal for anybody, but he showed interest in the part about the Good Samaritan.

"Well," I said, "I'm pretty tired. I'll get on back to the motel." The good assistant, bowing out, the job done.

"So soon?" he said.

"You're right, Dad. This calls for a celebration." I went to the fridge, a mere three steps from his living room, pulled out the bottle of ale stowed there on my last visit, and poured a couple of ounces into a glass for him and the rest into a glass for me. I opened the light-blocking drape to temporarily dispel the stuffy dimness his eyes preferred. He blinked, didn't complain.

We raised our glasses. "To a good outcome," he said companionably. He sipped, I gulped.

"I'm glad." I said.

Then he blinked again, ratcheting his way into seeing how the loss of his gun, even recouping but little of its value, was truly worth celebrating. "Yes, a fine outcome, Jean." He looked at me, really looked at me, and I met his now failing eyes as in the old days. I didn't know how well he could see me, but a twinkle spoke of past good times, making me recall a practical joke we'd shared in a time when we car-camped as a family. The odd squawk he'd devised, its pitch and volume slowly rising from a rumbly low, those big hands cupped at his mouth, tightly straining as if at a trumpet. Immediate silence in the next camp. "What was *that*?" we'd hear them whisper in the darkness, as my sisters, Mom, and I, allies in this improvisation, had squelched our laughter.

Sitting across from my father in the newly brightened room, I was once again the daughter he'd cherished first. The one for whom he'd quit smoking when she was born, and whose countless excited schoolgirl reports he'd listened to, stories that couldn't wait even for him to finish changing his clothes after the office. It was as though in these later years he'd been asking me to help him live forever. But what he enjoyed was having a junior colleague to discuss projects with. And if his ambitions didn't work out, or even when they did, he was still my faithful booster as well, ready to encourage my own dreams and hopes. The choice had always been mine, to not fear his falling apart, to make room for my own dreams. I said, "Dad, we're alright." And meant it.

Jean Waight is a Bellingham essayist and memoirist who formerly worked in communications for Group Health Cooperative. Her first-person account of the twists and turns in a snow rescue, "Through the Floor," appeared in Cirque: A Literary Journal *for the North Pacific Rim, winter 2015. The Bellingham Herald published her beach cleanup essay, and her sociological research into retirement's effect on income stratification was published in the journal* Research in Social Stratification and Mobility. *Her blog of life among the trees, full of shady opinions, is at greenteasympathy.blogspot.com.*

Abaldyeno

Jennifer Wilke

I descend into
my dream as into a quiet lake
and there, already there, I find
my kinships.

William Carlos Williams, *Russia*

WE BOARDED AN AEROFLOT JET IN WASHINGTON, DC, IN AUGUST OF 1988, and flew east nonstop for seven hours, crossing eight time zones. Stewardesses wearing dark blue uniforms and iridescent blue eye shadow served us ground meat sandwiches with fading lettuce and glasses of green lemonade. When we landed on the gray tarmac under cloudy skies, it was dawn of the next day. The stark terminal was redeemed by six giant neon letters in the Cyrillic alphabet: M-O-C-K-B-A. *Moskva.*

We were two hundred Americans who'd met each other the week before, volunteers to join the International Soviet-American Peace Walk. We were flying on to Odessa in the Soviet Republic of Ukraine, where two hundred Soviet citizens participating through the Soviet Peace Committee would join us. Together, we would walk and camp 450 miles to Kiev, through villages and orchards and vast communal farms. We would carry a banner that read, in Russian, *We are walking together with a mission of peace.* Мир *(Meer)* is the Russian word for peace, and the word for community, and the word for planet Earth.

The Cold War was in abeyance and *glasnost* was real, but our two countries still possessed a total of 50,000 nuclear weapons, "essential" to keeping the peace. Our countries were caught in an arms race no one could win. Destroying all the weapons wasn't a likely prospect, so peace initiatives reflected a strategy even President Reagan liked: make friends with the enemy.

When I was preparing for this trip to the Союз советской Социалистической Республики—the Union of Soviet Socialist Republics—more than one US friend asked me, "Aren't you afraid to go there?" Yes, that was what intrigued me most! I wanted to challenge the assumption that we should fear people in the USSR. I knew they didn't need to fear me. My hero was Capt. James Kirk of the Starship Enterprise. On *Star Trek* he explored "strange new worlds to boldly go where no man has gone before." Scary things were always happening but he never panicked—he kept thinking rationally and won the day. I didn't need a phaser weapon—I intended to use words. I'd brought hundreds of cards to give away, with the same phrase printed in Russian and English: Пустъ мир с меня начнется. *Let peace begin with me.* My Russian tutor in Los Angeles told me the best thing to say to anyone I met: *We are the same simple people as you.*

At last, our motley retinue of two hundred Americans descended Aeroflot's push-up jet stairs and set foot on Soviet soil in Moscow. Among us were peace activists and businessmen, journalists, teachers, students, housewives, ex-military men, a California surfer who brought his skateboard—all adventurers of goodwill. The youngest walker was ten years old, from Iowa, who persuaded her mother to come with her to learn about Russians. The oldest walker was over seventy and set the fastest pace.

We followed our American leaders through an unmarked door into the Moscow terminal, subdued by the prospect of passing through Soviet Customs. The windowless hallway opened into a vast room where people waited in countless lines to talk to uniformed men in glass booths. The glare of the lights high overhead made my eyes water. My pulse beat faster as I chose a line. During our week of preparation in the US, we had been warned about the many, many, many things that were not permitted in the Soviet Union, including pornography, drug paraphernalia, and numerous other unspecified items detrimental to the State. We had been strongly advised to be mindful of our conduct and do nothing defiant or disrespectful of Soviet authorities.

As the line inched forward, I remembered the Aeroflot barf bag I'd stolen from my seat pocket on the plane. Would the Customs officer ask me to empty my pockets? Would he accept my defense of innocently wanting a souvenir of the Russian language description of how to use a barf bag? Is a sense of humor allowed?

When it was my turn, I stepped up to the glass booth and faced a young man in a plain brown uniform that needed ironing. He wore no nametag or badges or medals. The stiff collar chafed one side of his neck. His visored cap was too large for his head. I smiled as I offered him my passport. He studied my photograph, then his dark eyes scrutinized my face. He looked at my bright homemade nametag that read "Jenny" in English and "*Dzheni*" in Russian. Still holding the passport with my Los Angeles address, he said, "I like see California." His wistful smile matched the impossibility in his voice.

"Maybe you will one day," I said, because I had brought my optimism with me from America. I'd often dreamed of seeing the Soviet Union—and at long last, here I was. A moment ago I'd been dreading this confrontation, and instead I'd met a boy who loved Disneyland.

He shrugged and turned away to write on the Customs form. With his head bowed, he looked like a man praying. I could give him my return ticket and find my own way home. The Ukrainians I knew in LA would greet him at LAX if I asked them to, be his hosts, teach him English, introduce him to a nice Ukrainian girl. Maybe he could get a job with US Customs and marry the girl and have a family and take them to the Santa Monica Pier and write happy letters home—

He pushed my passport back to me through the hole in the glass. Pointing to the Peace Walk ID badge around my neck, he gave me a thumbs up. In my simple Russian, I told truth to power: "Let peace begin with us."

He winked and pointed me toward the exit, then motioned

the person behind me to step forward. I was sad to leave him. He was my first real Russian. We both liked California and peace, a very good omen.

After waiting for hours in the Moscow airport, we flew to Odessa, landing in the middle of the night, or the middle of the night before, I didn't remember anymore. The only light was from our jet's floodlights as we descended the stairs to a vast, empty tarmac. The only sound was from skateboard wheels as the lanky blond surfer made slow circles around us, in and out of the light. Where were the Soviet walkers who were supposed to meet us? We were exhausted, hungry, and felt abandoned. Not even our leaders had any idea where to go without our hosts, so we waited in the dark.

Our salvation began with the distant sound of buses, then the bright flash of headlights coming toward us. Bus after bus after bus, twenty in all, pulled to a stop. Doors opened and people sprang down the steps, calling out greetings as they ran toward us. We ran toward them, calling back, happy to be found. Our skateboarder zoomed ahead, the first to cross the diminishing divide between our two converging groups. In the middle of an airfield in the dead of night, somewhere near the city of Odessa and the Black Sea, our apprehensions vanished in the eager welcome of the Soviets who'd been waiting for us for hours. Our laughter didn't need translation.

A short, blonde woman with a megawatt smile read my nametag, *"Dzheni! Dzheni!"* and grabbed my hand to claim me. Alla was her name. She was a journalism student at a university in Moldova, which I knew was next door to the Ukraine, so she wasn't far from home. Her head barely came up to my shoulder. I wanted to make a joke about Mutt and Jeff, but didn't know where to begin. Alla spoke no English so was thrilled by every Russian word I uttered, and complimented my accent. She told me in Russian she knew I'd be fluent by the time we reached Kiev.

Alla led me toward the bus we would share. Every Soviet walker had befriended an American and soon we filled the buses. I gratefully settled into a window seat that was surprisingly plush. Alla sat across the aisle with her friend Nagore, a young Asian beauty who had three gold teeth and came from Tashkent in Uzbekistan. I knew there were several "-istan" Republics in the east before getting to China. But if anyone had challenged me to recite them all, I'd have failed. Like trying to name the seven dwarves or all the reindeer. Alla and Nagore weren't sure where California was, either. Why in the world hadn't I brought a pocket atlas?

Our caravan of buses drove toward our shared campsite. In the darkness, I couldn't see the landscape out the bus window, just the escort of motorcycle policemen flanking each bus. When I expressed amazement at this special treatment, Alla assured me that we were important people. The Soviet Peace Committee was in charge, which assured our special care and the success of our journey.

Another woman left her seat and came toward me, with a smile. She was petite, with trim, wavy hair. She stopped in the aisle and asked in English, with a slight British accent, if she might be permitted to occupy the vacant seat next to mine.

"This would be my honor," I said, to match her formal manner.

Ludmila introduced herself as she settled in. Her bright blue eyes and boldness made her courtesy all the more disarming. She had two children, a boy and a girl. Her husband was a doctor and they lived together in Chelyabinsk, a long way north and east of Odessa. Her smile revealed the lines in her face, and I gauged that she must be in her forties. She accessorized her running suit with a string of pearls. Her nails were clean and polished. Perhaps she didn't know we would be camping.

She asked about my family. I told her I worked in the movie business in Los Angeles, was divorced, and had no children. A shadow crossed her brow, but her smile didn't falter. She changed the subject and admired my homemade nametag.

"How did you come to be on this Peace Walk?" I asked her.

She touched my arm and laughed. "You are the first American of my life, Jenny. Camping is a small price to pay to meet you."

Her acceptance of me was unconditional, and so was mine of her. "But I'm worried about your shoes," I told her. She wore simple canvas flats with thin soles. I had been a camper since I joined the Girl Scouts when I was seven, and had on a pair of the best walking shoes American money could buy.

She waved away my worries. "Shoes can always be found here, but not Americans. Tell me about where you live."

I took a deep breath and attempted to describe Los Angeles. The Soviets in the seats all around us were listening. The other Americans on the bus were asleep.

"Why did you come on this Peace Walk?" Ludmila wanted to know.

"To stop being afraid of you," I said in Russian. I used the formal, plural "you."

The listening Soviets all leaned closer, eyes wide. "Afraid of us?" Alla asked in Russian.

I nodded. "Of the Soviet Union. Of the Communists. Of your atom bombs."

As Ludmila translated what I'd said, even Alla grew silent. With Ludmila's help, I told them about the drills we had in elementary school, when we hid under our desks with our hands over our heads to protect us from a Soviet bomb. I told them that forty years ago a person's life could be ruined if people thought they were a Communist, or even had a friend who was.

A young man behind my seat said something in Russian and I saw Ludmila give him a disapproving shake of her head.

"What did he say?" I asked her.

She shrugged, but answered me. "He said that lives here are ruined if you are not a Communist."

When we reached our camp and disembarked, our baggage was waiting. Alla guided us to the wooden latrines set in a long outdoor row, so newly built they still smelled of fresh-cut pine. With the help of flashlights and pantomime, Alla and the three other women in her tent turned their bedding so that the five of us could lie across the four air mattresses for the night. Thanking them, I fell fast asleep.

I was the first to wake at dawn. I peeked through the tent flap and saw clear sky. Still in yesterday's clothes, I put on the shoes I'd broken in walking in the Hollywood Hills, and grabbed my ID tags and camera. I stepped out of the tent in the early morning light onto a dirt path between rows of tents identical to the one I'd exited—A-shaped fraying canvas tents that looked like military cast-offs. Communal living. I looked forward to my new Soviet friends' reaction tonight when I set up my own small and shiny tent, nothing communal about it. I hoped it translated that I wasn't unfriendly—I just wanted to get a good night's sleep.

The landscape was sparse, a few small trees, more dirt than grass. Some of the bushes looked like rhododendrons. The path led me out of the Soviet tent rows to an open meadow and the view made me laugh out loud. The tents here were every type and shape, in a rainbow of colors, pitched last night in the dark without any concern for straight lines or order—the American campers!

A woman I'd met from Nebraska entered the meadow from another path. She was in a swimsuit and drying her hair with a towel. I followed that trail over a slight dune to discover a curving sandy beach and the endless Black Sea. The vast expanse of water was velvet blue, not black. The faded moon was sinking into the watery horizon to let the sun take its place. I saw a bobbing head swimming toward shore. A man walked out and retrieved his towel from the beach. As he came closer, I recognized Meerzo from the night before, a small, muscled man whose enthusiasm for conversation with Americans wasn't hindered by his speaking no English. He was from an "-istan" country. He had a leathery look and laborer's hands. He grinned and gestured for me to follow. Together, we found breakfast.

A large, rough building in the center of the camp was filled with long rows of tables laid with linen tablecloths, napkins, silverware, and china set at every place. The orange juice was fizzy, like soda. Gorgeous brass samovars kept water hot for tea or instant coffee. Sliced tomatoes, ham, and thick pieces of rye bread were layered on serving plates. Sweet butter and jam nestled in china pots with silver serving spoons. I was famished. A perfect feast.

After we'd all had breakfast, I joined Alla and her pals for another walk to the sea. I took everyone's photograph and they all asked me to send them a copy. I should have brought a Polaroid. I stepped away from the happy group to watch the Black Sea taking on the day's colors. Two women stood together at the water's edge, in one-piece black swimming suits. Facing each other, profiled against the growing light, their fat bellies almost touched. I took their photograph without permission. If I showed it back home, I imagined that everyone would get a laugh at their immodesty and disregard of censure; no one that fat wears a bathing suit on a beach in Southern California. I watched the women tuck their short hair into tight rubber caps. They stepped out of their sandals and walked into the sea. A morning ritual, I assumed. Were they sisters? In-laws? Friends? They swam away from shore in parallel paths, each with powerful, steady strokes. They belonged here. I was the shallow American guest, ungraciously judging them. I put my camera away.

I rejoined the group with Alla. She put her arms around me and asked if I was having a good time. Welcoming her embrace, I assured her in Russian that I was very happy to be there. I saw a walker nearby who could translate and waved him over for help. I wanted to know the best Russian slang for "awesome."

He didn't know what "awesome" meant.

"In Los Angeles, it's slang for something brilliant, exciting, something that makes you very happy."

He consulted with everyone, and they reached an agreement. "Abaldyeno!" he announced.

"Abaldyeno," I repeated, making everyone laugh. They corrected my pronunciation to emphasize the third syllable. I repeated it several more times. They kept laughing.

"Why's it so funny?" I protested. "You're playing a trick on me!"

"*Nyet, nyet, nyet,*" Alla assured me in Russian, "we laugh because you sound so Russian, Jenny."

I grinned. "Abaldyeno!"

Jennifer Wilke's first trauma was realizing she could never read all the books in the library. She once threw over a boyfriend who thought a 700-page biography of Tolstoy was a better Christmas present than a novel by Tolstoy or a love poem. Her first published writing was a controversial newspaper column, when she had an opinion about everything. She once owned a coffeehouse in Alaska and still makes wonderful soup (pesto is the secret to great minestrone, and rosemary does wonders for split pea soup). She loves good movies and winning at charades. After studying screenwriting in LA and yada yada yada, she was relieved to return to the Pacific Northwest, find Red Wheelbarrow Writer pals in Bellingham, and complete a historical novel. "Abaldyeno" is an excerpt from a memoir in progress, After a Little Rain on Thursday, *about peace and war.*

The Great Moratorium

Diane Wood

First he said:
It is the woman in
Us that makes us write—
Let us acknowledge it—
Men would be silent
We are not men
Therefore we can speak

William Carlos Williams, *Transitional*

WHEN I WAS EIGHTEEN AND LIVING A HUMDRUM AND BORING LIFE, MY HOR-mone-soaked cells raced through my body screaming, "Let's get the hell out of here!" My mind overflowed with daydreams of an exciting, colorful life of freedom, self-determination, and independence. Bustin' out of the beige life was at the top of my to-do list. The big challenge was how to pull it off.

A month after graduation I eloped with my high-school sweetheart. The idea of being married was titillating. I reveled in finally being able to make my own decisions. Man and wife. What a heady experience. We lived with his family, which seemed a logical idea at the time, and shared a twin bed. Our wedding reception was held on a beautiful August evening in his parents' backyard. That was the first time I'd experienced a bunch of drunks physically fighting and swearing out loud at the neighbors. It was also the night I experienced my first split lip. So much for conjugal bliss. *Wow, this is just like in the movies!* ran through my mind.

The next morning my new mother-in-law took my hand, looked me in the eyes and said, "Well, you're married now, *mija*. You'll have to learn to take it."

As completely confused, shamed, and tenacious as I was at that age, I allowed this to become my hidden life. The last thing I wanted was to hear my family say, "You made your bed. Now lie in it." Polite conversation wouldn't include talking about one's abusive husband. I thought sooner rather than later everyone would figure it out anyway.

Friday night fights became the norm. Calm weekdays, payday, alcohol, insanity, apology, forgiveness. Repeat, repeat, repeat for three passionate, terrifying, exasperating years. One boy child. One girl child. Existing on hope and promises. Add one surprising miscarriage. A tiny, six-week-old fetus the size of an egg slid out of my body during one extremely traumatic weekend. I was done. The sign was clear—life was slipping out of me. We escaped that volatile relationship: my nineteen-month-old son, my four-month-old daughter and the will to change my life.

* * *

During the next fifteen years, my old dreams still included the white picket fence lifestyle. *If I could just find the perfect prince.* Two more short-lived marriages. *What's wrong with me? Is my picker that broken?*

There was a knowing deep inside me that something significant had to change in me before I would get this relationship thing right. I knew the answer wasn't outside myself. Drinking coffee one morning I read a tiny ad in the *Rocky Mountain News* about an upcoming volunteer training for the Domestic Violence Prevention Center in Colorado Springs. I saw the clouds part and heard the trumpets blare.

Helping battered women! I knew about that stuff! They needed me! I signed up.

A pathway to worldly enlightenment and blossoming feminism was being laid out before me. So many things I'd contemplated were being affirmed. My most profound awakening during that training was when I learned that what I'd experienced was called abuse. Abuse with a capital A. What a monumental epiphany that was. I had been one of them, one of *those* women, a victim of domestic violence. Only now I was called—a survivor. I gagged trying to swallow all of that truth at one time. That was when I began wiping the fog off the mirror of my life.

Armed with my new attitude, I became the program's Legal Advocate. My passion had planted me there. The right choices kept me growing there. Fortuitously, whatever it was, something kept pushing me to saturate myself with anything I could learn there. After three failed marriages, it was time to change my self-destructive relationship patterns before it would happen again.

During my first year at DVPC, a woman named Sandra, one of Colorado Springs' notable therapists, selected me to collaborate with her in developing weekend-long workshops for battered women. Whatever she'd seen in me wasn't obvious to me at the time, but I was more than willing to shed my cocoon.

Throughout the early 1980s, society as a whole was barely awakening to the issues of family violence, spousal abuse, or whatever terms were being created to describe domestic violence. The dynamics of DV began coming out of the closet. As a survivor, I was a poster child of lingering self-esteem issues and PTSD.

Once again, my higher power had gone to work for me by sending in my new female role model, Sandra. Despite my enormous insecurities, we became colleagues that summer. During one of our many dinner meetings we began sharing our personal lives. At some point I heard the words ". . . and that's when I declared a five-year moratorium on relationships."

Goosebumps covered my body. Could she see the stunned look on my face as I tried imagining life without a relationship for even a month? *For what earthly reason?* Something profound like, "Oh wow, I could never do anything like that," fell out of my mouth. Surely that would change her mind about working with me, the unenlightened one.

Sandra laughed. "You'd be surprised."

My parochial mind twisted her words into suggesting my joining a convent. I'd been raised Catholic, but please. No sex? What I hadn't realized at the time was this wise woman had offered me an option for changing my life, not a ticket to a celibate life. The seed was planted.

My formerly ingrained beliefs about gender roles in relationships had been undergoing a huge metamorphosis. Man was god, hunter-gatherer, provider, strong, protector, dirty. Woman was goddess, weak, seductive, nurturer, quiet, clean. This slippery relationship slope had been a precariously confusing place in my life. On days when my emotional health peaked I could see the harmful pattern of serial relationships. As if I were chain-smoking, I'd light a new flame off a dying one.

Yes, my consciousness was being raised. However, transforming into this new me, I couldn't open myself to sharing this undertaking. What if I failed? Not only would I have failed, but everyone would know I had failed.

Honestly, I wasn't convinced I could pull off this abstinence thing. On one hand, I believed that no other woman's picker had ever been as defective as mine in her search for the prince. Then, on the other hand, I still felt incomplete without one.

During the next meeting with Sandra, to nurture my curiosity, I surreptitiously drilled her for more details about this choice of hers . . . for research. I felt lightheaded and hollow. *What was happening to me?* It had to mean something. I'd never felt that way before. Sitting in Adam's Mountain Café in Manitou Springs, I was completely oblivious to my own process. As with any addiction mine was accompanied with brain fog. Clarity, the goal, would come later.

Although the idea of abstinence had me intrigued, I just didn't understand why one would choose it. Sandra, who had no investment in whether or not I took on this mission, gently nudged one end of my teeter-totter with, "Well, if you want to do it, you can always start out small, and recommit as you go. I'm getting ready to recommit in November, but I'm not sure for how long."

"Maybe I'll try it for a month," I said, wanting to be intrepid like her.

"No trying. Only commitment works."

On May 16, 1983, The Great Moratorium was launched. I literally X'd off the days on a calendar as I went along. My cool, new advocate girlfriends were astonished when I'd told them about my accomplishment. Months passed. I realized it hadn't been that bad not having a date for the weekends. It was gratifying to have set a goal and accomplished it. Friday—date night—just became another day of the week.

What does someone like me do instead of dating? I watched scary movies on a new-fangled VCR thing with my teenaged daughter. I enjoyed dinners with girlfriends. I explored women's spirituality and began a practice of Transcendental Meditation. I wrote a dream journal. I became a gourmet cook and even turned liver, nettles, and rice into health food for my kitties.

Buoyed by success I reenlisted for an additional two-month stretch, to test my mettle. Looking around my little Victorian mother-in-law cottage, I realized that a lot of my possessions held unhappy memories. All that stuff I lived with was only reminders from relationships I no longer needed to think about. I donated it all to the shelter. The next part of my process was to discover what I liked and what I didn't like, another hallmark of survivors. A part of survival was that the focus is always on the other's needs.

I discovered I liked the colors plum, black, and white. The textures of crisp cotton, warm wood, and cool, smooth stone soothed my soul. My spirit moved to sounds of the blues. I liked candlelight, solitude, meditation music, and yoga. Peaceful things.

The next two months flashed by. Thriving on my freedom and self-discovery, it became easier to overcome the irrational insecurity of being out alone in public. Women in my generation were indoctrinated into a world of coupledom worship. The first time I'd felt adventurous enough to go to a movie by myself, I went in the early evening so I would be surrounded by people. It wouldn't be quite as obvious that I was there alone.

Full of false bravado I plunked myself down in the middle of the theater knowing every couple in the room was looking at me and pitying this solitary female.

At this point my kids were worried that I'd turned gay. As if people were salt shakers, and everyone should be in a set. Some friends expressed concern with my choice. *Did they fear their husbands weren't safe around me?* They tried fixing me up with eligible, needy widowers or those nice, divorced guys with steady jobs and great personalities.

Six months passed. Not only was I alive and well, but my old skin was slipping away. I took ownership of my life, my Self. It was empowering and something I'd never experienced before. I was in charge. *Could I possibly make it six more months in solitary? Without sex?* I really liked sex. It was part of my ego, my existence, my self-expression, my way of being. *Should I be scared?* Celibacy was for priests and nuns, not warm-blooded women. *How long was this experiment of mine going to last? What if this meant I'd never ever have another relationship?*

Not needing to answer to anyone else and being able to make my own choices felt odd, but it was an excellent kind of odd. No one to check in with but myself. Popcorn for dinner and peanut butter toast for breakfast—how audacious. When someone asked me, "Don't you miss it?"—whatever they implied by "it," I'd tell them that what I missed the most was having someone else pick up the tab once in a while.

No one was more surprised than I was when I'd actually done this Great Moratorium thing for an entire year. Even more astonishing was my very conscious choice to commit for another year just for the hell of it. Why not? If Sandra could, why couldn't I? Autonomy was oozing out of my pores. Having survived the biggest challenge—the first month—was way over. Finished. I was Woman!

My mental, emotional, spiritual, and even physical self strengthened as the days, and then the months rolled by. I saved that calendar. 1984. Another year rolled by. I saved that calendar, too. 1985. My evolution was alive!

May 16 rolled around again. 1986. As if I'd developed invisible blinders, the opposite sex was no longer even on my radar. It had to be a self-preservation thing on my psyche's part. Three years passed. Occasionally, not often, I'd ponder how—and when—this would all end. Why wasn't I concerned that I had another yea/nay date approaching? Aside from relishing in the changes, why was I still doing this curious alone thing? Reflecting on the epic strides I'd made during those three years, I couldn't deny the process was fundamentally shifting who I'd thought I was—in the best of ways. It was impacting every facet of my being.

Working in the Victim Advocacy Program helped me begin to understand what had attracted me to unhealthy relationships, and vice-versa. We teach what we most need to learn. Right? I realized I could survive on my own—financially, physically, and emotionally. It was good. It was working.

I eventually came to realize I hadn't been the only person affected by my life choices. That was gut-wrenching. My relationships with my teenage kids needed focus. Filled with humility, love, and forgiveness, I was awed by who they'd grown into despite the years of chaos. They were strong, smart, passionate, and funny. I adored them. I began concentrating on my relationships with these uber-independent teenagers. The beginning of our healing journey wasn't exactly a love fest, but we pushed through it. Our relationships were given blessed do-overs. Gratitude filled my heart. Still a bit codependent, I became dedicated to their happiness.

Uncovering my inner strength came from overcoming obstacles on the path. That meant no more riding the waves and gripping the life raft. It was time for me to swim. I became engaged in their lives. There was so much I'd never been aware of when my life had been driven by a need to make unhealthy relationships into normal ones, whatever that was. The daydream of holding our family unit together at all costs was unrealistic. Keeping up appearances was an exhausting illusion that had held me and my children hostage in a precarious house of cards. Releasing that tenuous home-sweet-home façade allowed us to start living life. For me the only way to clarity meant eliminating the obsession of that mirage. The Great Moratorium continued.

As more years passed and May 16 approached, I'd examine my life and contemplate recommitment. I pondered how my first eighteen years had been spent in a nest with my parents dictating what to do, what to think, what to say, how to be. The next eighteen years, my serial relationships had done the same thing, trapped me in more boxes. Having to think for myself without imposed boundaries was unfamiliar.

I can't remember exactly at which juncture this lifestyle just became my way of being without a need for constant self-analysis. That was liberating in itself. I no longer worried about what the hell was wrong with me based on my choosing to be alone. I mused over what it would be like to spend the next eighteen years on this new journey of singlehood. My power had definitely been turned on while I'd grown deep, thick roots in these moratoria. The only time I'd ever think about it was each year as May rolled around. This was my wonderful, full, challenging, crazy life. By then the only time I'd ever noticed my lifestyle was unusual, besides May, was when someone made a comment like, "Gee, I've never even known you with a relationship. I have no idea what your taste in men is even like." Neither did I. *Was it still men?* What I did know was that it would certainly be different than before I'd first started down this path.

Each May 16 I'd celebrate in a happier, healthier, and more conscious me. Every year my life evolved even better than the year before. Ultimately, this did become my lifestyle of choice for eighteen years. Eighteen years! Occasionally I'd spend time reflecting on the enormous impact of that one illuminating conversation with Sandra. When I'd try to imagine where I'd be if she had not been such an inspiration to me, I'd draw a blank. I mused over the saying, "When the student is ready, the teacher appears."

Eventually I realized I'd never know how much I'd truly evolved as far as relationships went if I didn't take one out for a test drive. Excited terror filled my mind. Then I imagined it was like riding a bike—just get back on. Perhaps it was time to remove those blinders. Or was it? I told the Universe that if the right person were out there, send them in with some obvious divine intervention. I made it clear I was not looking, but would be open to possibilities.

Undeniably The Great Moratorium has influenced who I've become in allowing me the time and space for self-discovery. I certainly have a new attitude for navigating the rest of my life. Sometimes I feel as if everything I'd experienced in my life before The Great Moratorium I'd done in someone else's body. I see photographs of my past but I don't recognize that girl. After many years of twists and turns, that liberation, self-determination, and independence I'd been craving so much in my youth had finally arrived.

Without fanfare The Great Moratorium concluded in May 2000. A gentle, peaceful knowing that the time was right washed slowly over me. After four months of matchmaking prowess and persistence, my daughter-in-law presented me with the man who would eventually steal my heart and never give it back. Divine intervention? Close enough. With my re-built picker, I'd become a trusting, loving person able to embrace someone with the right stuff. My heart opened again. As life partners, we created an equal-opportunity relationship on a foundation of respect, humor, generosity, and profound love. The Universe had handed me the prince and the white picket fence gift-wrapped in one package.

I still like wearing wear black, white, and plum—only now they're being called ebony, snow, and aubergine.

Diane Wood has been writing as long as she can remem-
ber. When she was required to write a blurb for her high-school
yearbook she announced, "I will go out into the world and have
all kinds of exciting experiences. When I'm old I'll write about
them." Her life's experiences, told from a woman's world per-

spective, have intrigued and entertained friends and colleagues for decades. She's been published in small rags, won a few writing contests along the way, and written stories from experience about living with passion, humor, and redemption. Diane's background includes being a bar owner in Denver, a women's shelter director, a private chef to the rich and famous, and an elder care advocate. Stories abound. Now that she is actually retired she's writing about those personal experiences. Her current novel, Vital Signs, is in its anticipative final revision on its journey to publishing.

Acknowledgments

A special thank you to the following donors who helped make the publication of
Memory into Memoir a reality:

Nancy Adair	Carol McMillan
Debbie Brosten	Stephen Morrow
Nancy Canyon	Joe Nolting
Susan Chase-Foster	Mary Jo Olsen
Barbara Clarke	Cami Ostman
Lora Eckert	Victoria Ramos
Margaret/Barry Englestad	Laura/William Rink
Marian Exall	Richard Rink
Ben Frerichs	Betty Scott
Shannon Hager	Judith Shantz
Sky Hedman	RPP Smith, PhD
Francis Howard-Snyder	Jessica H. Stone
Laura Kalpakian	Diane Stowers
Dawn Landau	Jason Toews
Jonathan Lambert	Jean Waight
Linda Lambert	Jennifer Wilke

There are many people who put their hands to the plow in a practical way to see this volume come to fruition.

Gratitude to our executive editors and visionaries: Laura Kalpakian, Linda Lambert, Cami Ostman, Susan Tive.

Our thirteen team leaders each supported a small group of writers to polish and shape their work. Thanks to each of them: Linda Lambert, Linda Morrow, Victoria Doerper, Seán Dwyer, Susan Chase-Foster, Kate Miller, Joe Nolting, Frances Howard-Snyder, Marian Exall, Cami Ostman, Roy and Nancy Taylor, Rody Rowe, Susan Tive, Laura Kalpakian.

A huge bow to our publisher, project manager, point person, and administrator: Jessica H. Stone for keeping all of our plates spinning.

A hundred cheers to our hard-working, diligent editors Kari Neumeyer and Laura Rink. They are the Comma Queens! Thank you to our thank-you-notes-to-donors team: Linda Lambert and Jennifer Wilke.

And to our technical guru: Pam Helberg (Practical Genius).

The marketing committee strategized and organized our publicity and connection with the community, for which we are profoundly grateful: Nancy Adair, Janet Oakley, Ben Frerichs, and Jean Waight.

We're grateful as well to our awesome blog coordinator Diane Wood and to her merry band of bloggers.

Thanks, too, to our pals and legal advisers: Marian Exall and Richard Little.

Most importantly, we want to thank the writers themselves. Each contributor to this anthology collaborated with editors and team leaders to shape their material and to bring forward their best writing. Thanks for all your hard work!

So much depends upon community. Over the years, the following businesses and individuals have supported Red Wheelbarrow Writers in too many ways to name.

Thank you

• All of our children, partners, parents, therapists, and pets

• Charles and his team at Book Fare Café

• Dee, Chuck, Paul, Sam, and all the wonderful folks at Village Books

• Graphic artist and book designer, J. Allen Fielder

• Nerka Sea-Frozen Salmon for feeding us and cheering us

• Our other writing haunts: Tony's Coffee, Caffé Adagio

• Penchant Press International

• The Pickford Film Center

• The Whatcom Literacy Council

- Uisce Irish Pub and Johnny, the awesome bartender!

- Whatcom Community College

- Whatcom Writers and Publishers for their collaboration.